DIVINE LOVE
AND
WISDOM

DIVINE LOVE

AND

WISDOM

The Portable New Century Edition

EMANUEL SWEDENBORG

Translated from the Latin by George F. Dole

SWEDENBORG FOUNDATION

West Chester, Pennsylvania

Originally published as *Sapientia Angelica de Divino Amore*, Amsterdam, 1763

Revised second printing, 2015.

Printed in the United States of America

ISBN (library) 978-0-87785-480-7 (bound with *Divine Providence*)
ISBN (paperback) 978-0-87785-481-4
ISBN (portable) 978-0-87785-404-3

(The ISBN in the Library of Congress data shown below is from the previous printing of this Portable edition.)

Library of Congress Cataloging-in-Publication Data

Swedenborg, Emanuel, 1688–1772.
  [Sapientia angelica de divino amore. English]
  Divine love and wisdom / author, Emanuel Swedenborg ; translator, George F. Dole. — Portable ed.
    p. cm.
  ISBN 978-87785-402-9 (alk. paper)
  1. God (Christianity)—Love. 2. God (Christianity)—Wisdom. I. Title.

BX8712 .D3 2008
231'.6—dc22

                                                                        2008013017

Text designed by Joanna V. Hill
Ornaments from the first Latin edition, 1763
Typesetting by Alicia L. Dole
Cover designed by Karen Connor

For information contact:
Swedenborg Foundation
320 North Church Street
West Chester, PA 19380 USA
Telephone: (610) 430-3222
Web: www.swedenborg.com
E-mail: info@swedenborg.com

Contents

Part 2

Part 3

Part 4

Conventions Used in This Work

MOST of the following conventions apply generally to the translations in the New Century Edition Portable series. For introductory material on the content and history of *Divine Love and Wisdom,* and for annotations on the subject matter, including obscure or problematic content, and extensive indexes, the reader is referred to the Deluxe New Century Edition volume.

Section numbers Following a practice common in his time, Swedenborg divided his published theological works into sections numbered in sequence from beginning to end. His original section numbers have been preserved in this edition; they appear in boxes in the outside margins. Traditionally, these sections have been referred to as "numbers" and designated by the abbreviation "n." In this edition, however, the more common section symbol (§) is used to designate the section numbers, and the sections are referred to as such.

Citations of Swedenborg's text As is common in Swedenborgian studies, text citations of Swedenborg's works refer not to page numbers but to section numbers, which are uniform in most editions. In citations the section symbol (§) is generally omitted after the title of a work by Swedenborg. Thus *"Heaven and Hell* 56" refers to section 56 (§56) of Swedenborg's *Heaven and Hell,* not to page 56 of any edition. Where section numbers stand alone without titles, their function is indicated by the prefixed section symbol; for example, "§56".

Citations of the Bible Biblical citations in this edition follow the accepted standard: a semicolon is used between book references and between chapter references, and a comma between verse references. Therefore "Matthew 5:11, 12; 6:1; 10:41, 42; Luke 6:23, 35" refers to Matthew chapter 5, verses 11 and 12; Matthew chapter 6, verse 1; Matthew chapter 10, verses 41 and 42; and Luke chapter 6, verses 23 and 35. Swedenborg often incorporated the numbers of verses not actually represented in his text when listing verse numbers for a passage he quoted; these apparently constitute a kind of "see also" reference to other material he felt was relevant, and are generally retained in this edition. This edition also follows Swedenborg where he cites contiguous verses individually (for example, John 14:8, 9, 10, 11), rather than as a range (John 14:8–11). Occasionally this edition supplies a full, conventional Bible reference where Swedenborg omits one after a quotation.

Quotations in Swedenborg Some features of the original Latin text of *Divine Love and Wisdom* have been modernized in this edition. For example, Swedenborg's first edition relies on context or italics rather than on quotation marks to indicate passages taken from the Bible or from other works. The manner in which these conventions are used in the original suggests that Swedenborg did not feel it necessary to belabor the distinction between direct quotation and paraphrase of the Bible; neither did he mark his omissions from or changes to material he quoted, a practice in which this edition generally follows him.

Changes to and insertions in the text This translation is based on the first Latin edition, published by Swedenborg himself. Swedenborg made extensive cross-references within *Divine Love and Wisdom,* but often did not cite the number of the section or sections to which he was referring. These omitted cross-reference numbers have been inserted in square brackets [] in this edition. In a few cases Swedenborg supplied the section numbers, but they are obviously in error. Where a plausible correction has been found, it has been inserted in square brackets. These corrections have, furthermore, been italicized as an indication that they are intended to replace the preceding entry, not augment it. This system has also been applied to citations of the Bible and of Swedenborg's works that appear in the main text of the translation: that is, italicized brackets indicate a correction and roman brackets indicate an addition. Words not appearing in the first Latin edition, but necessary for the understanding of the text, also appear in roman brackets; this device has been used sparingly, however, even at the risk of some inconsistency in its application.

Chapter numbering Swedenborg numbered the parts of *Divine Love and Wisdom* but did not number the "chapters" within those parts. His decision not to do so seems to have been deliberate, and in accord with it chapter numbers are not included in the text. However, the table of contents provides such numbers in square brackets for the convenience of readers.

Biblical titles Swedenborg refers to the Hebrew Scriptures as the Old Testament and to the Greek Scriptures as the New Testament; his terminology has been adopted in this edition. As was the custom in his day, he refers to the Pentateuch (Genesis, Exodus, Leviticus, Numbers, and Deuteronomy) simply as "Moses." Similarly, in sentences or phrases introducing quotations he sometimes refers to the Psalms as "David"; for example, in §38 he writes "we read in David," and then quotes a passage from Psalm 89. Conventional references supplied in parentheses after such quotations specify their sources more precisely.

DIVINE LOVE
AND
WISDOM

ANGELIC WISDOM
ABOUT
DIVINE LOVE

PART 1

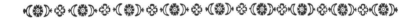

*L*OVE *is our life.* For most people, the existence of love is a given, but the nature of love is a mystery. As for the existence of love, this we know from everyday language. We say that someone loves us, that monarchs love their subjects, and that subjects love their monarch. We say that a husband loves his wife and that a mother loves her children, and vice versa. We say that people love their country, their fellow citizens, their neighbor. We use the same language about impersonal objects, saying that someone loves this or that thing.

Even though the word "love" is so commonly on our tongues, still hardly anyone knows what love is. When we stop to think about it, we find that we cannot form any image of it in our thoughts, so we say either that it is not really anything or that it is simply something that flows into us from our sight, hearing, touch, and conversation and therefore influences us. We are wholly unaware that it is our very life—not just the general life of our whole body and of all our thoughts, but the life of their every least detail. Wise people can grasp this when you ask, "If you take away the effects of love, can you think anything? Can you do anything? As the effects of love lose their warmth, do not thought and speech and action lose theirs as well? Do they not warm up as love warms up?" Still, the grasp of these wise people is not based on the thought that love is our life, but on their experience that this is how things happen.

2   We cannot know what our life is unless we know that it is love. If we do not know this, then one person may believe that life is nothing but sensation and action and another that it is thought, when in fact thought is the first effect of life, and sensation and action are secondary effects of life. Thought is the first effect of life, as just noted, but there are deeper and deeper forms of thought as well as more and more superficial ones. The deepest form of thought, the perception of ends, is actually the first effect of life. But more on this below [§§179–183] in connection with levels of life.

3   We can get some idea that love is our life from the warmth of the sun in our world. We know this warmth acts like the life shared by all earth's plants because when it increases in the spring, plants of all kinds sprout from the soil. They dress themselves in their leafy finery and then in their blossoms and eventually in fruit. This is how they "live." When the warmth ebbs away, though, as it does in fall and winter, they are stripped of these signs of life and they wither. Love works the same way in us because love and warmth correspond to each other. This is why love makes us warm.

4   *God alone—the Lord—is love itself, because he is life itself. Both we on earth and angels are life-receivers.* I will be offering many illustrations of this in works on divine providence and life. Here I would say only that the Lord, who is the God of the universe, is uncreated and infinite, while we and angels are created and finite. Since the Lord is uncreated and infinite, he is that essential reality that is called Jehovah and is life itself or life in itself. No one can be created directly from the Uncreated, the Infinite, from Reality itself and Life itself, because what is divine is one and undivided. We must be created out of things created and finite, things so formed that something divine can dwell within. Since we and angels are of this nature, we are life-receivers. So if we let ourselves be misled in thought so badly that we think we are not life-receivers but are actually life, there is no way to keep us from thinking that we are God.

Our sense that we are life and our consequent belief that we are life rests on an illusion: in an instrumental cause, the presence of its principal cause is only felt as something identical to itself. The Lord himself teaches that he is life in itself in John: "As the Father has life in himself, so too he has granted the Son to have life in himself" (John 5:26); and again in John (11:25 and 14:6) he teaches that he is life itself. Since life and love are one and the same, as we can see from the first two sections above, it follows that the Lord, being life itself, is love itself.

If this is to be intelligible, though, it is essential to realize that the Lord, **5** being love in its very essence or divine love, is visible to angels in heaven as a sun; that warmth and light flow from that sun; that the outflowing warmth is essentially love and the outflowing light essentially wisdom; and that to the extent that angels are receptive of that spiritual warmth and spiritual light, they themselves are instances of love and wisdom—instances of love and wisdom not on their own, but from the Lord.

Spiritual warmth and spiritual light flow into and affect not only angels but also us, precisely to the extent that we become receptive. Our receptivity develops in proportion to our love for the Lord and our love for our neighbor.

That sun itself, or divine love, cannot use its warmth and light to create anyone directly from itself. If it did, the creature would be love in its essence, which is the Lord himself. It can, however, create people out of material substances so formed as to be receptive of its actual warmth and light. In the same way, the sun of our world cannot use its warmth and light to bring forth sprouts in the earth directly. Rather, the sun uses substances in the soil in which it can be present through its warmth and light to make plants grow. (On the Lord's divine love being seen as the sun in the spiritual world, with spiritual warmth and light flowing from it, giving angels their love and wisdom, see *Heaven and Hell* 116–142.)

Since we are life-receivers, not life, it follows that our conception from **6** our parents is not the conception of life but simply the conception of the first and purest forms that can accept life. These forms serve as a nucleus or beginning in the womb, to which are added, step by step, material substances in forms suited, in their various patterns and levels, to the reception of life.

Divinity is not in space. Given the divine omnipresence—presence with **7** everyone in the world, with every angel in heaven, and with every spirit under heaven—there is no way a merely physical image can compass the thought that Divinity, or God, is not in space. Only a spiritual image will suffice. Physical images are inadequate because they involve space. They are put together out of earthly things, and there is something spatial about absolutely every earthly thing we see with our eyes. Everything that is large or small here involves space, everything that is long or wide or high here involves space—in a word, every measurement, every shape, every form here involves space. This is why I said that a merely physical image cannot compass the fact that Divinity is not in space when the claim is made that it is everywhere.

Still, we can grasp this with our earthly thinking if only we let in a little spiritual light. This requires that I first say something about spiritual concepts and the spiritual thinking that arises from them. Spiritual concepts have nothing to do with space. They have to do solely with state, state being an attribute of love, life, wisdom, desires, and the delights they provide—in general, an attribute of what is good and true. A truly spiritual concept of these realities has nothing in common with space. It is higher and looks down on spatial concepts the way heaven looks down on earth.

However, since angels and spirits see with their eyes the way we do on earth, and since objects can be seen only in space, there does seem to be space in the spiritual world where angels and spirits are, space like ours on earth. Still, it is not space but an appearance of space. It is not fixed and invariant like ours. It can be lengthened and shortened, changed and altered; and since it cannot be defined by measurement, we here cannot grasp it with an earthly concept, but only with a spiritual one. Spiritual concepts are no different when they apply to spatial distances than when they apply to "distances" of what is good and "distances" of what is true, which are agreements and likenesses as to state.

8   It stands to reason, then, that with merely earthly concepts we cannot grasp the fact that Divinity is everywhere and still not in space, and that angels and spirits understand this quite clearly. This means that we too could understand if we would only let a little spiritual light into our thinking. The reason we can understand is that it is not our bodies that think but our spirits; so it is not our physical side but our spiritual side.

9   The reason so many people do not grasp this is that they love what is earthly and are therefore reluctant to lift their thinking above it into spiritual light. People who are reluctant can think only spatially, even about God; and thinking spatially about God is thinking about the extended size of nature.

This premise is necessary because without a knowledge and some sense that Divinity is not in space, we cannot understand anything about the divine life that is love and wisdom, which are our present topic. This means there can be little if any understanding of divine providence, omnipresence, omniscience, omnipotence, infinity, and eternity, which are to be dealt with in sequence.

10   I have stated that in the spiritual world, just as in this physical world, we can see space and therefore distances as well, but that they are appearances, dependent on spiritual likenesses of love and wisdom, or of what is good and true. This is why even though the Lord is with angels everywhere in heaven, he still appears high overhead, looking like a sun. Further, since it is the acceptance of love and wisdom that causes likeness to him, if angels have a closer resemblance because of their acceptance, their heavens appear to be closer to the Lord than those of the angels whose resemblance is more remote. This is also why the heavens (there are three of them) are marked off from each other, as are the communities of each heaven. It is also why the hells underneath them are farther away in proportion to their rejection of love and wisdom.

It is the same for us. The Lord is present in us and with us throughout the whole world; and the reason for this is simply that the Lord is not in space.

God is the essential person. Throughout all the heavens, the only concept of **11** God is a concept of a person. The reason is that heaven, overall and regionally, is in a kind of human form, and Divinity among the angels is what makes heaven. Further, thinking proceeds in keeping with heaven's form, so it is not possible for angels to think about God in any other way. This is why all the people on earth who are in touch with heaven think about God in the same way when they are thinking very deeply, or in their spirit.

It is because God is a person that all angels and spirits are perfectly formed people. This is because of heaven's form, which is the same in its largest and its smallest manifestations. (On heaven being in a human form overall and regionally, see *Heaven and Hell* 59–87 *[59–86]*, and on thought progressing in keeping with heaven's form, see §§203–204 there.)

It is common knowledge that we were created in the image and likeness of God because of Genesis 1:26, 27 and from the fact that Abraham and others saw God as a person.

The early people, wise and simple alike, thought of God only as a person. Even when they began to worship many gods, as they did in Athens and Rome, they worshiped them as persons. By way of illustration, here is an excerpt from an earlier booklet.

> Non-Christians—especially Africans—who acknowledge and worship one God as the Creator of the universe conceive of that God as a person. They say that no one can have any other concept of God. When they hear that many people prefer an image of God as a little cloud in the center, they ask where these people are; and when they are told that these people are among the Christians, they respond that this is impossible. They are told, however, that Christians get this idea from the fact that in the Word God is called a spirit; and the only concept

they have of spirit is of a piece of cloud. They do not realize that every spirit and every angel is a person. However, when inquiry was made to find out whether their spiritual concept was the same as their earthly one, it turned out that it was not the same for people who inwardly recognized the Lord as the God of heaven and earth.

I heard one Christian elder say that no one could have a concept of a being both divine and human; and I saw him taken to various non-Christians, more and more profound ones. Then he was taken to their heavens, and finally to a heaven of Christians. Through the whole process people's inner perception of God was communicated to him, and he came to realize that their only concept of God was a concept of a person—which is the same as a concept of a being both divine and human.

12   The ordinary concept of God among Christians is a concept of a person because God is called a person in the Athanasian doctrine of the Trinity. The better educated, though, claim that God is invisible. This is because they cannot understand how a human God could have created heaven and earth and filled the universe with his presence, along with other things that pass the bounds of understanding as long as people do not realize that Divinity is not in space. Still, people who turn to the Lord alone think of one who is both divine and human, and therefore think of God as a person.

13   We may gather how important it is to have a right concept of God from the fact that this concept is the very core of the thinking of anyone who has a religion. All the elements of religion and of worship focus on God; and since God is involved in every element of religion and worship, whether general or particular, unless there is a right concept of God there can be no communication with heaven. This is why every nation is allotted its place in the spiritual world according to its concept of a human God. This [understanding of God as human] is where the concept of the Lord is to be found, and nowhere else.

We can see very clearly that our state after death depends on our avowed concept of God if we consider the opposite, namely that the denial of God, and in the Christian world, a denial of the Lord's divinity, constitutes hell.

14   *In the Divine-Human One, reality and its manifestation are both distinguishable and united.* Wherever there is reality, there is its manifestation:

the one does not occur without the other. In fact, reality *exists* through its manifestation, and not apart from it. Our rational capacity grasps this when we ponder whether there can be any reality that does not manifest itself, and whether there can be any manifestation except from some reality. Since each occurs with the other and not apart from it, it follows that they are one entity, but "distinguishably one."

They are distinguishably one like love and wisdom. Further, love *is* reality and wisdom is its manifestation. Love occurs only in wisdom, and wisdom only from love. So love becomes manifest when it is in wisdom. These two are one entity in such a way that although they can be distinguished in thought they cannot be distinguished in fact; and since they can be distinguished in thought and not in fact, we refer to them as "distinguishably one."

Reality and its manifestation are also distinguishably one in the Divine-Human One the way soul and body are. A soul does not occur without its body, nor a body without its soul. The divine soul of the Divine-Human One is what we mean by the divine reality, and the divine body of the Divine-Human One is what we mean by the divine manifestation.

The notion that a soul can exist and think and be wise without a body is an error that stems from deceptive appearances. Every soul is in a spiritual body after it has cast off the material skin that it carried around in this world.

The reason reality is not reality unless it is manifested is that before [15] that happens it has no form, and if it has no form it has no attributes. Anything that has no attributes is not really anything. Whatever is manifest on the basis of its reality is one with that reality because it stems from that reality. This is the basis of their being united into a single entity, and this is why each belongs to the other reciprocally, with each being wholly present in every detail of the other, as it is in itself.

It therefore stands to reason that God is a person and in this way is [16] God manifest—not manifest from himself, but manifest in himself. The one who is manifest in himself is the God who is the source of all.

In the Divine-Human One, infinite things are distinguishably one. It is rec- [17] ognized that God is infinite: he is in fact called the Infinite One. But he is called infinite because he is infinite. He is not infinite simply because he is intrinsically essential reality and manifestation, but because there are infinite things in him. An infinite being without infinite things within it would be infinite in name only.

The infinite things in him should not be called "infinitely many" or "infinitely all," because of our earthly concepts of "many" and "all." Our earthly concept of "infinitely many" is limited, and while there is something limitless about our concept of "infinitely all," it still rests on limited things in our universe. This means that since our concept is earthly, we cannot arrive at a sense of the infinite things in God by some process of shifting it to a higher level or by comparison. However, since angels enjoy spiritual concepts they can surpass us by changing to a higher level and by comparison, though they cannot reach infinity itself.

18   Anyone can come to an inner assurance about the presence of infinite things in God—anyone, that is, who believes that God is a person; because if God is a person, he has a body and everything that having a body entails. So he has a face, torso, abdomen, upper legs, and lower legs, since without these he would not be a person. Since he has these components, he also has eyes, ears, nose, mouth, and tongue. He also has what we find within a person, such as a heart and lungs and the things that depend on them, all of which, taken together, make us human. We are created with these many components, and if we consider them in their interconnections, they are beyond counting. In the Divine-Human One, though, they are infinite. Nothing is lacking, so he has an infinite completeness.

We can make this comparison of the uncreated Person, who is God, with us who are created, because that God is a person. It is because of [his being a person] that we earthly beings are said to have been created in his image and in his likeness (Genesis 1:26, 27).

19   The presence of infinite things in God is even more obvious to angels because of the heavens where they live. The whole heaven, made up of millions of angels, is like a person in its overall form. Each individual community of heaven, large or small, is the same; and therefore an angel is a person. An angel is actually a heaven in its smallest form (see *Heaven and Hell* 51–87 [*51–86*]).

Heaven is in this form overall, regionally, and in individuals because of the divine nature that angels accept, since the extent to which angels accept the divine nature determines the perfection of their human form. This is why we say that angels are in God and that God is in them, and that God is everything to them.

The multiplicity of heaven is indescribable; and since it is Divinity that makes heaven, and therefore Divinity is the source of that indescribable multiplicity, we can see quite clearly that there are infinite things in that quintessential Person who is God.

We can draw the same inference from the created universe if we turn our attention to its functions and the things that answer to them. However, this will not be comprehensible until some examples have been offered.   **20**

Since there are infinite things in the Divine-Human One, things that are, so to speak, reflected in heaven, in angels, and in us, and since the Divine-Human One is not in space (see §§7–10 above), we can see and understand to some extent how God can be omnipresent, omniscient, and omniprovident, and how, even as a person, he could have created everything, and how as a person he can forever keep everything he has created in its proper order.   **21**

Further, if we look at ourselves we can see a kind of reflection of the fact that these infinite things in the Divine-Human One are distinguishably one. There are many things within us—countless things, as already noted [§18]; yet we feel them as one. On the basis of our feelings, we have no sense of our brain or heart or lungs, of our liver or spleen or pancreas, of the countless components of our eyes, ears, tongue, stomach, sexual organs, and so on; and since we are not aware of them, we sense them as all one.   **22**

The reason is that all these organs are gathered into a form that precludes the absence of any one of them. It is a form designed to receive life from the Divine-Human One, as explained in §§4–6 above. The organization and connection of all these elements in this kind of form give rise to the feeling and therefore to the image of them not as many or countless but as one.

We may therefore conclude that the innumerably many components that constitute a kind of unity in us are distinguishably one—supremely so—in that quintessential Person who is God.

There is one human God who is the source of everything. All the elements of human reason unite in, and in a sense center on, the fact that a single God is the Creator of the universe. As a result, rational people, on the basis of their shared understanding, neither do nor can think in any other way. Tell people of sound reason that there are two creators of the universe and you will feel within yourself how they recoil from this notion,   **23** perhaps simply from the tone of their voice in your ear. This enables us to see that all the elements of human reason unite and center on the oneness of God.

There are two reasons for this. The first is that in its own right, our very ability to think rationally is not our own property. It is a property of God within us. Human rationality in general depends on this fact, and this general property causes our reason more or less spontaneously to see the oneness of God. The second is that through our rational ability either we are in heaven's light or we draw from it some general quality of its thought, and the all-pervading element of heaven's light is that God is one.

This is not the case if we have used our rational ability to skew our lower understanding. In this case we still possess the ability, but by the distortion of our lower abilities we have steered it off course, and our rationality is not sound.

24   We may not be aware of it, but we all think of an aggregation of people as a single individual. So we understand right away when someone says that monarchs are the head and that their subjects are the body, or when someone says that this or that individual has some particular role in the body politic, that is, in the realm. It is the same with the spiritual body as with the civil. The spiritual body is the church, whose head is the Divine-Human One. We can see from this what kind of person a church would look like under this construct if we were to think not of one God as creator and sustainer of the universe but of many gods instead. We would apparently be envisioning a single body with many heads on it—not a human being, then, but a monster.

If we were to claim that these heads have a single essence that made them all one head, then the only possible image would be either of a single head with many faces or of many heads with one face. In our perception, then, the church would look grotesque. In fact, one God is the head, and the church is the body that acts at the bidding of the head and not on its own, as is true of us as well.

This is also why there is only one monarch per realm. More than one would pull it apart; one holds it together.

25   It would be the same in the church that is spread throughout the world, which is called a communion because it is like a single body under a single head. It is recognized that the head governs the body beneath itself at will. The head is after all the locus of our discernment and our volition, and the body acts at the behest of our discernment and volition to the point that the body is pure obedience. The body is incapable of

doing anything except at the behest of the discernment and volition in the head; and in similar fashion we of the church can do nothing apart from God. It does seem as though the body acts on its own—as though hands and feet move of their own accord when we do something, as though mouth and tongue vibrate of their own accord when we say something—and yet nothing whatever is done "on its own." It is prompted by the stimulus of our volition and the consequent thinking of the discernment in the head.

Just think. If one body had many heads, and each head had its own agenda based on its mind and its volition, could the body survive? There could be no unanimity among them the way there is with a single head.

It is the same in the heavens, which consist of millions of angels, as it is in the church. Unless every single angel focused on one God, one angel would move away from another and heaven would fall apart. So an angel who even thinks about many gods instantly disappears, exiled to the very edge of heaven, and collapses.

Since the whole heaven and everything in it depend on a single God, **26** it is the nature of angelic speech to come to a close in a particular harmony that flows from heaven's own harmony. This is a sign that it is impossible for angels to think of more than one God. Their speech follows from their thought.

Surely everyone of sound reason perceives the fact that Divinity is **27** not divisible, that there is not a multiplicity of infinite, uncreated, omnipotent beings, or gods. Suppose some irrational soul were to say that there could be a multiplicity of infinite, uncreated, omnipotent beings, or gods, if only they had a single "same essence," and that this would result in one being who was infinite, uncreated, omnipotent, and god. Would not that single same essence have one "same identity"? And it is not possible for many beings to have the same identity. If this individual were to say that one is derived from the other, then the one that is derived from the other is not God in and of himself; yet God in and of himself is the source of all (see §16 above).

The true divine essence is love and wisdom. If you gather together every- **28** thing you know, focus your mind's insight on it, and look through it carefully from some spiritual height to discover what is common to everything, the only conclusion you can draw is that it is love and wisdom. These two are essential to every aspect of our life. Everything we deal with that is civic, everything moral, and everything spiritual depends on these two things. Apart from them, there is nothing. The same holds true for everything in the life of that composite person who is (as already noted [§24]) our larger and smaller community, our monarchy or empire, the church, and also the angelic heaven. Take love and wisdom away from these collective bodies and ask whether there is anything left, and you will be struck by the fact that without love and wisdom as their source, they are nothing.

29 No one can deny that in God we find love and wisdom together in their very essence. He loves us all out of the love that is within him, and he guides us all out of the wisdom that is within him.

Further, if you look at the created universe with an eye to its design, it is so full of wisdom from love that you might say everything taken all together is wisdom itself. There are things without measure in such a pattern, both sequential and simultaneous, that taken all together they constitute a single entity. This is the only reason they can be held together and sustained forever.

30 It is because the very essence of the Divine is love and wisdom that we have two abilities of life. From the one we get our discernment, and from the other volition. Our discernment is supplied entirely by an inflow of wisdom from God, while our volition is supplied entirely by an inflow of love from God. Our failures to be appropriately wise and appropriately loving do not take these abilities away from us. They only close them off; and as long as they do, while we may call our discernment "discernment" and our volition "volition," essentially they are not. So if these abilities really were taken away from us, everything human about us would be destroyed—our thinking and the speech that results from thought, and our purposing and the actions that result from purpose.

We can see from this that the divine nature within us dwells in these two abilities, in our ability to be wise and our ability to love. That is, it dwells in the fact that we are capable of being wise and loving. I have discovered from an abundance of experience that we have the ability to love even though we are not wise and do not love as we could. You will find this experience described in abundance elsewhere.

31 It is because the divine essence itself is love and wisdom that everything in the universe involves what is good and what is true. Everything that flows from love is called good, and everything that flows from wisdom is called true. But more on this later [§§83–102].

32 It is because the divine essence itself is love and wisdom that the universe and everything in it, whether living or not, depends on warmth and light for its survival. Warmth in fact corresponds to love and light corresponds to wisdom, which also means that spiritual warmth is love and spiritual light is wisdom. But more on this as well later [§§83–84, 89–92].

All human feelings and thoughts arise from the divine love and wis- **33** dom that constitute the very essence that is God. The feelings arise from divine love and the thoughts from divine wisdom. Further, every single bit of our being is nothing but feeling and thought. These two are like the springs of everything that is alive in us. They are the source of all our life experiences of delight and enchantment, the delight from the prompting of our love and the enchantment from our consequent thought.

Since we have been created to be recipients, then, and since we are recipients to the extent that we love God and are wise because of our love for God (that is, the extent to which we are moved by what comes from God and think as a result of that feeling), it therefore follows that the divine essence, the Creatress, is divine love and wisdom.

Divine love is a property of divine wisdom, and divine wisdom is a property **34** *of divine love.* On the divine reality and the divine manifestation being distinguishably one in the Divine-Human One, see §§14–16 above. Since the divine reality is divine love and the divine manifestation is divine wisdom, these latter are similarly distinguishably one.

We refer to them as "distinguishably one" because love and wisdom are two distinguishable things, and yet they are so united that love is a property of wisdom and wisdom a property of love. Love finds its reality in wisdom, and wisdom finds its manifestation in love. Further, since wisdom derives its manifestation from love (as noted in §15 *[14]* above), divine wisdom is reality as well. It follows from this that love and wisdom together are the divine reality, though when they are distinguished we call love the divine reality and wisdom the divine manifestation. This is the quality of the angelic concept of divine love and wisdom.

Because there is such a oneness of love and wisdom and of wisdom **35** and love in the Divine-Human One, the divine essence is one. In fact, the divine essence is divine love because that love is a property of divine wisdom, and it is divine wisdom because that wisdom is a property of divine love. Because of this oneness, the divine life is a unity as well: life is the divine essence.

The reason divine love and wisdom are one is that the union is reciprocal, and a reciprocal union makes complete unity. But there will be more to say about reciprocal union later [§§115–116].

36   There is a union of love and wisdom in every divine work as well. This is why it endures, even to eternity. If there were more divine love than divine wisdom or more divine wisdom than divine love in any created work, nothing would endure in it except what was equal. Any excess would pass away.

37   As divine providence works for our reformation, regeneration, and salvation, it shares equally in divine love and divine wisdom. We cannot be reformed, regenerated, and saved by any excess of divine love over divine wisdom or by any excess of divine wisdom over divine love. Divine love wants to save everyone, but it can do so only by means of divine wisdom. All the laws that govern salvation are laws of divine wisdom, and love cannot transcend those laws because divine love and divine wisdom are one and act in unison.

38   In the Word, "justice" and "judgment" mean divine love and divine wisdom, "justice" meaning divine love and "judgment" meaning divine wisdom; so in the Word justice and judgment are ascribed to God. For example, we read in David, "Justice and judgment are the foundation of your throne" (Psalms 79:15 *[89:14]*); and again, "Jehovah will bring out his justice like light and his judgment like noonday" (Psalms 37:6); in Hosea, "I will betroth myself to you forever in justice and judgment" (Hosea 2:19); in Jeremiah, "I will raise up a just branch for David who will rule as king and make judgment and justice in the land" (Jeremiah 23:5); in Isaiah, "He will sit on the throne of David and over his kingdom, to make it secure in judgment and in justice" (Isaiah 9:6 *[9:7]*); and again, "Let Jehovah be extolled, because he has filled the earth with judgment and justice" (Isaiah 33:5); in David, "When I shall have learned the judgments of your justice . . . seven times a day I will praise you over the judgments of your justice" (Psalms 119:7, 164). "Life" and "light" in John mean the same: "In him was life, and the life was the light of humanity" (John 1:4). "Life" here means the Lord's divine love, and "light" his divine wisdom. "Life" and "spirit" mean the same in John as well: "Jesus said, 'The words that I speak to you are spirit and life'" (John 6:63).

39   Even though love and wisdom seem to be two separate things in us, essentially they are distinguishably one. This is because the quality of our love determines the quality of our wisdom and the quality of our wisdom the quality of our love. Any wisdom that is not united to our love seems like wisdom, but it is not; and any love that is not united to our wisdom seems like wisdom's love even though it is not. Each gets its essence and its life from the other in mutual fashion.

The reason the wisdom and love within us seem to be two separate things is that our ability to understand can be raised into heaven's light, while our ability to love cannot, except to the extent that we act according to our understanding. So any trace of apparent wisdom that is not united to our love for wisdom relapses into the love with which it is united. This may not be a love for wisdom, and may even be a love for insanity. We are perfectly capable of knowing, from our wisdom, that we ought to do one thing or another, and then of not doing it because we have no love for it. However, to the extent that we do the bidding of our wisdom, from love, we are images of God.

Divine love and wisdom is substance and is form. The everyday concept of **40** love and wisdom is that they are something floating around in, or breathed out by, thin air or ether. Hardly anyone considers that in reality and in function they are substance and form.

Even people who do see that love and wisdom are substance and form sense them as something outside their subject, flowing from it; and they refer to what in their perceptions is outside the subject and flowing from it as substance and form even though they sense it as floating around. They do not realize that love and wisdom are the actual subject, and that what they sense as floating out from the subject is only the appearance of the inherent state of the subject.

There are many reasons why this has not come to light before. One of them is that appearances are the first things the human mind draws on in forming its understanding, and the only way to dispel these appearances is through careful probing into cause. If a cause is deeply hidden, we cannot probe into it unless we keep our discernment in spiritual light for a protracted period of time; and we cannot hold it there for a long time because of the earthly light that keeps pulling us back.

Still, the truth is that love and wisdom are the real and functional substance and form that make up the very subject.

Since this truth is counter to appearance, though, it may seem **41** unworthy of credence unless some evidence is supplied; and since the only way to supply evidence is with the kind of things we perceive with our physical senses, that is what I need to draw on.

We have five external senses, called touch, taste, smell, hearing, and sight. The subject of touch is the skin that envelops us: the very substance and form of the skin make it feel what comes into contact with it. The sense of touch is not in the things that come into contact with it but in the substance and form of the skin. That is the subject, and the sense itself is simply the way it is affected by contact.

It is the same with taste. This sense is simply the way a substance and form, this time of the tongue, are affected. The tongue is the subject. It is the same with smell. We recognize that odors affect the nostrils and are in the nostrils, and that smell is the way impinging aromas affect them. It is the same with hearing. It seems as though hearing were in the place where the sound originates, but hearing is in the ear and is the way its substance and form are affected. It is only an appearance that hearing happens at a distance from the ear.

This is true of sight as well. When we see objects at a distance, it seems as though our sight were where they are. However, sight is in the eye, which is the subject; and sight is the way the eye is affected, too. Distance is simply what we infer about space on the basis of intervening objects or on the basis of reduced size and consequent loss of clarity of an object whose image is being presented within the eye according to its angle of incidence. We can see from this that sight does not go out from the eye to the object, but that an image of the object enters the eye and affects its substance and form. It is the same for both sight and hearing. Hearing does not go out of the ear to seize on the sound, but the sound enters the ear and affects it.

It stands to reason, then, that the affecting of substance and form that constitutes a sense is not something separate from the subject. It is simply the effecting of a change within the subject, with the subject remaining the subject throughout and thereafter. It then follows that sight, hearing, smell, taste, and touch are not things that go floating out from their organs. They are the organs themselves, in respect to their substance and form. Sensation happens when they are affected.

42   It is the same with love and wisdom, the only difference being that the substances and forms that are love and wisdom are not visible to our eyes as are the organs of our external senses. Still, no one can deny that those matters of love and wisdom that we call thoughts, perceptions, and feelings are substances and forms. They are not things that go floating out from nothing, remote from any functional and real substance and form that are their subjects. There are in fact countless substances and forms in the brain that serve as the homes of all the inner sensation that involves our discernment and volition.

What has just been said about our external senses points to the conclusion that all our feelings, perceptions, and thoughts in those substances and forms are not something they breathe out; they themselves are functional and substantial subjects. They do not emit anything, but simply undergo changes in response to the things that touch and affect them. There will be more later [§§210, 273] on these things that touch and affect them.

This brings us to the point where we can see that divine love and wisdom in and of themselves are substance and form. They are essential reality and manifestation, and unless they were as much reality and manifestation as they are substance and form, they would be only theoretical constructs that in and of themselves are nothing. **43**

Divine love and wisdom are substance and form in and of themselves, and are therefore wholly "itself" and unique. I have just given evidence that divine love and wisdom is substance and form, and I have also said that the divine reality and its manifestation is reality and manifestation in and of itself. We cannot say that it is reality and manifestation derived from itself, because that would involve a beginning, a beginning from something else that had within it some intrinsic reality and manifestation; while true reality and its manifestation in and of itself exists from eternity. Then too, true reality and manifestation in and of itself is uncreated; and nothing that has been created can exist except from something uncreated. What is created is also finite; and what is finite can arise only from what is infinite. **44**

Anyone who can pursue and grasp inherent reality and its manifestation at all thoughtfully will necessarily come to grasp the fact that it is wholly itself and unique. We call it wholly itself because it alone exists; and we call it unique because it is the source of everything else. **45**

Further, since what is wholly itself and unique is substance and form, it follows that it is the unique substance and form, and wholly itself; and since that true substance and form is divine love and wisdom, it follows that it is the unique love, wholly itself, and the unique wisdom, wholly itself. It is therefore the unique essence, wholly itself, and the unique life, wholly itself, since love and wisdom is life.

All this shows how sensually people are thinking when they say that nature exists in its own right, how reliant they are on their physical senses and their darkness in matters of the spirit. They are thinking from the eye and are unable to think from the understanding. Thinking from the eye closes understanding, but thinking from understanding opens the eye. They are unable to entertain any thought about inherent reality and manifestation, any thought that it is eternal, uncreated, and infinite. They can entertain no thought about life except as something volatile **46** that vanishes into thin air, no other thought about love and wisdom, and no thought whatever about the fact that they are the source of everything in nature.

The only way to see that love and wisdom are the source of everything in nature is to look at nature on the basis of its functions in their sequence and pattern rather than on the basis of some of nature's forms, which register only on our eyes. The only source of nature's functions is life, and the only source of their sequence and pattern is love and wisdom. Forms, though, are vessels of functions. This means that if we look only at forms, no trace is visible of the life in nature, let alone of love and wisdom, and therefore of God.

47 *Divine love and wisdom cannot fail to be and to be manifested in others that it has created.* The hallmark of love is not loving ourselves but loving others and being united to them through love. The hallmark of love is also being loved by others because this is how we are united. Truly, the essence of all love is to be found in union, in the life of love that we call joy, delight, pleasure, sweetness, blessedness, contentment, and happiness.

The essence of love is that what is ours should belong to someone else. Feeling the joy of someone else as joy within ourselves—that is loving. Feeling our joy in others, though, and not theirs in ourselves is not loving. That is loving ourselves, while the former is loving our neighbor. These two kinds of love are exact opposites. True, they both unite us; and it does not seem as though loving what belongs to us, or loving ourselves in the other, is divisive. Yet it is so divisive that to the extent that we love others in this way we later harbor hatred for them. Step by step our union with them dissolves, and the love becomes hatred of corresponding intensity.

48 Can anyone fail to see this who looks into the essential nature of love? What is loving ourselves alone, really, and not loving someone else who loves us in return? This is more fragmentation than union. Love's union depends on mutuality, and there is no mutuality within ourselves alone. If we think there is, it is because we are imagining some mutuality in others.

We can see from this that divine love cannot fail to be and to be manifested in others whom it loves and who love it. If this is characteristic of all love, it must be supremely characteristic, infinitely characteristic, of love itself.

49 In regard to God, loving and being loved in return are not possible in the case of others who have some share of infinity or anything of the essence and life of intrinsic love or of Divinity. If there were within them any share of infinity or anything of the essence and life of intrinsic love—of Divinity, that is—it would not be *others* who would be loving God. He would be loving *himself*. What is infinite or divine is unique. If it were in others, it would still be itself; and it would be pure love for itself, of which there cannot be the slightest trace in God. This is absolutely opposite to the divine essence. For love to be mutual, then, it needs to be a love for others in whom there is nothing of intrinsic Divinity; and we will see below [§§55, 305] that it is a love for others who were created by Divinity.

For this to happen, though, there must be an infinite wisdom that is at one with infinite love. That is, there must be the divine love of divine wisdom and the divine wisdom of divine love discussed above (§§34–39).

On our grasping and knowing this mystery depends our grasping **50** and knowing God's manifestation or creation of everything and God's maintenance or preservation of everything—that is, all the acts of God in the created universe that I will be talking about in the following pages.

Please, though, do not muddle your concepts with time and space. **51** To the extent that there is time and space in your concepts as you read what follows, you will not understand it, because Divinity is not in time and space. This will become clear in the sequel to the present book, specifically on eternity, infinity, and omnipresence.

Everything in the universe was created by the divine love and wisdom of the **52** *Divine-Human One.* The universe, from beginning to end and from first to last, is so full of divine love and wisdom that you could call it divine love and wisdom in an image. This is clearly evidenced by the way everything in the universe answers to something in us. Every single thing that comes to light in the created universe has such an equivalence with every single thing in us that you could call us a kind of universe as well. There is a correspondence of our affective side and its consequent thought with everything in the animal kingdom, a correspondence of our volitional side and its consequent discernment with everything in the plant kingdom, and a correspondence of our outermost life with everything in the mineral kingdom.

This kind of correspondence is not apparent to anyone in our physical world, but it is apparent to observant people in the spiritual world. We find in this latter world all the things that occur in the three kingdoms of our physical world, and they reflect the feelings and thoughts of the people who are there—the feelings that come from their volition and the thoughts that come from their discernment—as well as the outermost aspects of their life. Both their feelings and their thoughts are visible around them looking much like the things we see in the created universe, though we see them in less perfect representations.

From this it is obvious to angels that the created universe is an image depicting the Divine-Human One and that it is his love and wisdom that are presented, in image, in the universe. It is not that the created universe is the Divine-Human One: rather, it comes from him; for nothing whatever in the universe is intrinsic substance and form or intrinsic life or intrinsic love and wisdom. We are not "intrinsic persons." It all comes from God, who is the intrinsic person, the intrinsic wisdom and love, and the intrinsic form and substance. Whatever has intrinsic existence is uncreated and infinite; while what comes from it, possessing nothing within itself that has intrinsic existence, is created and finite. This latter presents an image of the One from whom it derives its existence and manifestation.

53   Created, finite things may be said to have reality and manifestation, substance and form, life, and even love and wisdom, but all of these are created and finite. The reason we can say they have these attributes is not that they possess any divinity but that they are in Divinity and there is Divinity in them. Anything that has been created is intrinsically without soul and dead, but it is given a soul and brought to life by the presence of Divinity in it, and by its dwelling in Divinity.

54   The divine nature is not different in one subject than it is in another. Rather, one created subject is different from another: there are no two alike, so each vessel is different. This is why the divine nature seems to differ in appearance. I will be talking later [§275] about its presence in opposites.

55   *Everything in the created universe is a vessel for the divine love and wisdom of the Divine-Human One.* We acknowledge that everything in the universe, great and small, has been created by God. That is why the universe and absolutely everything in it is called "the work of Jehovah's hands" in the Word.

People do say that the whole world was created out of nothing, and they like to think of "nothing" as absolutely nothing. However, nothing comes from "absolutely nothing" and nothing can. This is an abiding truth. This means that the universe, being an image of God and therefore full of God, could be created by God only in God. God is reality itself, and everything that exists must come from that reality. To speak of creating something that exists from a "nothing" that does not exist is a plain contradiction of terms.

Still, what is created by God in God is not a continuation of him, since God is intrinsic reality and there is no trace of intrinsic reality in anything created. If there were any intrinsic reality in a created being, it would be a continuation of God, and any continuation of God is God.

The angelic concept involved is that anything created by God in God is like something within ourselves that we have put forth from our life, but the life is then withdrawn from it. It then agrees with our life, but still, it is not our life. In support of this, angels cite many things that happen in their heaven, where they say that they are in God and that God is in them, and yet that they have in their being no trace of God that is actually God. This may serve simply as information; more of the angels' evidence will be offered later [§116].

Everything created from this source is in its own nature suited to be **56** receptive of God not by continuity but by contact. Union comes through contact, not through continuity. What is created is suitable for this contact because it has been created by God in God. Because it has been created in this way, it is an analog; and because of the union, it is like an image of God in a mirror.

This is why angels are not angels in their own right but are angels **57** by virtue of their union with the Divine-Human One; and their union depends on their acceptance of what is divinely good and what is divinely true. What is divinely good and what is divinely true are God, and seem to emanate from him even though they are within him. Their acceptance depends on the way angels apply the laws of his design, which are divine truths, to themselves, using their freedom to think and intend according to their reason, a freedom given them by God as their own possession. This is what enables them to accept what is divinely good and divinely true in apparent autonomy; and this in turn is what makes possible the mutual element in their love, for as already noted [§48], love is not real unless it is mutual. It is the same with us here on earth.

All this enables us finally to see that everything in the created universe is a vessel for the divine love and wisdom of the Divine-Human One.

There are many things that need to be said about levels of life and **58** levels of vessels of life before I can give an intelligible explanation of the fact that other things in the universe, things that are not like angels and people, are also vessels for the divine love and wisdom of the

Divine-Human One—for example, things below us in the animal king-dom, things below them in the plant kingdom, and things below them in the mineral kingdom. Union with them depends on their functions. All useful functions have their only source in a related union with God that is, however, increasingly dissimilar depending on its level. As we come down step by step, this union takes on a nature in which there is no element of freedom involved because there is no element of reason. There is therefore no appearance of life involved; but still these are vessels. Because they are vessels, they are also characterized by reaction. It is actually by virtue of their reactions that they are vessels.

I will discuss union with functions that are not useful after I have explained the origin of evil [§§264–270].

59 We can conclude from this that Divinity is present in absolutely every-thing in the created universe and that the created universe is therefore the work of Jehovah's hands, as it says in the Word. That is, it is a work of divine love and wisdom, for this is what is meant by "Jehovah's hands." Further, even though Divinity is present in all things great and small in the created universe, there is no trace of intrinsic divinity in their own being. While the created universe is not God, it is from God; and since it is from God, his image is in it like the image of a person in a mirror. We do indeed see a person there, but there is still nothing of the person in the mirror.

60 I once heard a number of people around me in the spiritual world talking and saying that they did in fact want to recognize that there was something divine in absolutely everything in the universe because they saw God's wonders there, and the deeper they looked, the more wonder-ful were the things they saw. However, when they heard someone say that there actually *was* something divine in absolutely everything in the created universe, they resented it. This was a sign that they claimed the belief but did not actually believe it.

They were therefore asked whether they could not see this simply in the marvelous ability in every seed of generating its growth in sequence all the way to new seeds. In every seed, then, there is an image of some-thing infinite and eternal, an inherent effort to multiply and bear fruit without limit, to eternity.

Or they might see this in even the tiniest animals, realizing that they contain sensory organs, brains, hearts, lungs, and the like, along with arteries, veins, nerve fibers, muscles, and the activities that arise from them, to say nothing of incredible features of their basic nature that have had whole books written about them.

All these wonders come from God, though the forms that clothe them are of earthly matter. These forms give rise to plant life and, in due sequence, to human life. This is why humanity is said to have been created out of the ground, to be the dust of the earth with the breath of life breathed in (Genesis 2:7). We can see from this that the divine nature is not our possession but is joined to us.

All the things that have been created reflect the human in some respect. There **61** is evidence for this in every detail of the animal kingdom, in every detail of the plant kingdom, and in every detail of the mineral kingdom.

We can see ourselves reflected in every detail of the animal kingdom from the fact that all kinds of animal have in common with us members for locomotion, sensory organs, and the inner organs that support these activities. They also have their impulses and desires like our own physical ones. They have the innate knowledge proper to their desires, with an apparently spiritual element visible in some of them, more or less obvious to the eye in the beasts of the earth, the fowl of the heavens, bees, silkworms, ants, and the like. This is why merely earthly-minded people regard the living creatures of this kingdom as much like themselves, lacking only speech.

We can see ourselves reflected in every detail of the plant kingdom in the way plants grow from seeds and go through their successive stages of life. They have something like marriages with births that follow. Their vegetative "soul" is the function to which they give form. There are many other ways in which they reflect us, which some writers have described.

We can see ourselves reflected in every detail of the mineral kingdom simply in its effort to produce the forms that reflect us—all the details of the plant kingdom, as I have just noted—and to perform its proper functions in this way. The moment a seed falls into earth's lap, she nurtures it and from all around offers it resources from herself for its sprouting and emerging in a form representative of humanity. We can see this effort in solid mineral materials if we look at deep-sea corals or at flowers in mines, where they spring from minerals and metals. This effort toward becoming plant life and thereby performing a useful function is the outermost element of Divinity in created things.

Just as there is an energy in earth's minerals toward plant growth, **62** there is an energy in plants toward movement. This is why there are various kinds of insect that are responsive to the fragrances they give off. We will see later [§§157–158] that this is not caused by the warmth of our world's sun but comes through it, from life, according to the recipient vessels.

63   What has been cited thus far tells us that there is some reference to the human form in everything in the created universe, but it enables us to see this fact only obscurely. In the spiritual world, though, people see this clearly. Everything in the three kingdoms exists there as well, surrounding each angel. Angels see these things around themselves and also are aware that they are pictures of their own selves. In fact, when the very heart of their understanding is opened, they recognize themselves and see their own image in their surroundings, almost like a reflection in a mirror.

64   We can be quite certain, on the basis of all this and of many other things consistent with it (which it would take too long to include) that God is a person and that the created universe is an image of him. The overall totality offers a reflection of him, just as specific aspects offer reflections of us.

65   *The useful functions of everything created tend upward, step by step, from the lowest to us, and through us to God the Creator, their source.* As already stated [§52], these "lowest things" are all the elements of the mineral kingdom—various forms of matter, some stony substances, some saline, some oily, some mineral, some metallic, with the constant addition of a humus composed of plant and animal matter reduced to minute particles. Here lie hidden the goal and the beginning of all the functions that arise from life. The goal of all useful functions is the effort to produce [more] functions; the beginning of all functions is an active force that comes out of that effort. These are characteristics of the mineral kingdom.

The intermediate things are all the elements of the plant kingdom—grasses and herbs of all kinds, plants and shrubs of all kinds, and trees of all kinds. Their functions are in support of everything in the animal kingdom, whether flawed or flawless. They provide food, pleasure, and life. They nourish [animal] bodies with their substance, they delight them with their taste and fragrance and beauty, and they enliven their desires. This effort is inherent in them from their life.

The primary things are all the members of the animal kingdom. The lowest of these are called worms and insects, the intermediate ones birds and animals, and the highest humans; for there are lowest, intermediate, and highest things in each kingdom. The lowest are for the service of the intermediate and the intermediate for the service of the highest. So the useful functions of all created things tend upwards in a sequence from the lowest to the human, which is primary in the divine design.

There are three ascending levels in the physical world and three **66** ascending levels in the spiritual world. All animals are life-receivers, the more perfect ones receiving the life of the three levels of the physical world, the less perfect receiving the life of two levels of that world, and the least perfect the life of one level. Only we humans are receptive of the life not only of the three levels of the physical world but also of the three levels of the spiritual world. This is why we, unlike animals, can be lifted up above the physical world. We can think analytically and rationally about civil and moral issues within the material world and also about spiritual and heavenly issues that transcend the material world. We can even be lifted up into wisdom to the point that we see God. I will discuss in their proper place, though, the six levels by which the functions of all created things rise up all the way to God, their Creator.

This brief summary enables us to see that there is a ladder of all created things to that First who alone is life and that the functions of all things are the actual vessels of life, and so too, therefore, are the forms of those functions.

I need also to explain briefly how we climb—or rather, are lifted— **67** from the last level to the first. We are born on the lowest level of the physical world, and are lifted to the second level by means of factual knowledge. Then as we develop our discernment through this knowledge, we are lifted to the third level and become rational. The three ascending levels in the spiritual world are within this, resting on the three physical levels, and do not become visible until we leave our earthly bodies. When we do, the first spiritual level is opened for us, then the second, and finally the third. However, this last happens only for people who become angels of the third heaven. These are the ones who see God.

Angels of the second heaven and of the lowest heaven are people in whom the second and the lowest level can be opened. The opening of each spiritual level within us depends on our acceptance of divine love and wisdom from the Lord. People who accept some of this love and wisdom reach the first or lowest spiritual level; people who accept more reach the second or intermediate spiritual level; and people who accept a great deal reach the third or highest level. However, people who do not accept any divine love and wisdom stay on the physical levels, deriving from the spiritual levels only enough to allow them to think and therefore to talk and to intend and therefore to act—but not intelligently.

68   There is something else that we need to know about this lifting of the inner levels of our minds. Reaction is characteristic of everything created by God. Only life is action, while reaction is prompted by the action of life. This reaction seems to be proper to the created being because it becomes perceptible when that being is stirred; so when it happens in us, it seems to be our own. The reason is that even though we are only life-receivers, we have no sense that our life is anything but our own.

This is why we react against God as a result of our inherited evil. However, to the extent that we believe that all our life comes from God and that everything good about it comes from an act of God and everything bad about it from our own reaction, our reaction becomes a property of the action and we are then acting with God with apparent autonomy. The equilibrium of all things comes from action and immediate reaction, and everything must necessarily be in an equilibrium.

I mention these things to prevent any belief that we ourselves climb up to God on our own power. It is done by the Lord.

69   *Divinity fills all space in the universe nonspatially.* Nature has two basic properties: space and time. In this physical world, we use them to form the concepts of our thinking and therefore the way we understand things. If we stay engaged with them and do not raise our minds above them, there is no way we can grasp anything spiritual and divine. We entangle such matters in concepts drawn from space and time, and to the extent that we do, the light of our discernment becomes merely earthly. When we use this light to think logically about spiritual and divine matters, it is like using the dark of night to figure out things that can be seen only in the light of day. Materialism comes from this kind of thinking.

However, when we know how to raise our minds above images of thought derived from space and time, we pass from darkness into light and taste things spiritual and divine. Eventually we see what is inherent in them and what they entail; and then we dispel the darkness of earthly lighting with that [new] light and dismiss its illusions from the center to the sides.

People who possess discernment can think on a higher level than these properties of nature—can think realistically, that is—and see with assurance that Divinity, being omnipresent, is not within space. They can also see with assurance the other things already mentioned. If they deny divine omnipresence, though, and attribute everything to nature, then they do not want to be lifted up even though they could be.

These two properties of nature—the space and time just mentioned— **70** are left behind by everyone who dies and becomes an angel. At that time, people come into a spiritual light in which the objects of their thought are truths, and the objects of their vision—even though those objects look like things in this physical world—are actually responsive to their thoughts.

The objects of their thought, which as just noted are truths, are not at all dependent on space and time. While the objects of their sight do seem to be in space and in time, angels do not use them as the basis for their thinking. The reason is that in the spiritual world intervals of space and time are not fixed the way they are in our physical world, but are changeable in response to their states of life. This means that states of life take the place of space and time in the concepts of their thinking. Issues related to states of love are in place of spatial intervals and issues related to states of wisdom are in place of temporal intervals. This is why spiritual thought and the consequent spiritual speech are so different from earthly thought and its speech that they have nothing in common. They are alike only as to the deeper aspects of their subject matter, which are entirely spiritual. I need to say more about this difference later [§§163, 295, and 306].

Since angels' thoughts do not depend at all on space and time, then, but on states of life, we can see that angels do not understand when someone says that Divinity fills space. They do not know what spatial intervals are. They understand perfectly, though, when someone says that Divinity fills everything, with no reference to any image of space.

The following example should illustrate how merely earthly people **71** think in spatial terms about matters spiritual and divine, while spiritual people do so without reference to space. When merely earthly people think, they use images they have garnered from things they have seen. There is some shape to all of these involving length, breadth, and height, some angular or curved form bounded by these dimensions. These dimensions are clearly present in the mental images people have of visible, earthly things; and they are present as well in their mental images of things they do not see, such as civic and moral matters. They do not actually see these dimensions, but they are still present implicitly.

It is different for spiritual people, and especially for heaven's angels. Their thinking has nothing to do with form and shape involving spatial length, breadth, and height. It has to do with the state of the matter as it follows from a state of life. This means that in place of length they consider how good something is as a result of the quality of the life from which it stems; in place of breadth they consider how true something is because of the truth of the life from which it stems; and in place of height they consider the level of these qualities. They are thinking on the basis of correspondence, then, which is the mutual relationship between spiritual and earthly things. It is because of this correspondence that "length" in the Word means how good something is, "breadth" means how true it is, and "height" means the level of these qualities.

We can see from this that the only way heaven's angels can think about divine omnipresence is that Divinity fills everything, but nonspatially. Whatever angels think is true, because the light that illumines their understanding is divine wisdom.

72   This is a foundational thought about God, since without it, while readers may understand what I am going to say about the creation of the universe by the Divine-Human One and about God's providence, omnipotence, omnipresence, and omniscience, they still will not retain it. This is because even when merely earthly people do understand these things, they still slip back into the love of their life that is their basic volition. This dissipates their previous thought and plunges their thinking into space, where they find the light that they call "rational." They do not realize that to the extent that they deny what they have understood, they become irrational.

You may confirm the truth of this by looking at the concept of the truth that God is human. Please read carefully what I wrote above in §§11–13 and thereafter, and you will understand that it is true. Then bring your thoughts back into the earthly lighting that involves space. Will these things not seem paradoxical to you? And if you bring your thoughts all the way back, you will deny them.

This is why I said that Divinity fills all space in the universe and did not say that the Divine-Human One does. If I were to say this, merely earthly light would not accept it, though it can accept the notion that Divinity fills all space because this agrees with the standard language of theologians. They say that God is omnipresent, and hears and knows everything. There is more on this subject in §§7–10 above.

73   *Divinity is in all time, nontemporally.* Just as Divinity is in all space nonspatially, it is in all time nontemporally. Nothing proper to the physical world can be attributed to Divinity, and space and time are proper to the physical world. Space in the physical world can be measured, and so can time. Time is measured in days, weeks, months, years, and centuries; days are measured in hours; weeks and months in days; years in the four seasons; and centuries in years. The physical world gets these measurements from the apparent circuit and rotation of earth's sun.

It is different in the spiritual world. Life does seem to go on in time there in much the same way. People live with each other the way we do on earth, which cannot happen without some appearance of time. However, time there is not divided into segments the way it is in our world because their sun is always in its east. It never moves. It is actually the Lord's divine love that angels see as their sun. This means that they do not have days, weeks, months, years, or centuries, but states of life instead. It provides them with divisions that cannot be called divisions into time segments, only divisions of state. This is why angels do not know what time is, and why they think of state when time is mentioned. Further, when it is state that determines time, time is only an appearance. A pleasant state makes time seem brief, and an unpleasant one makes it seem long. We can therefore see that time in the spiritual world is simply an attribute of state.

This is why hours, days, weeks, months, and years in the Word mean states and their sequences, viewed either serially or comprehensively. When the church is described in terms of time, its morning is its initial state, its noon is its fulfillment, its evening is its decline, and its night is its end. The same holds true for the four seasons of the year: spring, summer, fall, and winter.

We can see from this that time is the equivalent of thought from feeling. This is in fact the source of our basic quality as people. **74**

There are many examples of the fact that as people move through space in the spiritual world, distances are equivalent to progress through time. Paths there are actually or correspondingly lengthened, in response to eagerness, which is a matter of thought from affection. This is also why we speak of "stretches of time." In other situations, though, such as in dreams, where thought is not coordinated with our actual feelings, time is not in evidence.

Now, since the segments of time that are proper to nature in its world are nothing but states in the spiritual world, and since these states come to view sequentially because angels and spirits are finite, it stands to reason that they are not sequential in God, because God is infinite. The infinite things in God are all one, in keeping with what has been **75** explained above in §§17–22. It then follows from this that Divinity is present in all time, nontemporally.

76 If people do not know about God beyond time, if they cannot think about such a God with some insight, then they are totally incapable of seeing eternity as anything but an eternity of time. They cannot help getting caught in crazy thoughts about God from eternity, thinking about some beginning; and a beginning has to do with nothing but time. This leads to the fantasy that God emerged from himself, and promptly degenerates into nature originating from itself. The only way out of this notion is through a spiritual or angelic concept of eternity, one that does not involve time. Once time is excluded, eternity and Divinity are one and the same; Divinity is Divinity in and of itself, and not from itself. Angels say that while they can conceive of God from eternity, there is no way they can conceive of nature from eternity, let alone nature from itself; by no means whatever can they conceive of nature that is intrinsically nature. This is because anything that has intrinsic existence is the reality itself that is the source of everything else. That intrinsic reality is the "life itself" that is the divine love that belongs to divine wisdom and the divine wisdom that belongs to divine love.

This, for angels, is eternity, which transcends time the way the Uncreated transcends the creature or the Infinite one transcends the finite. There is no ratio whatever between them.

77 *Divinity is the same in the largest and smallest things.* This follows from the two preceding sections, from Divinity being nonspatially present in all space and nontemporally present in all time. There are larger and larger and smaller and smaller spaces; and since as already noted [§74] space and time are indistinguishable, the same holds true for segments of time. The reason Divinity is the same in all of them is that Divinity is not changeable or inconsistent like everything that involves space and time, or nature. It is constant and unchanging, so it is everywhere and always the same.

78 It does seem as though Divinity were not the same in one person as in another, as though it were different in a wise person than in a simple one, for example, or different in an elderly one than in a child. This is just the deceptive way things seem, though. The person may be different, but Divinity within is not. The person is a receiver, and the receiver or vessel will differ. A wise person is a more adequate receiver of divine love and wisdom than a simple one, and therefore a fuller receiver. An elderly and wise individual is more receptive than a child or youth. Still, Divinity is the same in the one as in the other.

Outward appearance also gives rise to the illusion that Divinity is different in heaven's angels than it is in people on earth because heaven's angels enjoy indescribable wisdom and we do not. However, this apparent difference is in the subjects and depends on their openness to Divinity. It is not in the Lord.

We may also use heaven and an individual angel to illustrate the fact that Divinity is the same in the largest and smallest things. Divinity in the whole heaven and Divinity in an individual angel is the same. This is why all heaven can be seen as a single angel.   **79**

The same holds true for the church and for the individual member of it. The largest entity in which Divinity is present is all of heaven and the whole church together; the smallest is an individual angel or an individual member of the church. On occasion I have seen a whole heavenly community as a single angelic person, and I have been told that this may look like an immense, gigantic individual or like a little, childlike one. This is because Divinity is the same in the largest and smallest things.

Divinity is also the same in the largest and smallest of inanimate created things. It is actually present in every benefit of the function that they serve. The reason they are not alive is that they are forms of functions rather than forms of life, and the form will vary depending on the benefit of the function. I will be explaining how Divinity is present in them later, when we get to the subject of creation.   **80**

Take away space and absolutely rule out vacuum, and then think about divine love and wisdom as ultimate essence once space has been taken away and vacuum has been ruled out. Then think in terms of space, and you will see that Divinity is the same in the largest and the smallest instances of space. Once you remove space from essence, there is no "large" or "small." It is all the same.   **81**

I need to say something about vacuum at this point. I once heard some angels talking with Newton about vacuum, saying that they could not stand the notion of vacuum. This was because in their world, which is a spiritual one, within or above the space and time of our earthly world, they were still feeling, thinking, being moved, loving, intending, and breathing, and still talking and acting, which could not possibly happen in a vacuum that was "nothing" because nothing is nothing, and we cannot attribute anything to nothing.   **82**

Newton said he knew that Divinity, the One who is, fills everything, and that he was aghast at the notion of a vacuum as nothing because this was a totally destructive notion. He urged the angels who were discussing vacuum with him to beware the notion of nothing, calling it a fantasy because there is no mental activity in nothing.

ANGELIC WISDOM
ABOUT
DIVINE LOVE

PART 2

IN the spiritual world, divine love and wisdom look like a sun. There are **83** two worlds, one spiritual and one physical; and the spiritual world does not derive anything from the physical one, nor does the physical one derive anything from the spiritual one. They are completely distinct from each other, communicating only by means of correspondence, whose nature has been amply explained elsewhere. The following example may be enlightening. Warmth in the physical world is the equivalent of the good that thoughtfulness does in the spiritual world, and light in the physical world is the equivalent of the truth that faith perceives in the spiritual world. No one can fail to see that warmth and the goodness of being thoughtful, and light and the truth of faith, are completely distinct from each other.

At first glance, they seem as distinct as two quite different things. That is what comes to the fore when we start thinking about what the goodness of being thoughtful has in common with warmth and what the truth of faith has in common with light. Yet spiritual warmth is that very "goodness," and spiritual light is that very "truth."

In spite of the fact that they are so distinct from each other, though, they still make a single whole by means of their correspondence. They are so united that when we read about warmth and light in the Word, the spirits and angels who are with us see thoughtfulness in the place of warmth and faith in the place of light.

I include this example to make it clear that the two worlds, the spiritual one and the physical one, are so distinct from each other that they have nothing in common, and that still they have been created in such a way that they communicate with each other and are actually united through their correspondences.

84 Because these two worlds are so distinct from each other, it is quite obvious that the spiritual world is under a different sun than is the physical world. There is just as much warmth and light in the spiritual world as there is in the physical world, but the warmth there is spiritual and so is the light. Spiritual warmth is the good that thoughtfulness does and spiritual light is the truth that faith perceives.

Now, since the only possible source of warmth and light is a sun, it stands to reason that there is a different sun in the spiritual world than there is in the physical world. It also stands to reason that because of the essential nature of the spiritual world's sun, spiritual warmth and light can come forth from it, while because of the essential nature of the physical world's sun, physical warmth [and light] can come forth from it. The only possible source of anything spiritual—that is, anything that has to do with what is good and true—is divine love and wisdom. Everything good is a result of love and everything true is a result of wisdom. Any wise individual can see that this is their only possible source.

85 People have not realized before that there is another sun besides the sun of our physical world. This is because our spiritual nature has become so deeply involved in our physical nature that people do not know what the word "spiritual" means. So they do not realize that there is a spiritual world other than and different from this physical one, a world where angels and spirits live.

Because that spiritual world has become so completely hidden from people in this physical world, the Lord has graciously opened the sight of my spirit so that I can see things in that world just the way I see things in this physical world, and then provide descriptions of that spiritual world. This I have done in the book *Heaven and Hell,* which has a chapter on the sun of the spiritual world. I have in fact seen it, and it seemed about the same size as the sun of this physical world. It had a similar fiery look, but was more reddish. I was given to understand that the whole angelic heaven lies beneath this sun and that angels of the third heaven see it constantly, angels of the second heaven often, and angels of the first or most remote heaven occasionally.

It will be made clear in what follows that all their warmth and all their light—everything people see in that world—comes from that sun.

That sun is not the Lord himself, though it is from the Lord. What **86** looks like the sun in the spiritual world is the emanating divine love and wisdom. Since love and wisdom are one in the Lord (see part 1), we say that this sun is divine love. Divine wisdom is actually an attribute of divine love, so it too is love.

The reason that sun looks like fire to angels' eyes is that love and fire **87** are interactive. Angels cannot see love with their eyes, but instead of love they see what answers to it. They have inner and outer natures just as we do. It is their inner self that thinks and is wise, that intends and loves, and their outer self that feels, sees, speaks, and acts. All these outer functions of theirs are responsive to the inner ones, but the responsiveness is spiritual and not earthly.

To spiritual beings, divine love feels like fire. This is why fire means love when it is mentioned in the Word. That is what "sacred fire" used to mean in the Israelite church, and that is why we often ask in our prayers to God that heavenly fire (meaning divine love) should kindle our hearts.

Since there is the kind of distinction described in §83 between what **88** is spiritual and what is physical, not a trace of anything from the sun of the physical world can cross over into the spiritual world—that is, not a trace of its light and warmth or of any object on earth. The light of the physical world is darkness there, and its warmth is death there. Still, our world's warmth can be brought to life by an inflow of heaven's warmth, and our world's light can be brightened by an inflow of heaven's light. This inflow happens by means of correspondences, and cannot happen as a result of continuity.

Warmth and light emanates from the sun that arises from divine love and **89** *wisdom.* In the spiritual world where angels and spirits live, there is just as much warmth and light as there is in the physical world where we live. The warmth feels just like warmth and the light looks just like light, as well. Still, the warmth and light of the spiritual world and the warmth and light of the physical world are so different that they have nothing in common, as I have already mentioned [§83]. They are as different as life and death. The warmth of the spiritual world is essentially alive, and so is the light; while the warmth of the physical world is essentially dead, and so is the light. The warmth and the light of the spiritual world come from a sun that is nothing but love, while the warmth and light of the physical world come from a sun that is nothing but fire. Love is alive, and divine love is life itself. Fire is dead, and solar fire is death itself. We may call it that because it has absolutely no life in it.

90   Since angels are spiritual beings, they cannot live in any warmth or any light that is not spiritual. We, on the other hand, cannot live in any warmth or any light that is not physical. This is because what is spiritual suits what is spiritual, and what is physical suits what is physical. If angels were to depend on physical warmth and light to even the least extent, they would be destroyed. It is absolutely wrong for their life.

Each of us is a spirit, as far as the inner levels of our minds are concerned. When we die, we leave this world of nature completely behind. We give up everything it has to offer and enter a world that contains nothing proper to the world of nature. In that world we live so completely distanced from nature that there is no communication along a continuum, that is, nothing like degrees of purity or coarseness. It is a case of before and after, with no communication except by correspondences.

It stands to reason, then, that spiritual warmth is not a purer form of physical warmth, that spiritual light is not a purer form of physical light, but that they are completely different in essence. Spiritual warmth and light derive their essence from a sun that is nothing but love, a sun that is life itself, while physical warmth and light derive their essence from a sun that is nothing but fire, containing no life whatever, as I have already stated [§89].

91   Given this kind of difference between the warmth and light of the two worlds, it is obvious why people who live in one of the worlds cannot see people who are living in the other. Our eyes, which see in physical light, are made of substances of their own world, and angels' are made of substances of their world. In other words, in each case they are designed for adequate sensitivity to their own light.

We can see from this what ignorance underlies the thinking of people who exclude from their faith any notion that angels and spirits are people, simply because they do not see them with their own eyes.

92   It has not been known before that angels and spirits are in a completely different light and warmth than we are. It has not even been known that there was a different light and warmth. Human thought has not penetrated beyond the deeper or purer aspects of nature. As a result, many people have located the dwellings of angels and spirits in the ether or even in the stars—within nature, that is, and not above or beyond it. In fact, though, angels and spirits are wholly above or beyond nature. They are in their own world, one that is under a different sun. Further,

since spatial intervals are only apparent in that world, as I have explained earlier [§7], we cannot say that they are in the ether or in the stars. They are right with us, united to our own spirits in feeling and thought. Each of us is a spirit. That is the source of our thinking and intending. This means that the spiritual world is right where we are, not distanced from us in the least. In short, as far as the deeper levels of our minds are concerned we are all in that world, surrounded by angels and spirits there. We think because of the light of that world and love because of its warmth.

That sun is not God. Rather, it is an emanation from the divine love and wisdom of the Divine-Human One. The same is true of warmth and light from that sun. "The sun that angels see" (the sun that gives them warmth and light) does not mean the Lord himself. It means that first emanation from him that is the highest form of spiritual warmth. The highest form of spiritual warmth is spiritual fire, which is divine love and wisdom in its first correspondential form. This is why that sun looks fiery and also is fiery for angels, though it is not for us. What we experience as fire is not spiritual but physical, and the difference between these two is like the difference between life and death. The spiritual sun, then, brings spiritual people to life with its warmth and maintains spiritual things, while the physical sun does the same for physical people and things. It does not do this with its own power, though, but by an inflow of spiritual warmth that provides it with effective resources. **93**

The spiritual fire where light dwells in its origin becomes a spiritual warmth and light that decrease as they emanate, with the decrease occurring by levels that will be discussed later. The ancients pictured this as brightly gleaming circles of reddish fire around the head of God, a form of representation that is still common today when God is portrayed as human in paintings. **94**

It is obvious from actual experience that love generates warmth and wisdom generates light. When we feel love, we become warmer, and when we think from wisdom, it is like seeing things in the light. We can see from this that the first thing that emanates from love is warmth and that the first thing that emanates from wisdom is light. **95**

We can also see that these are correspondences, since the warmth does not occur within the love itself but as a result of it, in our volition and therefore in our bodies. The light does not occur within the wisdom, but in the thinking of our discernment and therefore in our speaking. That is, love and wisdom are the essence and life of warmth and light;

and warmth and light are emanations from love and wisdom. Because they are emanations from them, they are also responsive to them.

96 If you observe carefully the thoughts of your own mind, you can recognize that there is a spiritual light completely distinct from physical light. When a mind is thinking, it sees its objects in light, and people who think spiritually see truths as readily at midnight as in daytime. This is why we attribute light to our discernment and talk about "seeing." One person may hear what someone else says and say, "I see that this is true," meaning "I understand." Since this understanding is spiritual, it cannot see by physical light. Physical light does not last, but departs with the sun. We can see from this that our discernment enjoys a light other than that of our eyes, and that this light comes from a different source.

97 Take care not to think that the spiritual world's sun is actually God. The real God is a person. The first emanation from his love and wisdom is something fiery and spiritual that looks like a sun to angels. When the Lord makes himself visible to angels in person, then, he does so in human form, sometimes within the sun, sometimes outside it.

98 It is because of this correspondence that in the Word the Lord is called not only the sun but also fire and light. "The sun" refers to him as divine love and wisdom together; "the fire" refers to him as divine love, and "the light" refers to him as divine wisdom.

99 *The spiritual warmth and light that result from the emanation from the Lord as the sun form a single whole just as his divine love and wisdom do.* Part 1 explains how divine love and wisdom form a single whole in the Lord. Warmth and light form a similar whole because they are emanations, and emanations constitute a whole by reason of their correspondence. The warmth answers to love, and the light to wisdom.

It therefore follows that since divine love is the divine reality and divine wisdom is the divine manifestation (see §§14–16 above), spiritual warmth is Divinity emanating from the divine reality and spiritual light is Divinity emanating from the divine manifestation. This means that just as divine love is a property of divine wisdom and divine wisdom is a property of divine love because of this union (see §§34–39 above), spiritual warmth is a property of spiritual light and spiritual light is a property of spiritual warmth. As a result of this kind of oneness, it follows that warmth and light are a single whole as they emanate from the Lord as the sun.

We will see later, though [§125], that they are not accepted as a single whole by angels or by us.

The warmth and light that emanate from the Lord as the sun are **100** what we call "spiritual"; and they are referred to as spiritual in the singular because they are a single whole. In the following pages, therefore, when it says "spiritual" it will mean both as a single whole. It is because of this spiritual [energy] that the whole other world is called "spiritual." Everything in that world has its source in that spiritual [energy] and takes its name from it as well.

The reason the warmth and light are called "spiritual" is that God is called "the Spirit," and God as the Spirit is that emanation. As to his very essence, God is called Jehovah; but he enlightens and gives life to heaven's angels and to us of the church through that emanation. This is why it is said that giving life and bringing about enlightenment are acts performed by the spirit of Jehovah.

The oneness of [spiritual] warmth and light (that is, of the spiritual **101** [energy] that emanates from the Lord as the sun) can be illustrated by the warmth and light that emanate from the sun of our physical world. These "two" are also a single whole as they radiate from the sun. The reason they are not a single whole on earth is to be found in the earth itself, not in the sun. The earth rotates daily on its axis and follows its annual ecliptic orbit. This is why its warmth and light do not seem to be a single whole, why there is more warmth than light in midsummer and more light than warmth in midwinter. The same thing happens in the spiritual world. While the earth there does not rotate or follow an orbit, angels do turn more and less toward the Lord. The ones who turn more toward him accept more of the warmth and less of the light; while the ones who turn less toward the Lord accept more of the light and less of the warmth. This is why the heavens, which are made up of angels, are marked off into two kingdoms, one called "heavenly" and the other called "spiritual." Heavenly angels accept more of the warmth and spiritual angels accept more of the light.

The regions where angels live also look different depending on their acceptance of the warmth and light. The correspondence is exact, provided we think of angels' change of state instead of earthly motion.

We will see later [§124] that in their own right, all the spiritual phe- **102** nomena that stem from the warmth and light of their sun constitute a single whole in the same way, though they do not do so if we regard them as coming from the feelings that angels have. When the warmth and light are a single whole in the heavens, it is like springtime for angels. When they are not a single whole, it is like either summer or winter—not like winter in cold latitudes but like winter in warm latitudes. The essence of angelic nature is a balanced acceptance of love and wisdom, so angels are angels of heaven depending on the oneness of their love and wisdom. The same holds true for us of the church, if our love and wisdom, or charity and faith, are fully united.

103 *The sun of the spiritual world is seen at a middle elevation, as far from angels as our physical world's sun is from us.* Many people bring with them from our world an image of God as high overhead and of the Lord as being in heaven among its angels. The reason they bring an image of God as high overhead is that God is called "most high" in the Word, and it says that he lives "on high." This is why we lift up our eyes and our hands when we pray and worship, unaware that "highest" means "inmost."

The reason people bring along an image of the Lord as being in heaven among its angels is that they think of him only as being like any other individual, or like an angel. They do not realize that the Lord is the real and only God, the one who rules the universe. If he were living in heaven among the angels, he could not keep the universe under his sight and hold it in his care and keeping. If he were not shining like the sun on the people in the spiritual world, angels could not have any light. Angels, that is, are spiritual beings, so only spiritual light is suited to their essence. When I discuss levels later [§182], we will see that there is a light in the heavens that is far, far greater than our light on earth.

104 As for the sun that is the source of angels' warmth and light, they see it at about a forty-five degree angle above the lands where they live, at a middle elevation. It also seems to be about as far from angels as this world's sun is from us.

They see the sun at that height and distance constantly; it does not move. This is why angels do not have stretches of time marked off into days and years or any daily progression from morning through noon to evening and on into night. They do not have a yearly sequence from spring through summer to autumn and on into winter, either. Instead, they have a constant daylight and constant springtime; which means that instead of "times" they have states, as already noted [§§70, 73].

105 The following are the primary reasons why the sun of the spiritual world is seen at a middle elevation. First, this means that the warmth and light that emanate from that sun are at their median level—they are of equal proportions, therefore, and appropriately moderate. That is, if the sun appeared above that middle elevation, angels would perceive more warmth than light, while if it appeared lower, they would perceive more light than warmth, as happens on earth when the sun is above or below the middle of the sky. When it is above, the warmth increases more than the light; and when it is below, the light increases more than the warmth. The light actually stays the same in summer and winter, but the warmth increases or decreases depending on the degree of the sun's height.

A second reason that the spiritual world's sun appears at a middle height above the angelic heaven is that this results in a constant springtime for all the angelic heavens. Consequently, angels are in a state of peace, for this state corresponds to springtime on earth.

A third reason is that it enables angels to turn their faces toward the Lord constantly and to see him with their eyes. For angels, the east—and therefore the Lord—is in front of them no matter which way they turn their bodies, which is a unique feature of their world. This would not happen if the sun of their world were above or below middle height, and it would be absolutely impossible if it were directly overhead.

If the spiritual world's sun did not seem to be as far from angels as the physical world's sun is from us, the whole angelic heaven, the hell underneath it, and our globe of lands and seas below them could not be under the Lord's watchful guidance, omnipresence, omniscience, omnipotence, and providence. In the same way, if our world's sun were not at the distance from the earth where we see it to be, it could not be present and effective with its warmth and light in all our lands, so it could not provide its subsidiary resources to the spiritual world's sun. **106**

It is of critical importance to realize that there are two suns, a spiritual one and a physical one, the spiritual sun for people who are in the spiritual world and the physical sun for people who are in the physical world. Unless this is recognized, there can be no real comprehension of creation or of humanity, subjects we are about to deal with. True, some effects can be seen, but unless the causes behind the effects are seen at the same time, it is like looking at the effects in the night. **107**

The distance between the sun and angels in the spiritual world is an apparent distance that depends on their acceptance of divine love and wisdom. All the illusions that are prevalent among evil people and simple people come from appearances that have been taken as facts. As long as appearances remain appearances, they are virtual truths, and it is all right for anyone to think and talk in terms of them. However, when they are taken to be actual truths, which happens when they are defended as facts, then the virtual truths become falsities and fallacies. **108**

For example, it seems as though the sun travels around the earth every day and also follows its yearly ecliptic path. As long as this is not taken as fact, this is a virtual truth, and anyone may think and talk in such terms. We can say that the sun rises and sets, causing morning, noon, evening, and night. We can say that the sun is at this or that point on the ecliptic, or at this or that elevation, causing spring, summer, autumn, and winter. However, when these appearances are defended as the real truth, then the person who defends them is thinking and speaking falsity based on illusion.

The same holds true for countless other appearances, not only in earthly, civic, and moral matters, but also in spiritual ones.

109 It is the same with the distance of the spiritual world's sun, the sun that is the first emanation of the Lord's divine love and wisdom. The truth is that there is no distance. Rather, the distance is an appearance that depends on angels' acceptance of divine love and wisdom on their own level. It makes sense that distances in the spiritual world are appearances when we consider what has been presented already, like the material in §§7–9 *[7–10]* on Divinity not being in space and in §§69–72 on Divinity filling all space nonspatially. If there are no segments of space, then there are no distances either; or in other words, if segments of space are appearances, so are distances, since distances are a matter of space.

110 The reason the spiritual world's sun appears at a distance from angels is that they accept divine love and wisdom at an appropriate level of warmth and light. Since angels are created and finite, they cannot accept the Lord at the prime level of warmth and light, as it is in the sun. That would mean being totally consumed; so they accept the Lord at the level of warmth and light that matches their own love and wisdom.

The following may serve to illustrate. Angels of the lowest heaven cannot rise up to angels of the third heaven. If they were to rise up and enter their heaven, they would collapse in a kind of faint, as though their life were struggling against death. This is because their love and wisdom is at a lower level, and so is the warmth of their love and the light of their wisdom. What would happen, then, if an angel were to rise up toward the sun and enter its fire?

As a result of the differences in angels' acceptance of the Lord, the heavens appear to be marked off from each other. The highest heaven, called the third heaven, seems to be over the second, and the second over the first. It is not that the heavens *are* distant from each other, but that they seem to be. In fact, the Lord is just as present with people in the most remote heaven as he is with people in the third heaven. What causes the appearance of distance is in the subjects, the angels, and not in the Lord.

It is almost impossible to grasp this in any earthly image, since that **111** would involve space. It can be grasped in a spiritual image, though, since there is no space involved. That is the kind of image angels have.

This much can be grasped in an earthly image, though—love and wisdom, or in other words the Lord who is divine love and wisdom, cannot move through space but is with every one of us depending on our acceptance. The Lord teaches in Matthew 28:20 that he is with everyone; and in John 14:21 [14:23] he says that he makes his home with those who love him.

This may seem like a matter of higher wisdom since it is being sup- **112** ported by reference to heavens and angels. However, the same holds true for us. As far as the deeper levels of our minds are concerned, we are warmed and enlightened by that same sun, warmed by its warmth and enlightened by its light, to the extent that we accept love and wisdom from the Lord. The difference between angels and us is that angels are under that [spiritual] sun only, while we are not only under that sun but also under the sun of our world. Our bodies could not take form and endure if they were not under both suns. It is different for angels' bodies because they are spiritual.

Angels are in the Lord and the Lord is in them; and since angels are vessels, **113** *the Lord alone is heaven.* Heaven is called God's dwelling and God's throne, so people think that God lives there like a monarch in a realm. However, God—that is, the Lord—is in the sun above the heavens and is in the heavens by means of his presence in warmth and light, as I have explained in the last two sections. Further, even though the Lord is present in heaven in this apparently distant way, he is still also intrinsically present there, so to speak, since as I have just explained in §§103–112 the distance between the sun and heaven is not a distance but a virtual distance. Given the fact that this distance is only apparent, then, it follows that the Lord himself is in heaven. He is in the love and wisdom of heaven's angels; and since he is in the love and wisdom of all the angels and the angels make up heaven, he is in all of heaven.

The reason the Lord is not only *in* heaven but actually *is* heaven itself **114** is that love and wisdom make an angel, and these two are properties of the Lord in the angels. It therefore follows that the Lord is heaven.

Angels are not angels because of anything that belongs to them. What belongs to them is just like what belongs to us—evil. The reason this is what belongs to angels is that all angels were once earthly people, and this attribute clings to them from their birth. It is simply moved aside, and to the extent that it is, they accept love and wisdom, or the Lord, into themselves.

With a little elevation of understanding, everyone can see that it is quite impossible for the Lord to dwell with angels in anything but what is his, that is, what belongs to him, which is love and wisdom. He cannot dwell in anything that belongs to the angels, which is evil. This is why the Lord is in them, and they are angels, to the extent that evil is moved aside. The actual angelic essence of heaven is divine love and wisdom. This divine reality is called "angelic" when it is in angels; so again we can see that angels are angels because of the Lord and not on their own. The same therefore holds true for heaven as well.

115 Still, there is no understanding how the Lord is in an angel and an angel is in the Lord except through knowing what kind of union is involved. It is a union of the Lord with the angel and of the angel with the Lord, so it is a reciprocal union. On the angel's side, it is like this. Angels, like us, simply feel as though they participate in love and wisdom on their own, and therefore that love and wisdom are theirs, their very own. If they did not feel this way there would be no union, so the Lord would not be in them, nor they in the Lord. It cannot happen that the Lord is in any angels or people unless they, as subjects of his presence in love and wisdom, sense and feel this as their own. This enables them not only to accept but also to retain what they have accepted, and to love in response. This, then, is how angels become wise and remain wise. Can people decide to love God and their neighbor, can people decide to gain wisdom, unless they feel and sense that what they love, learn, and gain is their own? Can they retain anything in themselves otherwise? If it were not for this, then the inflowing love and wisdom would have no seat. They would flow right through without making any difference; and as a result angels would not be angels and people would not be human. They would be virtually lifeless.

It makes sense, then, that if there is to be union, there must be reciprocity.

116 However, this calls for an explanation of how angels can feel and sense this as their own and so accept and retain it when in fact it is not theirs, given the statement that angels are not angels on their own but by virtue of what is within them from the Lord. The essence of the matter is this. There is freedom and rationality in every angel. These two qualities are there so that angels can be open to love and wisdom from the Lord. Neither of these, though—neither the freedom nor the rationality—belongs to the angels. They are in them but belong to the Lord. However, since these two elements are intimately united to angels' life, so intimately united that you could call them linked to their life, it seems as though they belong to the angels. Freedom and rationality enable them to think and intend and to speak and act; and what they think, intend, speak, and act as a result seems to be done on their own. This gives rise to the reciprocal element that is the means to union.

Still, the more that angels believe that love and wisdom are within them and claim them for themselves as their own, the more there is nothing angelic within them. To the same extent, then, there is no union with the Lord for them. They are outside the truth; and since truth is identical with heaven's light, they are correspondingly unable to be in heaven. This leads to a denial that they live from the Lord and a belief that they live on their own and therefore that they possess some divine essence. The life called angelic and human consists of these two elements—freedom and rationality.

This leads to the conclusion that angels have a reciprocal ability for the sake of their union with the Lord, but that the reciprocal element, seen as an ability, is the Lord's and not theirs. As a result, angels fall from angelhood if they abuse this reciprocal element that enables them to feel and sense what is the Lord's as their own by actually claiming it for themselves. The Lord himself teaches us in John 14:20–24 and 15:4, 5, 6 that union is reciprocal, and in John 15:7 that the Lord's union with us and ours with him occurs in things that belong to him, things called "his words."

117 There are people who think that Adam had a kind of freedom or ability to choose that enabled him to love God and be wise on his own, and that this freedom to choose was lost in his descendants. This, however, is wrong. We are not life, but life-receivers (see §§4–6 and 54–60 [55–60] above); and people who are life-receivers cannot love and be wise from their own resources. So when Adam wanted to love and be wise from his own resources, he fell from wisdom and love and was cast out of the garden.

118 We can say much the same about the heaven that is made up of angels as we have said about individual angels, since Divinity is the same in the largest and smallest things (see §§77–82 above). What we have said about angels and heaven needs to be said about us and the church as well, since angels of heaven and we of the church act in consort because of our union. Further, as to the inner reaches of our minds, we of the church are angels—but "we of the church" means people who have the church within themselves.

119 *The east in the spiritual world is where the Lord is seen as the sun, and the other directions follow from that.* Now that I have discussed the spiritual world's sun and its essence, its warmth and light, and the Lord's consequent presence, I need to talk as well about the regions of that world. The reason for talking about the sun and that world is that our subject is God, and love and wisdom. To discuss these apart from their *origin* would be to start from effects and not from their causes. Yet effects teach us nothing but effects. When only they are highlighted, they do not show us any cause; rather, causes show us effects. Knowing about effects on the basis of their cause is being wise, but exploring causes on the basis of their effects is not being wise; because when we do, various illusions present themselves that we as investigators identify as causes. To do this is to make foolishness of wisdom. Causes precede and effects follow. We cannot see preceding things from following things, but we can see following things from preceding things. That is the pattern.

This is why we are dealing with the spiritual world first here. That world is where all the causes are. Later [§§134, 154] we will discuss the physical world, where everything we see is an effect.

120 At this point, then, we need to discuss the regions in the spiritual world. There are regions there just as there are in the physical world; but the regions of the spiritual world, like that world itself, are spiritual, while the regions of the physical world, like this world itself, are physical. This means that they are so different that they have nothing in common.

There are four regions in each world, called the east, the west, the south, and the north. In the physical world, these four regions are static, determined by the sun in the south. The north is behind, with the east on one side and the west on the other. These regions are determined by the south wherever you go, since the sun's position at noon is always the same and therefore static.

It is different in the spiritual world. There the regions are determined by the sun, which always appears in its own place; and where it appears is the east. So the assignment of regions in that world is not from the south as it is in the physical world but from the east. The west is behind, with the south on one side and the north on the other. We will see below, however, that the regions are not caused by its sun but by the inhabitants of that world, the angels and spirits.

Since these regions are spiritual because of their source (the Lord as 121
the sun), the places where angels and spirits live are spiritual as well, since
the places all depend on these regions. The places are spiritual because
their locations depend on the angels' acceptance of love and wisdom
from the Lord. People who are at a higher level of love live in the east,
while people who are at a lower level of love live in the west. People who
are at a higher level of wisdom live in the south, while people who are at
a lower level of wisdom live in the north.

This is why "the east" in the Word, in its highest sense, means the
Lord, while in a secondary sense it means a love for him, while "the west"
means a waning love for him. "The south" means wisdom in the light
and "the north" wisdom beclouded. There are some variations of these
meanings as they relate to the state of the people under discussion.

Since the east is the basis on which all the regions in the spiritual 122
world are laid out, and since the east in the highest sense means the Lord
and divine love, we can see that the Lord and love for him is the source of
everything. We can also see that to the extent that people do not share in
that love, they are far from him and live either in the west or in the south
or in the north, with the distance depending on their openness to love.

Since the Lord as the sun is always in the east, early people—for 123
whom all the elements of worship were symbolic of spiritual realities—
faced the east when they worshiped. Further, to be sure that they did this
in all their rituals, they faced their temples in the same direction. This is
the reason churches are built in the same way at present.

The regions in the spiritual world are not caused by the Lord as the sun but 124
by the angels, depending on their receptivity. I have stated that angels live in
distinct regions, some in the east, some in the west, some in the south,
and some in the north. I have also stated that the ones who live in the
east are engaged in a higher level of love, those in the west in a lower level
of love, those in the south in the light of wisdom, and those in the north
in the shadow of wisdom.

This variation of place seems to be caused by the Lord as the sun, yet
it is actually caused by the angels. The Lord is not at a greater or lesser
degree of love and wisdom; as the sun, he is not at a greater or lesser level
of warmth and light for one person than for another. He is everywhere
the same. However, he is not accepted at the same level by one person
as by another, and this makes it seem as though they are more or less
distant from each other, in a variety of regions. It follows from this that
the regions in the spiritual world are simply variations in the receptivity

of love and wisdom and therefore of the warmth and light of the Lord as the sun. If you look at what was explained in §§108–112 about distances in the spiritual world being apparent only, you will see that this is true.

125   Since the regions are variations in the way angels accept love and wisdom, I need to say something about the variety that gives rise to the appearance.

As I explained in the preceding section, the Lord is in each angel, and each angel is in the Lord. However, since it looks as though the Lord as the sun were outside angels, it also looks as though the Lord is seeing them from the sun and that they are seeing the Lord in the sun. This is much like seeing an image in a mirror. So if we talk on the basis of the way things seem, that is how it is. The Lord sees and examines angels face to face, but angels do not see the Lord in the same way. When they are engaged in the love for him that comes from him, they do see him straight ahead, so they are in the east or the west. When they are more engaged in wisdom, though, they see the Lord off to the right, and when they are less engaged in wisdom they see him off to the left, so they are in the north or the south.

The reason they have an oblique view is that love and wisdom emanate from the Lord as a single whole, but they are not accepted that way by angels, as I have already noted [§99]. Any wisdom that goes beyond love may look like wisdom, but it is not, since there is no life from love in that excess wisdom.

We can see from this where the differences in receptivity come from, the differences that cause the appearance that angels live in the different regions in the spiritual world.

126   It makes sense that a particular openness to love and wisdom establishes a region in the spiritual world, given the fact that angels change their location in response to any increase or decrease of love in them. We can see from this that the location is not caused by the Lord as the sun but by angels, according to their receptivity.

The same holds true for us as far as our spirits are concerned. In spirit, each of us is in some particular region of the spiritual world no matter where we may be in the physical world. That is, the regions of the spiritual world have nothing in common with those of the physical world, as already stated [§120]. We are in the one as to body and in the other as to spirit.

127   For love and wisdom to be a single whole in angels and in us, there are pairs throughout our bodies. Our eyes, ears, and nostrils are paired, our hands, sides, and feet are paired, our brains are divided into two hemispheres, our heart into two chambers, our lungs into two lobes, and so on. So for both angels and for us there is a right side and a left side; and all the right side parts have to do with the love that gives rise to wisdom, while all the left side parts have to do with the wisdom of that love. We could also say, which amounts to the same thing, that all the right side parts have to do with the good that gives rise to the true and all the left side parts with what is true because of that goodness.

Both we and angels have these pairs so that love and wisdom, or what is good and what is true, may act in unison and focus on the Lord in unison—but there will be more on this later [§§384, 409].

We can see from this how caught up in illusion and consequent distortion people are if they think that the Lord parcels heaven out arbitrarily, or arbitrarily enables one person to be wiser and more loving than another. No, the Lord intends that one person should be just as wise and just as saved as another. He offers all of us the means. To the extent that we accept them and live by them, we are wise and we are saved, because the Lord is the same with one person as with another. The receivers, though, the angels and the people on earth, are different because of their differing receptivity and life. **128**

This fits with what has already been said [§124] about the regions and about the way angels' locations depend on them, namely that the differences stem from the recipients and not from the Lord.

Angels always face the Lord as the sun, so south is on their right, north on their left, and west behind them. All these statements about angels and the way they face the Lord as the sun should also be understood as applying to us spiritually, since we are spirits as to our minds, and angels if we are engaged in love and wisdom. So after death, when we shed the outer forms we have derived from the physical world, we become spirits or angels. Since angels do constantly face the sunrise (the Lord), we say of people who are engaged in love and wisdom from the Lord that they see God, that they look to God, and that they have God before their eyes, meaning that they are living like angels. We say these things in this world both because that is what is really happening in heaven and because that is what is actually happening in our spirits. Do we not all look straight ahead at God when we pray, no matter which way we are facing? **129**

The reason angels constantly face the Lord as the sun is that angels are in the Lord and the Lord is in them. The Lord exercises an inner guidance of their feelings and thoughts and constantly turns them toward **130** himself. This means that they cannot help but look toward the east where they see the Lord as the sun. We can see from this that angels do not turn themselves toward the Lord—the Lord turns them toward himself. When angels are thinking about the Lord inwardly, they think of him simply as in themselves. This deeper thought itself does not create any distance, while more outward thought does, the thought that acts in unison with eyesight. The reason is that the outward thought is in space, while the inward thought is not, though even when it is not in space (as in the spiritual world) it is still in an appearance of space.

It is hard for people to understand this, though, if they think spatially about God. God is actually everywhere and yet not in space. So he is both within and outside angels, which enables them to see him both inside and outside themselves—inside themselves when they are thinking from love and wisdom, and outside themselves when they are thinking about love and wisdom. This topic will be discussed in greater detail, though, in works on the Lord's omnipotence, omniscience, and omnipresence.

Everyone should beware not to slip into the terrible heresy that God pours himself into us and is in us and no longer in himself. God is everywhere, within us and outside us, being in all space nonspatially, as I have already explained in §§7–10 and 69–72. That is, if he were in us he would be not only divided up but enclosed in space, and we could then even think that we were God. This heresy is so loathsome that in the spiritual world it stinks like a corpse.

131 Angels' turning toward the Lord is like this: no matter which way they turn their bodies, they are looking at the Lord as the sun in front of themselves. Angels can turn this way and that and can thus see the various things that surround them, but still the Lord as the sun seems to be constantly in front of them.

This may seem remarkable, but it is the truth. I too have been allowed to see the Lord as the sun like this. I have been seeing him in front of me for a number of years; whatever direction I turned to, I saw him like this.

132 Since the Lord as the sun and therefore the east is in front of all heaven's angels, it follows that the south is to their right, the north to their left, and the west behind them, again no matter which way they turn their bodies. That is, all the regions in the spiritual world are based on the east, as already stated [§120]. This means that people who have the east before their eyes are in those very regions and actually set their boundaries; since, as I have just explained in §§124–128, the regions are not caused by the Lord as the sun but by the angels, according to their receptivity.

Now, since heaven is made up of angels, and since this is what angels **133** are like, it follows that the whole heaven faces the Lord and that because it does, heaven is governed by the Lord as though it were a single individual—which is what heaven looks like in the Lord's sight. On heaven looking like a single individual in the Lord's sight, see *Heaven and Hell* 59–87 *[59–86]*. This is the cause of heaven's regions as well.

Since these regions are virtually written on each angel and on all of **134** heaven, angels, unlike us in our world, know their homes and houses no matter where they travel. The reason we do not know our homes and houses instinctively, from their regions, is that we are thinking in terms of space and therefore in terms of this physical world's geography, which has nothing in common with the geography of the spiritual world.

However, birds and animals have this kind of knowledge by instinct. They know their homes and dwellings instinctively, as much experience testifies. This is a clue to the nature of the spiritual world, since everything that happens in the physical world is an effect and everything that happens in the spiritual world is a cause of such effects. Nothing happens in nature that does not have its cause in the spiritual realm.

Everything in the deeper reaches of angels' minds and bodies alike is turned **135** *toward the Lord as the sun.* Angels have discernment and volition, and they have faces and bodies. Further, there are deeper levels of discernment and volition and deeper contents of their faces and bodies. The deeper levels of their discernment and volition are activities of their deeper feeling and thought. The deeper contents of their faces are their brains, and the contents of their bodies are their viscera, headed by heart and lungs. In a word, angels have everything we on earth have. This is what makes them human. An outward form apart from these inner elements would not make them human; only an outward form with its inner elements and even constituted by them would do so. Otherwise they would be only images of people with no life in them because there was no form of life within.

It is recognized that volition and discernment control the body com-**136** pletely. The mouth says what discernment thinks and the body does what volition intends. We can see from this that the body is a form responsive to discernment and volition. Further, since we attribute form to discernment and volition, we can say that the body's form is responsive to the form of discernment and volition. This is not the place, however, to describe the nature of either form. There are countless components in each, and those countless components act in unison in each because they are responsive to each other. This is why the mind (or volition and discernment) controls the body completely, just as though it were controlling itself.

It follows from this that the deeper levels of the mind act in unison with the deeper levels of the body, and that the outer levels of the mind act in unison with the outer levels of the body. I need to discuss the deeper levels of the mind later, when we deal first with levels of life, and then in the same vein with the deeper levels of the body [§§236–241 and 277–281].

137 Given the fact that the deeper levels of the mind act in unison with the deeper levels of the body, it follows that when the deeper levels of the mind turn toward the Lord as the sun, the deeper levels of the body do the same. Further, since the outer levels of both body and mind depend on their inner levels, they behave in the same way. The outer does what it does at the prompting of the inner, since a collective body derives its whole nature from its specific components. We can see from this that because an angel is turning face and body toward the Lord as the sun, the inner levels of that angel's mind and body have been turned in that direction as well.

It is the same with us. If we constantly keep the Lord before our eyes (which happens if we are engaged in love and wisdom), then it is not only our eyes and face that turn to him, it is our whole mind and our whole heart. That is, it is everything in our intention and mind and everything in our body at the same time.

138 This turning toward the Lord is an active turning—it is a kind of lifting up. We are actually lifted into heaven's warmth and light, and this is accomplished by an opening of our inner reaches. When these have been opened, love and wisdom flow into the deeper reaches of our minds and heaven's warmth and light flow into the deeper reaches of our bodies. This results in a lifting, as though we were brought out of the mist into clear air, or out of the air into the ether. Further, love and wisdom, together with their warmth and light, are the Lord with us, the Lord who, as already noted [§130], turns us toward himself.

The opposite holds for people who are not engaged in love and wisdom, and all the more for people who resist love and wisdom. The deeper reaches of their minds and bodies alike are closed; and when they are closed, then their outer natures resist the Lord because this is their inherent nature. This is why such people turn away from the Lord, and this "turning away" is a turning toward hell.

139 This active turning toward the Lord comes from love and wisdom together, not from love alone or wisdom alone. Love alone is like a reality with no manifestation, since love makes itself manifest in wisdom; and wisdom without love is like a manifestation with no reality, since wisdom is the manifestation of love.

There is actually a kind of love apart from wisdom, but it is ours and not the Lord's. There is also wisdom apart from love, but while it comes from the Lord, it does not have the Lord within it. It is like sunlight in winter that does of course come from the sun but does not have within it the essence of the sun, its warmth.

Every kind of spirit turns toward her or his ruling love in the same way. **140** First I need to define "angel" and "spirit." Immediately after death we come into a world of spirits that is halfway between heaven and hell. There we work through our stretches of time, or our states, and are prepared either for heaven or for hell, depending on the way we have lived. As long as we stay in this world, we are called "spirits." Anyone who has been brought up from this world into heaven is called an angel, and anyone who has been cast into hell is called a satan or a devil. As long as we are in the world of spirits, people who are being readied for heaven are called angelic spirits, and people who are being readied for hell are called hellish spirits. All the while, angelic spirits are united to heaven and hellish spirits to hell.

All the spirits who are in the world of spirits are together with us because we are similarly between heaven and hell as to the deeper levels of our minds. Through these spirits we are in touch with either heaven or hell, depending on the way we are living.

It should be clear that "the world of spirits" is not the same thing as "the spiritual world." The world of spirits is the one I have just been talking about, while the spiritual world includes that world, heaven, and hell.

Something also needs to be said about loves, since we are talking **141** about how angels and spirits turn toward their loves because of their loves.

Heaven as a whole is laid out in communities depending on all the differences in loves. So is hell, and so is the world of spirits. Heaven, though, is laid out in communities according to differences in heavenly loves, while hell is laid out in communities according to differences in hellish loves, and the world of spirits is laid out in communities according to differences in both heavenly and hellish loves.

There are two loves that are at the head of all the rest, and two loves that lie behind all the rest. The head of all heavenly loves, the love basic to them all, is love for the Lord. The head of all hellish loves, or the love that underlies them all, is a love of controlling prompted by self-love. These two loves are absolute opposites.

Since these two loves—love for the Lord and love of controlling **142** prompted by self-love—are absolute opposites, and since everyone who is caught up in love for the Lord turns toward the Lord as the sun, as explained in the preceding section, it stands to reason that everyone who is caught up in a love of controlling prompted by self-love turns away from the Lord. The reason people turn in opposite directions is that those who are caught up in love for the Lord love being led by the Lord more than anything else, and want the Lord alone to be in control. In contrast, if people are caught up in a love of controlling prompted by self-love, there is nothing they love more than leading themselves. They want to be the *only* ones who are in control.

The reason we refer to "a love of controlling prompted by self-love" is that there is a love of controlling out of a love of service. Since this love acts in unison with love for our neighbor, it is a spiritual love. In fact, it cannot truly be called a love of being in control: it should be called a love of service.

143 The reason spirits of all kinds turn toward their ruling loves is that for all of us, love is life (as explained in §§1–3 of part 1), and life turns its vessels, called members, organs, and viscera—the whole person, therefore—toward the particular community that is engaged in a similar love, the community where our own love is.

144 Since a love of controlling prompted by self-love is the absolute opposite of love for the Lord, spirits caught up in this love of controlling turn away from the Lord. So their eyes are looking toward that world's west; and since their bodies are turned around, the east is behind them, the north is on their right, and the south is on their left. The east is behind them because they harbor a hatred of the Lord; the north is on their right because they love illusions and the consequent distortions; and the south is on their left because they have no use for the light of wisdom. They can turn this way and that, but still everything they see around themselves looks like their love.

They all are oriented toward outward nature and their senses. They are the kind of people who think they are the only ones who are really alive and who see others as unreal. They think they themselves are wiser than anyone else, even though they are insane.

145 In the spiritual world, you can see roads laid out like roads in our physical world. Some of them lead to heaven and some to hell. The roads that lead to hell are not visible to people who are going to heaven, and the roads that lead to heaven are not visible to people who are going to hell. There are more such roads than you can count, roads leading to each heavenly community and to each hellish community. Each individual spirit sets out on the road that leads to the community of his or her own love and does not even see the roads that lead in other directions. As a result, when spirits turn toward their ruling love, they also travel.

The divine love and wisdom that emanate from the Lord as the sun and con- **146**
stitute heaven's warmth and light is the emanating Divinity that is the Holy
Spirit. I explained in *Teachings for the New Jerusalem on the Lord* that
God is one in both person and essence, consisting of a trinity, and that
this God is the Lord. I also explained that his trinity is called Father,
Son, and Holy Spirit. Divinity as source is the Father, Divinity as human
is the Son, and Divinity as emanating is the Holy Spirit.

We say "Divinity as emanating," and yet no one knows why we say
"emanating." The reason for this ignorance is that people have not known
before that the Lord looks like a sun to angels and that from that sun there
issues a warmth that is essentially divine love and a light that is essentially
divine wisdom. As long as this remains unknown, people cannot help
"knowing" that Divinity as emanating is intrinsic Divinity because it says
in the Athanasian doctrine of the Trinity that the Father is one Person,
the Son another, and the Holy Spirit another. Now that we know that the
Lord looks like a sun, though, we can have an appropriate image of the
"Divinity as emanating" that is called the Holy Spirit. We can realize that
while it is one with the Lord, it emanates from him the way warmth and
light emanate from the sun. This is also why angels are in divine warmth
and light to the extent that they are caught up in love and wisdom.

Without this recognition that the Lord looks like a sun in the spiritual world and that his Divinity emanates from him in this way, there is
no way for anyone to know what "emanating" means—whether it means
simply sharing what belongs to the Father and the Son or simply enlightening and teaching. However, it does not come from enlightened reason
if we acknowledge the Holy Spirit as intrinsic Divinity, call it "God,"
and draw boundaries around it when we know as well that God is both
one and omnipresent.

I explained above [§126] that God is not in space and is therefore **147**
omnipresent and that Divinity is everywhere the same, but that there is
an apparent variation of divinity in angels and in us because of our differences in receptivity. Since divinity as emanating from the Lord as the
sun takes place in light and warmth, then, and since light and warmth
flow first of all into those universal vessels that are called "atmospheres"
in our world, and since these are what contain clouds, it stands to reason
that the way the deeper levels of angels' minds, or of our own, are veiled

by such clouds determines how open we are to Divinity as emanating. By these "clouds," I mean spiritual clouds. These are thoughts that are in harmony with divine wisdom if they are based on true perceptions and that disagree if they consist of false ones. So when they are represented visually in the spiritual world, thoughts based on true perceptions look like bright clouds and thoughts based on false perceptions look like black clouds.

We may therefore conclude that Divinity as emanating is actually within all of us, but that it is variously veiled by us.

148 Since Divinity itself is present with angels and with us through its spiritual warmth and light, we look at people who are caught up in the truth of divine wisdom and the goodness of divine love, who are moved by them, and who are therefore in heartfelt thought, and we say that they are being "warmed by God." Sometimes this happens so openly that it can be noticed and felt, as when a preacher speaks with passion. We also say of such people that they are being "enlightened by God" because with his emanating divinity, the Lord not only kindles human intentions with spiritual warmth but also floods human minds with spiritual light.

149 We can see from the following passages in the Word that the Holy Spirit is the same as the Lord and is the very truth that is the source of our enlightenment. "Jesus said, 'When the spirit of truth has come, he will lead you into all truth. He will not speak on his own, but will say what he has heard'" (John 16:13). "He will glorify me because he will receive from me and will proclaim to you" (John 16:14, 15). He will be with the disciples and in them (John 15:26 *[14:17]*). "Jesus said, 'The things I am telling you are spirit and life'" (John 6:63). We can see from these passages that the very truth that emanates from the Lord is called the Holy Spirit, which enlightens us because it is in the light.

150 While the enlightenment attributed to the Holy Spirit actually comes from the Lord, it happens through the agency of spirits and angels. I cannot yet describe what kind of agency it is, but can say only that in no way can angels and spirits enlighten us on their own because they, like us, are enlightened by the Lord. Since they are enlightened in this same way, it follows that all enlightenment is from the Lord alone. It happens through angels and spirits because when we are receiving enlightenment we are surrounded by the angels and spirits who are receiving more enlightenment than others from the Lord alone.

151 *The Lord created the universe and everything in it by means of that sun that is the first emanation of divine love and wisdom.* "The Lord" means God from eternity or Jehovah, who is called the Father and the Creator, because as explained in *Teachings for the New Jerusalem on the Lord,* the Lord and the Father are one. When I return to the topic of creation below [§§282–357], therefore, I will refer to "the Lord."

I gave ample evidence in part 1 that everything in the universe was created by divine love and wisdom (see particularly §§52–53 *[52–54]*). The point here is that this was done by means of the sun that is the first emanation of divine love and wisdom.

No one who can see how effects follow from causes and how causes lead to effects in due order and sequence can deny that the sun is the beginning of creation. Everything in our world is sustained by it, and because everything is sustained by it, everything arose from it—the one fact follows from the other and bears witness to it. Everything, that is, is watched over by the sun because the sun has determined its being, and the act of watching over it is an ongoing determination of that thing's being. This is why we say that being sustained is a constant coming into being. If anything were totally removed from the inflow of the sun through our atmospheres, it would instantly dissipate. It is the atmospheres with their different degrees of purity, empowered by the sun, that hold everything together. Since the universe and everything in it is sustained by the sun, then, we can see that the sun is the beginning of creation, the source.

We say "by the sun" but we mean "by the Lord through the sun," since the sun too was created by the Lord.

There are two suns by means of which the Lord created everything, the sun of the spiritual world and the sun of the physical world. The Lord created everything by means of the spiritual world's sun, but not by means of the physical world's sun, since this latter sun is far beneath the former one. It is at a midpoint, with the spiritual world above it and the physical world below it. The physical world's sun was created to play a supporting role, a role that will be discussed below [§157].

The reason the Lord created the universe and everything in it by means of the spiritual world's sun is that this sun is the first emanation of divine love and wisdom, and as explained above (§§52–82), everything comes from divine love and wisdom.

There are three components of everything that has been created, no matter how large or small it is: a purpose, a means, and a result. There is nothing created that lacks these three components. In the largest instance, the universe, these three components arise in the following pattern: the purpose of everything is in that sun that is the first emanation of

152

153

154

divine love and wisdom; the means of everything is in the spiritual world; and the result of everything is in the physical world. I will describe below [§§167–172] how these three components occur in both first and last forms.

Since there is nothing created that lacks these three components, it follows that the universe and everything in it has been created by the Lord by means of the sun where the purpose of everything resides.

155 Creation itself cannot be described intelligibly unless you banish space and time from your thoughts; but it can be understood if you banish them. If you can, or to the extent that you can, banish them and keep your mind on an image that is devoid of space and time. If you do, you will notice that there is no difference between the largest expanse and the smallest, and you will inevitably have the same image of the creation of the universe and of the creation of any particular feature of the universe. You will see that the diversity in created things arises from the fact that there are infinite things in the Divine-Human One and therefore unlimited things in that sun that is the first emanation from him, and those unlimited things emerge in the created universe as their reflections, so to speak. This is why there cannot be one thing identical to another anywhere. This is the cause of that variety of all things that meet our eyes in the context of space in this physical world, and in the appearance of space in the spiritual world. The variety is characteristic of both aggregates and details.

I presented the following points in part 1: Infinite things are distinguishably one in the Divine-Human One (§§17–22); everything in the universe was created by divine love and wisdom (§§52–53 *[52–54]*); everything in the created universe is a vessel for the divine love and wisdom of the Divine-Human One (§§54–60 *[55–60]*); Divinity is not in space (§§7–10); Divinity fills all space nonspatially (§§69–72); and Divinity is the same in the largest and smallest things (§§77–82).

156 We cannot say that the creation of the universe and everything in it happened from one place to another or from one moment in time to another, that is, gradually and sequentially. We must say that it happened from eternity and from infinity, and not from an eternity of time, since there is no such thing, but from a nontemporal eternity that is the same as Divinity, and not from an infinity of space, since there is no such thing, but from a nonspatial infinity that is also the same as Divinity.

I know that all this transcends any mental images that arise in physical light, but they do not transcend mental images that arise in spiritual light. There is no trace of space and time in these latter images. Actually, this does not completely transcend images that arise in physical light, since everyone would agree on the basis of reason that there is no such thing as an infinity of space. The same holds for eternity, which is an infinity of time. If you say "to eternity," this can be understood in temporal terms; but if you say "from eternity," that is incomprehensible unless you banish time.

The physical world's sun is nothing but fire and is therefore dead; and since **157** *nature has its origin in that sun, nature is dead.* In no respect whatever can creation itself be attributed to the physical world's sun: it is due entirely to the spiritual world's sun. This is because the physical world's sun is totally lifeless, while the spiritual world's sun is alive, being the first emanation of divine love and wisdom. Anything that is lifeless does not effect anything on its own, but is activated; so to attribute any aspect of creation to a lifeless sun would be to attribute the work of an artisan to the tool in the artisan's hand.

The physical world's sun is nothing but fire, with all its life removed. The spiritual world's sun is a fire that has divine life within it.

The angelic concept of the fire of the physical world's sun and the fire of the spiritual world's sun is like this: divine life is internal to the fire of the spiritual world's sun and external to the fire of the physical world's sun. We can see from this that the activity of our physical sun is not autonomous but stems from a living force that emanates from the spiritual world's sun. Consequently, if the living force of that sun were withdrawn or removed, our sun would fail. This is why the worship of the sun is the lowest of all forms of worship of God. It is just as dead as the sun itself; so in the Word it is called an abomination.

Since the physical world's sun is nothing but fire and is therefore life- **158** less, the warmth that emanates from it is also lifeless, and so is the emanating light. By the same token, the atmospheres called ether and air that receive this sun's warmth and light and bring them down into our embrace are lifeless as well. Since all these are lifeless, absolutely all the earthly things beneath them called soils are lifeless. However, they are all surrounded by spiritual realities that emanate and flow out from the spiritual world's sun. If they were not surrounded in this way, soils could not be activated to bring forth the forms of use called plants and the forms of life called animals, and they could not provide the substances that enable us to come into being and to survive.

Now since nature begins from this sun, and since everything that arises **159** from it and is sustained by it is called "natural," it follows that nature and absolutely everything in it is dead. Nature seems to be alive in us and in animals because of the life that visits it and animates it.

160 Since the lowest elements of nature that constitute our soils are dead and not varied and changeable in response to our states of feeling and thought the way they are in the spiritual world, but are unchangeable and stable, we have space and various spatial distances here. They have this stable nature because this is where creation comes to a close and remains at rest. We can see from this that space is proper to nature; and since space here is not an appearance of space responsive to states of life, the way it is in the spiritual world, we can refer to it as "dead."

161 Since times are similarly stable and constant, they too are proper to nature. The length of a day is always twenty-four hours and the length of a year is always three hundred and sixty-five days. The actual states of light, darkness, warmth, and cold that make these differences are constantly returning as well. The states that return every day are morning, noon, evening, and night; the states of the year are spring, summer, fall, and winter. Then too, the states of the year are constantly altering the states of the days. All of these states, since they are not states of life like the ones in the spiritual world, are lifeless. That is, in the spiritual world there is a constant light and a constant warmth. The light is responsive to the state of wisdom among the angels, and the warmth to the state of their love. As a result, these states are alive.

162 From this we can see the folly of people who attribute everything to nature. If we decide in nature's favor, we adopt a state in which we no longer want to raise our minds above nature. So our minds are closed upward and open downward, and we become focused on nature and our senses—spiritually dead. Further, since all we can think about is based on the kind of information we get through our physical senses, or from the world through those senses, at heart we deny God.

The result is a union with hell because our union with heaven has been broken. All we have left is the ability to think and intend—the ability to think coming from our rationality and the ability to intend coming from our freedom, two abilities the Lord gives every one of us and never takes away. Demons and angels alike have these abilities, but demons use them for madness and malice, while angels use them for wisdom and good.

163 *There would be no creation if it were not for this pair of suns, one living and one dead.* Generally speaking, the universe is divided into two worlds, a spiritual one and a physical one. Angels and spirits are in the spiritual world, and we are in the physical world. These two worlds are exactly alike in outward appearance, so much alike that there is no way to tell them apart; but as to inner appearance, they are completely different. The very people who are in the spiritual world (who are called angels and spirits, as I have just said) are spiritual beings; and since they are spiritual beings, they think spiritually and talk spiritually. On the other hand, we who are in the physical world are physical, so we think physically and talk physically. Spiritual thought and speech and physical thought and speech have nothing in common. We can see from this that the two worlds, the spiritual one and the physical one, are completely distinct from each other, so much so that there is no way for them to be in the same place.

Since these two worlds are so distinct, then, it is necessary that there **164** be two suns, one the source of everything spiritual and the other the source of everything physical. Further, since everything spiritual is alive in origin and everything physical is dead in origin, and the suns are the origins, it follows that the one sun is alive and the other dead, and that the sun that is actually dead was created by the Lord by means of the sun that is living.

The reason for the creation of the dead sun is so that in final forms **165** everything may be set and stable and lasting, so that it can give rise to things that last through the years. This is the only way creation can have a foundation. Our globe of lands and seas, with things like this in and on and around it, is like a solid base, since it is the final work in which everything comes to a close, on which everything rests. I will discuss later [§171] how it is also a kind of matrix from which are produced the effects that are the goals of creation.

As evidence that everything was created by the Lord by means of the **166** living sun and nothing by means of the dead sun, there is the fact that what is living arranges what is dead as it pleases. It shapes it for the forms of service that are its goals. The process does not happen the other way around.

Only someone deprived of reason can think that everything comes from nature, that it is even the source of life. People like this do not know what life is. Nature cannot arrange life for anything. In its own right, nature is completely lifeless. It is totally contrary to the design for something dead to activate something living, for a dead force to activate a living one, or—which amounts to the same thing—for something physical to activate something spiritual. Thinking along such lines is therefore contrary to the light of sound reason.

True, something dead or physical can be distorted or changed in many ways by external impingements, but it still cannot activate life. Rather, life activates it according to any change of form that has been imposed on it. The same holds for any physical inflow into the spiritual workings of the soul. We realize that this does not happen because it cannot happen.

167 *The goal of creation—that everything should return to the Creator and that there should be a union—becomes manifest in outermost forms.* First of all, I need to say something about "ends." There are three, which follow in sequence: They are called the first end, the mediate end, and the final end; and they are also called the purpose, the means, and the result. These three must all be present in anything in order for it to be something, since no first end occurs without an intermediate end and a final one at the same time. This is the same as saying that no purpose occurs apart from its means and result, or no means by itself, without a purpose as its source and a result that contains it, or no result by itself without a means and a purpose.

You can see the truth of this if you consider that a purpose apart from its result or separated from its result is nothing that in fact comes into being, so it is nothing but a word. For a purpose effectively to be a purpose, that is, it must be defined, and it finds its definition in its result. That is where it is first called a purpose, because this is its purpose. It looks as though the active or effective element arose spontaneously, but this is an appearance caused by the fact that it is in its result. If it is separated from its result, though, it promptly dissipates.

We can therefore see that this trio of purpose, means, and result needs to be in every entity if it is to be anything.

168 We also need to realize that the purpose is the sum and substance of the means and also the sum and substance of the result. This is why we call the purpose, the means, and the result the first, intermediate, and final ends. For the purpose to be the sum and substance of the means, though, there needs to be something from the purpose in which it exists; and for it to be the sum and substance of the result there must be something from the purpose through the means in which it exists. A purpose cannot exist in itself alone, but must exist in something that takes place because of it, something in which it can dwell with its total being, something which it can accomplish by its effort as long as it lasts. The reality in which it "lasts" is that final end that is called its result.

Throughout the created universe, in its largest and smallest instances **169** alike, we find these three—purpose, means, and result. The reason we find them in the largest and smallest instances of the created universe is that these three are in God the Creator, who is the Lord from eternity. Since he is infinite, though, and since in one who is infinite there are infinite things in a distinguishable oneness (as explained in §§17–22 above), these three are a distinguishable oneness in him and in the infinite things that belong to him. This is why the universe, being created from his reality and (if we look at its functions) being an image of him, retains these three in each of its constituent details.

The grand purpose, or the purpose of all elements of creation, is an **170** eternal union of the Creator with the created universe. This does not happen unless there are subjects in which his divinity can be at home, so to speak, subjects in which it can dwell and abide. For these subjects to be his dwellings and homes they must be receptive of his love and wisdom apparently of their own accord, subjects who will with apparent autonomy raise themselves toward the Creator and unite themselves with him. In the absence of this reciprocity, there is no union.

We are those subjects, people who can raise themselves and unite with apparent autonomy. I have already explained several times [§§4–6, 57, 68, 116] that we are subjects of this sort and that we are receptive of Divinity with apparent autonomy.

Through this union, the Lord is present in every work he has created, since in the last analysis everything has been created for our sake. As a result, the functions of all created things rise level by level from the lowest things to us, and through us to God the Creator, their source, as explained in §§65–68 above.

Creation is constantly pressing toward this final goal by means of this **171** trio of purpose, means, and result, because these three elements are in God the Creator, as just stated. Further, Divinity is in all space nonspatially (§§69–72) and is the same in the largest and smallest things (§§77–82). We can see from this that the entire creation, in its general tending toward its final goal, is the intermediate end, relatively speaking. God the Creator is constantly drawing up out of the earth forms of service in their sequence, a sequence that culminates in us, who are from the earth as far as our bodies are concerned. By accepting love and wisdom from the Lord, we are then raised up and furnished with all the means for the acceptance of love and wisdom. Moreover, we are so created that we can accept them if we are only willing to.

What has now been said enables us to see, if only in a general way so far, that the goal of creation becomes manifest in final things, the goal being the return of all things to their Creator, and union.

172   The presence of this trio of purpose, means, and result in absolutely everything created is evidenced also by the fact that all the results that we call final goals become fresh new goals in an endless series, from the First, who is the Lord the Creator, to the last, which is our union with him. We can see that all final goals become fresh new goals from the fact that there is nothing so lifeless and dead that it has no trace of effectiveness in it. Even from sand there breathes something that provides a resource for accomplishing something, and therefore for having some effect.

ANGELIC WISDOM
ABOUT
DIVINE LOVE

PART 3

◆(❀)◆❀◆(❀)◆❀◆(❀)◆❀◆(❀)◆❀◆(❀)◆❀◆(❀)◆❀◆(❀)◆❀◆(❀)◆❀◆(❀)◆

THERE are atmospheres, liquids, and solids in the spiritual world just as **173** *there are in the physical world, but they are spiritual, while ours are physical.* I have already noted (and in the book *Heaven and Hell* illustrated) the fact that the spiritual world and the physical world are similar to each other, the only difference being that every single thing in the spiritual world is spiritual and every single thing in the physical world is physical. Because these two worlds are similar to each other, there are atmospheres, liquids, and solids in each. These are the general elements that provide the means and substances for all the infinite variety of phenomena that arise.

As for the atmospheres that we refer to as "ethers" and "airs," there **174** are similar forms in each world, the spiritual and the physical, the difference being that in the spiritual world they are spiritual, while in the physical world they are physical. They are spiritual because they come from a sun that is the first emanation of the Lord's divine love and wisdom and accept into themselves the divine fire from him that is love and the divine light from him that is wisdom, bringing each down to the heavens where angels live. They bring about the presence of that sun in everything there, from the largest things to the smallest.

The spiritual atmospheres are distinct substances or elemental forms that arise from the sun. Since they accept the sun individually, the sun's fire becomes a warmth that is ultimately adapted to the love of angels in heaven and spirits under heaven by being separated into a corresponding number of substances, enfolded in them, and tempered by being enfolded. The same holds true for the sun's light.

In this respect, our physical atmospheres are like the spiritual ones. They too are distinct substances and elemental forms, arising from the physical world's sun. They too accept the sun individually and conceal its fire within themselves, temper it, and bring it down as warmth to earth where we are; and the same holds true for light.

175 The difference between spiritual atmospheres and physical atmospheres is that spiritual atmospheres are vessels of divine fire and light, of love and wisdom, then. They bear these things within themselves. Physical atmospheres, though, are not vessels of divine fire and light; they are vessels of the fire and light of their own sun, which is intrinsically dead, as explained above [§§89, 157–159]. As a result, there is nothing from the spiritual world's sun within them. However, they are surrounded by the spiritual atmospheres that come from that sun.

This differentiation between spiritual atmospheres and physical atmospheres is a matter of angelic wisdom.

176 It stands to reason that there are atmospheres in the spiritual world just as there are in the physical world, given the fact that angels and spirits breathe and talk and hear just the way we do in this physical world. Breathing involves that lowest atmosphere that we call "air," as do speech and hearing. We may also cite the fact that angels and spirits see just as we do in this physical world, and sight would not be possible without a medium purer than air. Then there is the fact that angels and spirits think and are moved just as we are in this physical world, and thought and feeling would not be possible without the aid of still purer atmospheres. Finally, there is the fact that every part of angels' and spirits' bodies, both the inner and the outer parts, is held closely together, the outer parts by an airlike medium and the inner parts by ethereal ones. Clearly, if it were not for the active pressure of these atmospheres, the inner and outer forms of their bodies would disintegrate.

Since angels are spiritual beings, then, and since everything about their bodies is held together, given form, and organized by these atmospheres, it follows that the atmospheres are spiritual. They are spiritual too because they come from the spiritual sun that is the first emanation of the Lord's divine love and wisdom.

177 I have already presented (and in *Heaven and Hell* illustrated) the fact that there are bodies of water and there are lands in the spiritual world

just as there are in the physical world, with the difference that the bodies
of water and lands in the spiritual world are spiritual. Because they are
spiritual, they are moved and affected by the warmth and light of the spiritual sun through its atmospheres just as the bodies of water and lands in
our physical world are moved and affected by the warmth and light of
the sun of our world through its atmospheres.

We speak of atmospheres, liquids, and solids here because these are **178**
the three basics through which and from which everything arises, with
infinite variety. The atmospheres are active factors, the liquids intermediate factors, and the solids passive factors from which all results arise. The
arrangement of three such factors in this sequence comes solely from the
life that emanates from the Lord as the sun and enables them to be active.

There are levels of love and wisdom, consequent levels of warmth and light, **179**
and also levels of atmosphere. Without a knowledge that there are levels,
what they are and what they are like, what is to follow will be incomprehensible, since there are levels in everything that has been created; therefore they exist in every form. Consequently, I need to discuss levels in
this part of *Angelic Wisdom.*

We can tell clearly from the angels of the three heavens that there are
levels of love and wisdom. Angels of the third heaven so surpass angels of
the second heaven in love and wisdom, and these in turn so surpass
angels of the farthest heaven, that they cannot live in the same place.
Their levels of love and wisdom mark them off and separate them. This
is why angels of the lower heavens cannot climb up to angels of the
higher heavens, and why if they are allowed to climb up they do not see
anyone or anything around them. The reason they do not see anyone is
that the love and wisdom of the higher angels is on a higher level, a level
beyond their perception. Every angel actually is her or his love and wisdom; and love together with wisdom is human in form because God,
who is love itself and wisdom itself, is human.

Occasionally I have been allowed to see angels of the farthest heaven
go up to angels of the third heaven. When they managed to get there, I
heard them complain that they could not see anyone; and yet they
were surrounded by angels. They were afterwards told that these angels
had been invisible to them because they could not perceive their love
and wisdom, and it is love and wisdom that give angels their human
appearance.

It is even clearer that there are levels of love and wisdom if we com- **180**
pare angels' love and wisdom with our love and wisdom. It is generally

acknowledged that the wisdom of angels is unutterable, relatively speaking. You will see later [§§267, 416] that it is also incomprehensible to us when we are wrapped up in our earthly love. The reason it seems unutterable and incomprehensible is that it is on a higher level.

181 Since there are levels of love and wisdom, there are levels of warmth and light—warmth and light here meaning spiritual warmth and light as angels experience them in the heavens and as they exist for us in the deeper levels of our minds. This is because we do have a warmth of love and a light of wisdom like that of angels.

It is like this in the heavens. The quality and amount of angels' love determines the quality and amount of their warmth, with the same relationship between their wisdom and their light. This is because there is love in their warmth and wisdom in their light, as I have already described [§§5, 32, 84]. The same holds true for us on earth, but with the difference that angels feel the warmth and see the light, while we do not, the reason being that we are focused on physical warmth and light; and as long as we are, we feel spiritual warmth only as a kind of pleasure of love and see spiritual light only as a kind of sense of what is true.

Since people know nothing about the spiritual warmth and light within them as long as they are focused on physical warmth and light, and since they can know about this only through experience offered by the spiritual world, I need first of all to talk about the warmth and light that surround angels and their heavens. This is the one and only way to shed some light on this matter.

182 However, the levels of spiritual warmth cannot be described on the basis of experience because the love to which spiritual warmth corresponds does not fit into the images of our thought. Still, the levels of spiritual light can be described because light does fit. It is actually an attribute of thought. On the basis of levels of light, we can understand levels of spiritual warmth, since warmth and light are on comparable levels.

As for the spiritual light that surrounds angels, I have been allowed to see this with my own eyes. For angels of the higher heavens, the light is so brilliant that it is indescribable, even by comparison with the brilliance of snow; and it also has a glow that defies description, even by comparison with the radiant glory of our world's sun. In short, this light is a thousand times greater than the light at noon on earth. The light of angels of the lower heavens can in some measure be described by comparisons, though. Even so, it surpasses the highest level of light on earth.

The reason the light of angels of the higher heavens defies description is that this light is integral to their wisdom. Since their wisdom, relative to ours, is inexpressible, so is their light.

We can tell from these few facts that there are levels of light; and since wisdom and love occur on comparable levels, it follows that there are similar levels of warmth.

Since the atmospheres are what receive and hold warmth and light, it follows that there are as many levels of atmosphere as there are of warmth and light—as many, that is, as there are levels of love and wisdom. An abundance of experience in the spiritual world has shown me that there are several atmospheres, distinguished from each other by level. One kind of experience was especially convincing, namely that angels of lower heavens cannot breathe in the realm of higher angels. They seem to labor for breath like creatures taken out of the air into the ether, or like creatures taken out of the water into the air. Then too, the spirits below heaven look as though they were in a cloud. **183**

On the existence of several atmospheres distinguished from each other by levels, see §176 above.

There are two kinds of levels, vertical levels and horizontal levels. Knowing about levels is a kind of key to unlocking the causes of things and probing into them. In the absence of this knowledge, hardly anything can be known about causes. In the absence of this knowledge, the objects and subjects of both worlds look so simple that there seems to be nothing within them beyond what meets the eye. Actually, though, in comparison to what lies hidden within, this surface is like one feature compared to a thousand or ten thousand. **184**

There is no way to uncover these deeper, invisible features without a knowledge of levels. We move from outer to inner and then to inmost by levels, and not by gradual levels but by distinct ones. "Gradual levels" is the name we give to declines or decreases from coarser to finer or denser to rarer, or better, to gains or increases from finer to coarser or from rarer to denser. They are just like going from light to darkness or from warmth to cold.

In contrast, distinct levels are totally different. They are like antecedent, subsequent, and final events, or like the purpose, the means, and the result. We refer to them as "distinct" because the antecedent event exists in its own right, the subsequent event in its own right, and the final event in its own right; and yet taken together they constitute a single whole.

Our atmospheres from top to bottom, from sun to earth, the atmospheres called ethers and airs, are marked off in levels of this kind. They are like the elements, compounds, and compounds of compounds that, taken all together, constitute a complex entity. These levels are distinct because they arise separately. They are what we mean by "vertical levels." The other levels, though, are gradual because they increase evenly. These are what we mean by "horizontal levels."

185 Absolutely everything that happens in the spiritual world and in the physical world results from a confluence of distinct and gradual levels, or of vertical and horizontal levels. We call the dimension constituted by distinct levels "height" and the dimension constituted by gradual levels "width." Their position relative to our eyesight does not change their labels.

Without a recognition of these levels, nothing can be known about the differences between the three heavens or about the differences of the love and wisdom of angels there, nothing about the differences of the warmth and light that surround them, nothing about the differences of the atmospheres that encompass and envelop them. Without a recognition of these levels, nothing can be known about differences of the inner abilities of our own minds, which means that nothing can be known about our states of reformation and regeneration, nothing about the differences of the outer, bodily abilities of both us and angels, nothing whatever about the difference between what is spiritual and what is physical and nothing therefore about correspondences, nothing about any difference between the life of humans and that of animals or between higher and lower animals, nothing about differences in the forms of the plant kingdom or the substances of the mineral kingdom.

We can tell from this that people who do not know about these levels do not see causes clearly and fairly. They see only effects and form judgments about causes on that basis—usually by tracing a string of effects. Yet causes produce effects not by simple continuity but by a distinct step. The cause is one thing and the effect another, and the difference between them is like the difference between an antecedent event and a subsequent one, or like the difference between what forms and what is formed.

186 The angelic heavens may serve as an example for better comprehension of the reality and nature of distinct levels and of how they differ from gradual levels. There are three heavens marked off by vertical levels so that one is underneath another. The only way they communicate is by an inflow that comes from the Lord through the heavens in sequence down to the lowest, and not the other way around.

Each heaven on its own, though, is marked off not by vertical levels but by horizontal ones. The people in the middle or center are in the light of wisdom, while those around them all the way to the borders are in the shadow of wisdom. That is, wisdom wanes all the way to ignorance as the light declines into shadow, which happens gradually.

It is the same with us. The inner realms of our minds are marked off into as many levels as are the angelic heavens, with one level over another. So the inner realms of our minds are marked off in distinct or vertical levels. This is why we can be engaged in the lowest level, a higher level, or the highest level depending on the level of our wisdom. It is why the higher level is closed when we are exclusively engaged in the lowest one, and why the higher one is opened as we accept wisdom from the Lord. There are also gradual or horizontal levels in us just as there are in heaven.

The reason we resemble the heavens is that we are miniature heavens as to the deeper realms of our minds when we are engaged in love and wisdom from the Lord. (On our being miniature heavens as to the deeper realms of our minds, see *Heaven and Hell* 51–58.)

We can tell from this sample that people who know nothing about **187** distinct or vertical levels cannot know anything about our state when it comes to reformation and regeneration, processes that are effected by our acceptance of love and wisdom from the Lord and a consequent opening of the deeper levels of our minds in due sequence. They cannot know, either, about the inflow through the heavens from the Lord or about the design into which they themselves were created. Anyone who ponders these subjects on the basis of gradual or horizontal levels rather than distinct or vertical ones can see them only in terms of effects and not at all in terms of causes. Seeing things solely in terms of effects is basing thought on illusions, which leads to one error after another. By inductive reasoning we can multiply these errors so much that ultimately grotesque distortions are labeled truths.

I am not aware that anything about distinct or vertical levels has yet **188** come to people's attention—only things about gradual or horizontal levels. Yet nothing about causes can come to light in truth without familiarity with both kinds of level. That is why this whole part is devoted to this subject. After all, the purpose of this modest work is to uncover causes and to see effects on that basis, thereby dispelling the darkness that envelops people in the church concerning God, the Lord, and the divine matters in general that we refer to as "spiritual."

This I can relate, that angels are struck with sorrow at the darkness on earth. They say that they hardly see any light anywhere and that people are latching onto illusions and "proving" them so that they pile distortion on distortion. In order to prove their distortions, they use reasoning based on illusions and on distorted truths to investigate things that cannot be cleared up because of the darkness that surrounds causes and because of their ignorance of truths. Angels expressed the greatest grief over their "proof" of faith separated from charity and over justification by faith, as well as over [mistaken] concepts of God, angels, and spirits, and over ignorance of the nature of love and wisdom.

189 *Vertical levels are matched in kind, with one following from another in sequence like a purpose, a means, and a result.* Since horizontal or gradual levels are like levels of light to shade, warmth to cold, hard to soft, dense to sparse, coarse to fine, and so on, and since we are familiar with these levels from our sensory and visual experience while we are not familiar with vertical or distinct levels, I need to give particular attention to these latter in this part. Without familiarity with these levels, that is, we cannot see causes.

It is in fact recognized that a purpose, a means, and a result follow in sequence like antecedent, subsequent, and final events. It is recognized that the purpose produces the means and then produces the result through the means so that the purpose can be realized; and much more is recognized along the same lines. Knowing such things without seeing them by applying them to actual events, however, is only abstract knowledge. It lasts only as long as we are engaged in analytical thought on the basis of metaphysical principles. As a result, even though a purpose, a means, and a result do progress by distinct levels, still there is little if any knowledge of those levels in the world. Thinking only about abstractions is like something ethereal that dissipates; but if these abstract principles are applied to things of an earthly nature, then they are like something we see with our own eyes on earth, and they stay in our memory.

190 Everything in the world characterized by three dimensions, that is, everything we call a compound, is constituted by three vertical or distinct levels. Some examples may make this clear. We know from visual experience that every muscle in the human body is made up of tiny fibers and that these, gathered into bundles, make up the larger fibers we call motor fibers. From these bundles come that compound entity called a muscle.

It is the same with our nerves. The smallest fibers in them are woven together into larger ones that look like threads, and gatherings of these are woven together into nerves. It is the same with the rest of the weavings, bundlings, and gatherings that make up our organs and viscera. They are compounds of fibers and vessels in various arrangements, depending on similar levels.

It is the same as well in all the members of the plant kingdom and all the members of the mineral kingdom. There are threefold gatherings of filaments in wood and threefold conglomerates of elements in metals and rocks as well.

We can see from this what distinct levels are like, namely that one level is made from another and a third from the second, the third being called a compound. Each level is distinct from the other.

On this basis we can draw conclusions about things not visible to our eyes, since their arrangement is similar—for example about the organized substances that are the vessels and dwellings of the thoughts and feelings in our brains, about the atmospheres, about warmth and light, and about love and wisdom. The atmospheres are vessels of warmth and light, and warmth and light are vessels of love and wisdom. So if there are levels of the atmospheres, then there are similar levels of warmth and light and similar levels of love and wisdom. There is not one set of relationships in one case and a different set in another. **191**

We can tell from what has just been said that these levels are consistent, of the same character and nature. The smallest, larger, and largest motor fibers of our muscles have the same basic nature. The smallest, larger, and largest nerve fibers match; the woody filaments match from their smallest forms to their compounds; and the parts of rocks and metals match in the same way. The organized substances that are vessels and dwellings of our thoughts and feelings match, from the very simplest to their overall compound, the brain. The atmospheres match, from pure ether to air. The levels of warmth and light that parallel those of the atmospheres in their sequence match; and therefore so do the levels of love and wisdom. **192**

Things that are not of the same character and nature do not match and do not harmonize with things that do. This means that they cannot combine with them to make up distinct levels. They can combine only with their own kind, with things of the same character and nature, things that match.

Clearly, these levels are in a sequence like that of a purpose, a means, and a result, since the first or smallest promotes its cause through the intermediate and achieves its result through the last. **193**

It is important to realize that each level is delineated from the other by its own membrane, with all the levels together being delineated by a **194** common membrane. This common membrane communicates with the deeper and deepest levels in proper sequence, which is what makes possible the union and concerted action of all of them.

195 *The first level is the sum and substance of all the levels.* This is because the levels of every subject and every object are matched in kind, and they are matched in kind because they have been produced by the first level. The way they are formed is that the first level produces a second by folding together or congregating—in short, by gathering; and through this second level, it produces a third. Further, it marks each level off from the other by a surrounding membrane. We can see from this that the first level is in primary and sole control of the subsequent ones, and that in fact the first level is the sum and substance of all the levels.

196 While we talk about the relationships of the levels to each other, this principle really applies to the substances that exist on their levels. The language of levels is an abstract language that is universal and therefore applicable to any subject or object that may have levels in its own particular way.

197 We can apply this principle to everything that was listed in the previous section—to muscles and nerves, for example, to the substances and components of both the plant and mineral kingdoms, to the organized substances that are the subjects of our own thoughts and feelings, to the atmospheres, to warmth and light, and to love and wisdom. In each instance the first is the only controlling reality in things subsequent and is in fact their only content; and since it is their only content, it is all there is to them.

We can see the truth of this from what we have already recognized, namely that the purpose is the whole of the means and through the means is the whole of the result. This is why we refer to a purpose, a means, and a result as a first end, an intermediate end, and a final end. It is why the cause of a cause is also the cause of what is caused. It is why there is nothing essential within the means except the purpose and nothing essential in motion except energy. It is also why there is only one substance that is substance in its own right.

198 This makes it clear that Divinity, being substance in its own right or the unique and sole substance, is the source of absolutely everything that has been created. This means that God is the sum and substance of the universe, in accord with what was presented in part 1: divine love and wisdom is substance and form (§§40–43); divine love and wisdom is substance and form in its own right, and is therefore wholly itself and unique (§§44–46); everything in the universe was created by divine love and wisdom (§§54–60 *[52–60]*); the created universe is therefore an image of him (§§61–65 *[61–64]*); and [in part 2,] the Lord alone is the heaven where angels live (§§113–118).

All processes of perfection increase and rise by and according to levels. I have **199** already explained that there are two kinds of level, horizontal and vertical, in §§184–188 above. I have explained that the horizontal levels are like levels of light tending toward darkness or wisdom tending toward ignorance, while vertical levels are like those of a purpose, a means, and a result, or like something antecedent, something subsequent, and something final. These latter levels are described as rising and falling, since they involve height; while the former are described as waxing and waning because they involve width.

These levels are so different from each other that they have nothing in common; so they need to be grasped clearly and not confused with each other in any way.

The reason all processes of perfection increase and rise by and accord- **200** ing to levels is that all attributes are secondary to their substances, and perfection and imperfection are general attributes. We attribute them to life, to forces, and to forms.

Perfection of life is perfection of love and wisdom, and since volition and discernment are their vessels, perfection of life is also perfection of volition and discernment and therefore of feelings and thoughts. Further, since spiritual warmth is the vehicle of love and spiritual light is the vehicle of wisdom, their perfection too can be traced back to perfection of life.

Perfection of forces is perfection of everything that is activated and set in motion by life, though life is not inherent in the forces. Such forces are the atmospheres in regard to what they do, also our own inner and outer organized substances and those of all kinds of animal. Such forces also are all the things in the physical world that get their activities directly or indirectly from its sun.

Perfection of forms and perfection of forces constitute a single entity, since the nature of the forces determines the nature of the forms. The only difference is that the forms are forms of substance while the forces are what the substances do. Consequently, the two have similar levels of perfection. Even forms that are not doing anything at a given time have their kinds of perfection according to levels.

There is no need at this point to discuss the way processes of perfec- **201** tion of life, forces, and forms rise and fall by horizontal or gradual levels because these levels are familiar in our world. There is, however, a need to discuss the way processes of perfection of life, forces, and forms rise and fall by vertical or distinct levels, because these levels are not familiar in our world. From what we can see in this physical world, it is almost impossible to understand how these processes rise and fall by distinct levels, but it is quite clear in what we can see in the spiritual world. All we discover from what we see in the physical world is that the deeper we look, the more wondrous are the things we run into—in our eyes, for example, or our ears, tongue, muscles, heart, lungs, liver, pancreas, kidneys, and the rest of our internal organs, as well as in seeds, fruits, and flowers and even in metals, minerals, and rocks. It is widely known that we run into more wondrous things in all these phenomena the deeper we probe; but little attention has been paid to the fact that the deeper perfection increases by vertical or distinct levels. Our ignorance of these levels has kept this hidden.

Since these levels are openly visible in the spiritual world, though, with that whole world clearly marked off by them from top to bottom, we can gain familiarity with these levels on that basis and then draw conclusions about the processes of perfection of forces and forms that occur on comparable levels in this physical world.

202 There are three heavens in the spiritual world, arranged by vertical levels. The angels in the highest heaven are better in every respect than those of the intermediate heaven, and the angels in the intermediate heaven are better in every respect than those of the lowest heaven. Because of these levels of perfection, angels of the lowest heaven cannot even approach the threshold of the perfection of angels of the intermediate heaven, and these latter in turn cannot approach the threshold of the perfection of angels of the highest heaven. This may appear paradoxical, but it is the truth. The reason is that they are grouped by distinct levels and not by gradual ones.

Experience has taught me that there is such a difference between angels of the higher and lower heavens in feelings and thoughts and therefore in speech that they have nothing in common. Communication happens only by the correspondences that arise through the Lord's direct inflow into all the heavens and the indirect inflow through the highest heaven to the lowest.

Because of the nature of these distinctions, they cannot be expressed in earthly language, so I cannot describe them. Angels' thoughts do not fit into earthly concepts because they are spiritual. They can only be expressed and described by angels in their own language and words and writing, but not in human ones. This is why it says that people have heard and seen indescribable things in the heavens.

The following may afford some understanding of these differences. The thoughts of angels of the highest or third heaven are thoughts of purposes; the thoughts of angels of the intermediate or second heaven are thoughts of means; and the thoughts of angels of the lowest or first heaven are thoughts of results. It is important to realize that it is one thing to think on the basis of purposes and another to think about purposes, one thing to think on the basis of means and another to think about means, one thing to think on the basis of results and another to think about results. Angels of the lower heavens do think about means and about purposes; but angels of the higher heavens think on the basis of means and on the basis of purposes. Thinking on the basis of such things comes from a higher level of wisdom, while thinking about them comes from a lower level. Thinking on the basis of purposes comes from wisdom; thinking on the basis of means comes from intelligence; and thinking on the basis of results comes from being informed.

We can see from this that all processes of perfection rise and fall by and according to levels.

Since the deeper reaches of our own minds, of our volition and discernment, are like the heavens as far as levels are concerned (we are actually miniature heavens as to the deeper reaches of our minds), their processes of perfection are similar. However, these processes are not perceptible to any of us as long as we are living in this world, since we are then on the lowest level; and the higher levels are unrecognizable from the lowest level. After death, though, we can identify them, since then we are on whatever level answers to our love and wisdom. Then we become angels and think and say things that are indescribable to our physical self. The raising up of everything in our minds then is not by some simple ratio but by the threefold ratio that is the ratio of vertical levels. The simple ratio applies to horizontal levels.

The only people who rise or are brought up to those levels, though, are the ones who have been attentive to truths in this world and have applied them to their lives.

It may seem as though antecedent things are less perfect than subsequent ones and constituent things are less perfect than compounds, but in fact the antecedent things that give rise to subsequent ones are more perfect, as are the constituents from which compounds are formed. This is because the antecedent or constituent things are less covered, less shrouded by lifeless substances and materials. They are more divine, so to

203

204

speak, and as such are closer to the spiritual sun where the Lord is. Perfection itself is in the Lord and therefore in the sun that is the first emanation of his divine love and wisdom. It comes from there into things that are next in sequence, and so on in order down to the lowest things, which are more imperfect as they are more remote.

If it were not for this supreme perfection in things antecedent and constituent, neither we nor any living creature could arise from seed and then continue in existence. The seeds of trees and shrubs could not sprout and spread, either. The more antecedent a thing is, or the more whole it is, the more immune it is to harm because of its greater perfection.

205 *In a sequential arrangement, the first level is the highest and the third the lowest, while in a simultaneous arrangement, the first level is the center and the third level is the circumference.* There is a sequential arrangement and a simultaneous one. The sequential arrangement of these levels is from highest to lowest or from top to bottom. This is the arrangement of the angelic heavens, with the third heaven as the highest, the second in between, and the first as the lowest. These are their relative locations.

The same sequential arrangement applies to states of love and wisdom among angels in heaven, to warmth and light, and to spiritual atmospheres. The same arrangement applies to all the processes of perfection of forces and forms there.

When the vertical or distinct levels are in this sequential arrangement, they are like a tower divided into three floors so that one can go up or down. The most perfect and lovely things are on the top floor, less perfect and lovely things on the middle floor, and still less perfect and lovely things on the lowest floor.

In a simultaneous arrangement of the same levels, though, it looks different. Then the highest elements of the sequential arrangement—as I have mentioned, the most perfect and lovely ones—are in the center, the lower ones in an intermediate region, and the lowest on the outside. It is as though there were a solid object made up of these three levels with the finest substances in the middle or center, less fine particles around that, and on the outside, forming a kind of envelope, parts composed of these and therefore coarsest. It is as though the tower we were talking about had settled into a plane, with the top floor becoming the center, the middle floor an intermediate region, and the lowest floor the outside.

206 Since the highest thing in sequential arrangement is the central thing in simultaneous arrangement and the lowest is the outermost, "higher" in the Word means more internal and "lower" means more external. The same holds for "upward" and "downward" and for "high" and "low."

In every final form there are distinct levels in simultaneous arrange- **207** ment. This is the arrangement of the motor fibers in every muscle, the fibers in every nerve, the fibers and tiny vessels in all our viscera and organs. At the heart of each are the simplest and most perfect substances, while the outside is formed from their compounds.

The same arrangement of these levels is found in every seed, every fruit, even in every metal and rock. This is the nature of the parts that constitute their totality. Their central, intermediate, and outermost parts are on these levels, and they themselves are successive compounds, aggregates, or masses of these simple components that are their primary substances and materials.

In short, there are levels like this in every final form and therefore **208** in every effect, since every final form consists of antecedents that in turn consist of things primary to them. Likewise every result comes from a means and every means from a purpose, the purpose being the whole essence of the means and the means the whole essence of the result, as I have just explained [§§168, 197]. Further, the purpose constitutes the center, the means the intermediate, and the result the final outcome.

We will see later [§§224, 231, 232, 235, 236–241] that the same holds for levels of love and wisdom, warmth and light, and for the organized forms of feelings and thoughts within us. I have discussed the sequence of these levels in sequential and simultaneous arrangements in *Teachings for the New Jerusalem on Sacred Scripture* 38 and elsewhere, showing that there are similar levels in all the details of the Word.

The final level is the composite, vessel, and foundation of the prior levels. **209** Examples of the principle of levels that is under discussion in this part have thus far been drawn from various things that occur in our two worlds—levels of the heavens where angels live, for example, levels of the warmth and light that surround them, of the atmospheres, of various parts of the human body, and of things in the animal and mineral kingdoms. The principle of levels has a wider range, though. Its range includes not only physical phenomena but also societal, moral, and spiritual ones in all their detail.

There are two reasons why the principle of levels includes such matters. The first is that there is a trine in everything that can be said to have attributes, a trine called purpose, means, and result; and these three are related to each other by vertical levels. The second reason is that no societal, moral, or spiritual phenomenon is abstract or disembodied. They are matters of substance, for just as love and wisdom are not abstractions but substances (as I have explained above in §§40–43), so are all the things we refer to as societal, moral, and spiritual. We can of course think about them in the abstract, as disembodied, but in their own right they are not abstractions. Take feeling and thought, for example, or charity and faith, or volition and discernment. What applies to love and wisdom applies to them as well, namely that they do not happen apart from subjects that are substantial. They actually have to do with the state of those subjects or substances. We will see later [§§273, 316] that they are shifts of state that give rise to change. "Substance" means form as well, since there is no such thing as a formless substance.

210 Since we can think about volition and discernment, about feeling and thought, and about charity and faith apart from the substantial realities that are their subjects, and since we have thought about them in this way, we have lost any appropriate concept of them, any realization that they refer to the states of substantial realities or forms. Exactly the same principle applies to sensations and actions, which are not things in the abstract apart from our sensory and motor organs. In the abstract, or apart from their organs, they are theoretical constructs only. They are like sight with no eye, hearing with no ear, taste with no tongue, and so on.

211 Since all societal, moral, and spiritual events, like all physical ones, happen not only by gradual levels but also on distinct levels, and since processes on distinct levels are like the processes of purpose to means and means to result, I should like to illustrate and demonstrate the present topic (that the final level is the composite, vessel, and foundation of the prior levels) by what I have just mentioned, namely instances of love and wisdom, of volition and discernment, of feeling and thought, and of charity and faith.

212 We can tell quite clearly that the final level is the composite, vessel, and foundation of the prior ones by looking at the way purpose and means progress to result. Enlightened reason can grasp the fact that the effect is the composite, vessel, and foundation of the means and the purpose, but cannot grasp as clearly the fact that the purpose in all fullness and the means in all fullness are actively present in the result, with the result being completely inclusive of them.

This follows from what has already been said in this part, especially from the fact that one level comes from another in a three-stage sequence and that a result is simply a purpose in its final form. Since the final form is this kind of composite, it follows that the final form is their vessel and also their foundation.

As for love and wisdom, love is the purpose, wisdom the means, **213** and service the result. Further, service is the composite, vessel, and foundation of wisdom and love, such a composite and such a vessel that every bit of love and every bit of wisdom is actively present in it. It is their total presence. We need to be absolutely clear, though, that in keeping with what was presented in §§189–194 above, what are present in service are all the elements of love and wisdom that are of the same kind, harmonious.

Desire, thought, and act occur on a sequence of similar levels, since **214** every desire has to do with love, every thought with wisdom, and every act with service. Charity, faith, and good works occur on the same sequence of levels, since charity is a matter of desire, faith of thought, and good works of act. Volition, discernment, and practice occur on the same sequence of levels as well, since volition is a matter of love and therefore of desire, discernment of wisdom and therefore of faith, and practice of service and therefore of deeds. Just as all the elements of wisdom and love dwell within service, all the elements of thought and desire dwell within act, and all the elements of faith and charity dwell within deeds, and so on. This means all the elements that are of the same kind, that are harmonious.

People have not yet recognized that the last member of each **215** sequence—service, act, deed, and practice—is the composite and vessel of all the earlier members. It seems as though there were nothing more within service, act, deed, or practice than there is within motion. However, all these prior stages are actively present within, so completely present that nothing is missing. They are enclosed within it the way wine is enclosed in a bottle or furnishings in a house.

The reason this is not noticed is that we look at acts of service from the outside only, and things seen from the outside are simply events and motions. It is like seeing our arms and hands move and not knowing that a thousand motor fibers are cooperating in each movement, with a thousand elements of thought and desire answering to those thousand motor fibers and stimulating them. Since these things are happening far inside, they are not visible to any of our physical senses. This much is known, that nothing is done in or through the body except from volition and through thought; and since these two are acting, every element of volition and thought must necessarily be present within the act. They cannot be separated. This is why we draw conclusions on the basis of deeds or works about each other's purposeful thought, which we refer to as "intent."

I have learned that angels can sense and see from someone's single deed or work everything about the intention and thought of the one who is doing it. From the person's volition, angels of the third heaven see the purpose for which it is being done, and angels of the second heaven see the means through which the purpose is working. This is why deeds and works are so often mandated in the Word, and why it says that we are known by our works.

216 According to angelic wisdom, unless volition and discernment, or desire and thought, or charity and faith, devote themselves to involvement in works or deeds whenever possible, they are nothing but passing breezes, so to speak, or images in the air that vanish. They first take on permanence in us and become part of our life when we perform and do them. The reason is that the final stage is the composite, vessel, and foundation of the prior stages.

Faith apart from good works is just this kind of airy nothing or image, and so are faith and charity apart from their practice. The only difference is that people who put faith and charity together know what is good and are able to intend and do it, but not people who are devoted to faith apart from charity.

217 *The vertical levels find their full realization and power in their final form.* I explained in the preceding section that the final level is the composite and vessel of the prior levels. It follows from this that the prior levels find their full realization in their final level. That is where they are in their effect, and every effect is a summary of its causes.

218 Everything I have already cited from what we can sense and perceive may be used in support of the proposition that the rising and falling levels, the ones we call antecedent and subsequent or vertical and distinct levels, find their power in their final stage. At this point, though, I want to cite only energy, force, and motion in lifeless and living entities.

It is common knowledge that energy does not accomplish anything by itself, but only through forces responsive to it, using them to cause motion. This is why energy is the whole essence of force, and through force, the whole essence of motion. Since motion is the final stage of energy, energy exercises its power through motion. The only way energy, force, and motion are united is by vertical levels, a union that is not one of continuity, since the levels are distinct, but of responsiveness. Energy, that is, is not force, and force is not motion. Rather, force is produced by energy, and force is energy being exercised; and motion is produced by force. This means that there is no power in pure energy or pure force, but in the motion that they produce.

The truth of this may appear debatable because I have not illustrated it by application to things we can sense and perceive in the physical world. Still, this is the nature of stages that culminate in power.

Let me apply these principles to living energy, living force, and living motion. Living energy in us, who are the living subjects, is our volition in union with our discernment. The living forces in us are what make up the inner parts of our bodies, throughout which there are motor fibers interconnected in various ways. Living motion in us is the action that is produced by volition in union with discernment through the agency of these forces. The deeper levels of volition and discernment constitute the first level, the inner parts of the body constitute the second level, and the whole body, their composite, constitutes the third level. It is common knowledge that the deeper levels of the mind are not empowered except through forces in the body, and that the forces become powerful and effective only through the action of the body.

219

These three stages do not act by continuity but by distinct levels, and acting by distinct levels is acting by responsiveness. The deeper levels of the mind answer to the inner parts of the body and the inner parts of the body answer to those outer parts that give rise to actions; so the two prior stages are empowered through the outer parts of the body.

It might seem as though our inner energy and forces had some power even in the absence of action—in dreams, for example, or when we are at rest—but at such times the energy and forces find definition in our general physical motions, those of heart and lungs. Once these stop, however, the forces stop as well, and with them the energy.

Since the whole being or body focuses its powers primarily in the arms and hands, which are the extremities, arms and hands in the Word mean power, with the right hand meaning the greater power. Since this is how the levels unfold and express themselves in power, the angels who are with us and are sensitive to everything in us can tell simply from a single action of our hand what we are like in discernment and intent, in charity and faith, and therefore in the inner life of our minds and the outer life in our bodies, which comes from the inner life.

220

I have often been astounded by the kind of recognition angels have simply from the physical action of a hand, but it has been shown to me often enough and by personal experience. I have also been told that this is why induction into ministry is done by the laying on of hands and why touching with the hand means sharing, among other things. This leads to the conclusion that the whole of charity and faith is in works and that charity and faith without works are like halos around the sun that dissipate and vanish when a cloud passes by. So time after time the Word talks about works and doing and says that our salvation depends on such things. Then too, the one who does something is called wise and the one who does not is called foolish.

We should realize, though, that "works" means deeds of service that are put into action. The whole of charity and faith is in them and depends on them. The correspondence is with acts of service because while the correspondence is spiritual, it happens through the substances and materials that are its subjects.

221 I am now allowed to disclose two secrets that can be brought within comprehension through what has just been said.

The first is that the Word finds its fullest expression and power in its literal meaning. There are three meanings in the Word answering to the three levels—a heavenly meaning, a spiritual meaning, and an earthly meaning. Since the Word contains these three meanings by the three vertical levels and their union is through correspondence, the final meaning, the earthly one that we call the literal meaning, is not only the composite, vessel, and foundation of the deeper, corresponding meanings, it is also the Word in its fullest expression and its full power. There is an abundance of evidence and support for this in *Teachings for the New Jerusalem on Sacred Scripture* 27–35 [27–36], 36–49 [37–49], 50–61, and 62–69.

The second secret is that the Lord came into the world and took on a human nature in order to gain access to the power to conquer the hells and bring everything in the heavens and on earth back into order. He put on this human nature over the human nature he had before. The human nature he put on in the world was like our own worldly nature, but each nature was still divine and therefore infinitely transcendent of our own and angels' finite human nature. Further, since he completely transformed his physical human level all the way to its limits, he, unlike anyone else, rose from death with his whole body. By taking on this human nature he clothed himself with a divine omnipotence not only for the conquest of the hells and the reordering of the heavens but also for keeping the hells subject forever and saving us. This power is what is meant by his sitting at the right hand of the power and might of God.

Since the Lord made himself divine truth in ultimate form by taking on a physical human nature, he is called "the Word," and it says that the

Word was made flesh. Divine truth in its ultimate form is the Word in its literal meaning. He made himself that Word by fulfilling everything about himself in the Word, in Moses and the prophets.

Everyone is his or her own good and true nature. Nothing else makes us human. Because he took on a physical human nature, the Lord is divine good and divine truth itself, or in other words, divine love and divine wisdom itself, in both their primal and their ultimate forms. This is why he looks like a sun in the angelic heavens with greater glory and fuller brilliance after his coming into the world than before his coming. This is a secret that can be brought within comprehension by the principle of levels.

I will be discussing later [§233] his omnipotence before his coming into the world.

There are levels of both kinds in everything that has been created, no matter how large or small. There is no way to offer visible examples of the fact that the largest and smallest things of all are made up of distinct and gradual, or vertical and horizontal, levels, because the smallest things that occur are not visible to our eyes and the largest do not seem to be marked off into levels. The only available way to explain this principle, then, is by looking to universal phenomena; and since angels are engaged in wisdom on the basis of universal principles and derive knowledge about details on that basis, I may offer some of the things they have said on the subject.

Angelic pronouncements on the subject are as follows. There is no thing so small that it does not contain levels of both kinds—not the smallest thing in any animal, not the smallest thing in any plant, not the smallest thing in any mineral, not the smallest thing in the ether or the air. Further, since the ether and air are vessels of warmth and light, this holds for the smallest trace of warmth and light, and since spiritual warmth and spiritual light are vessels of love and wisdom, there is not the smallest bit of these in which there are not levels of both kinds.

Another pronouncement of angels is that every least bit of desire, every least bit of thought, even every least bit of a mental image, is made up of levels of both kinds, and that any least thing that is not made up of these levels is actually nothing. It has no form, so it has no characteristics, no state that can shift and change so that it becomes manifest.

Angels support this by the truth that the infinite things in God the Creator, who is the Lord from eternity, are "distinguishably one," with infinite things within those infinite things of his and levels of both kinds

222

223

within those infinitely infinite things that are also distinguishably one in him. Since these are within him, then, and since everything was created by him and everything so created offers a kind of image of what is within him, it follows that there is not the smallest finite thing that does not have these levels in it. The reason these levels are in the smallest and the largest things alike is that Divinity is the same in the largest and smallest things.

On infinite things being distinguishably one in the Divine-Human One, see §§17–22 above; and on Divinity being the same in the largest and smallest things, §§77–82. There are further examples in §§155, 169, and 171.

224 The reason there is not the slightest trace of love and wisdom or of desire and thought or of a mental image that does not have levels of both kinds in it is that love and wisdom, and likewise desire and thought, are substance and form (as I have explained in §§40–43 above). As I have already stated [§223] there is no form that does not involve levels of both kinds. It follows that they involve these same levels. To separate love and wisdom or desire and thought from substance-in-form is to annihilate them, because they do not occur apart from their subjects. They are actually manifested by the states of these subjects as we perceive them when they change.

225 The largest things that involve levels of both kinds include the universe in all its fullness and the physical world in all its fullness. They include the spiritual world in its fullness, every empire and every monarchy in its fullness and their every moral and spiritual feature in its fullness, the whole animal kingdom, the whole plant kingdom, and the whole mineral kingdom, each in all its fullness. Then there are the atmospheres of each world taken as a whole, and their forms of warmth and light. The same holds for less inclusive entities, such as ourselves in our fullness, every animal in its fullness, every tree and shrub in its fullness, even every stone and metal in its fullness.

Their forms are similar in this respect, namely that they are made up of levels of both kinds. This is because the Divinity by which they were created is the same in the largest and smallest things, as noted above in §§77–82. All their details, no matter how minute, resemble their shared aspects—no matter how widely shared those aspects are among them—in being forms made up of levels of both kinds.

226 The fact that the largest and smallest things are forms made up of levels of both kinds results in their being connected from beginning to end; their likeness actually unites them. Still, there is not the least thing that is identical to something else, which is why there is a distinctiveness of everything, down to the least detail.

The reason there are no identical elements in any form or between different forms is that there are the same kinds of levels in the largest entities, and the largest entities are made up of the smallest ones. When the largest entities are made up of these levels, with corresponding constant distinctions from top to bottom and from center to circumference, it follows that there is nothing in them involving these levels, nothing lesser or least, that is identical.

It is also an item of angelic wisdom that the perfection of the created **227** universe comes from a resemblance in regard to levels between inclusive forms and their particular constituents, or between the largest and smallest things. This means that each thing sees the other as a kindred with which it can unite in its whole function and with which it can realize its whole purpose in actual results.

All this may seem paradoxical, true, because it has not been presented **228** with application to things we can see. Still, since abstract principles are universal, they are often easier to grasp than the applications. The applications vary constantly, and the variation is confusing.

Some people say that there is a substance so simple that it is not a **229** form made up of lesser forms, and that by putting enough of this substance together, secondary substances or compounds come into being, eventually leading to the substances that we refer to as "matter." However, there is no such thing as these "simplest substances." What would a substance be without some form? It would be something without attributes, and nothing can be constituted by putting together things that have no attributes.

Later, when I discuss forms, we will see that there are countless elements in the very first created substances, the very smallest and simplest ones.

There are three infinite and uncreated vertical levels in the Lord, and three **230** *finite and created levels in us.* The reason there are three infinite and uncreated vertical levels in the Lord is that the Lord is love itself and wisdom itself, as explained above [§§28–33]. Since the Lord is love itself and wisdom itself, he is also usefulness itself, since love has useful functions as its goal and puts them into effect by means of wisdom. Apart from usefulness, love and wisdom have no definition or boundary, no dwelling. This means that we cannot say they exist or are present unless there is a useful function in which they occur.

These three elements constitute three vertical levels in agents of life. These three are like the first end, the intermediate end that we refer to as the means, and the ultimate end that we refer to as the result. I have already [§§167–169, 184] explained and amply documented the fact that purpose, means, and result constitute three vertical levels.

231 We can tell that there are these three levels in us from the way human minds are raised all the way into those levels of love and wisdom that angels of the second and third heaven enjoy. All those angels were born human; and in regard to the inner reaches of our minds, each of us is a miniature form of heaven. Count the number of heavens and you have the number of vertical levels within each of us, from our creation. Each of us is an image and likeness of God; so these three levels are written into us because they are in the Divine-Human One—that is, in the Lord.

We can tell that these levels in the Lord are infinite and uncreated while ours are finite and created on the basis of what I presented in part I, for example from the principle that the Lord is intrinsic love and wisdom, that we are recipients of love and wisdom from the Lord, that only what is infinite can be attributed to the Lord, and that only what is finite can be attributed to us.

232 For angels, these three levels are called heavenly, spiritual, and earthly; and for them, the heavenly level is the level of love, the spiritual level the level of wisdom, and the earthly level the level of useful functions. The reason for giving the levels these names is that the heavens are divided into two kingdoms, one called the heavenly kingdom and the other the spiritual kingdom, with a third kingdom added where we in the world are, called the earthly one.

Then too, the angels who make up the heavenly kingdom are focused on love, while the angels who make up the spiritual kingdom are focused on wisdom and we in this world are focused on useful functions. This is why the kingdoms are united. I will be describing in the next part how to understand the statement that we are focused on useful functions.

233 I have received information from heaven that before the Lord from eternity (who is Jehovah) took on a human nature in the world, the first two levels in him were actual while the third level was potential, which is the way things are for angels. After he took on a human nature in our world, though, he clothed himself with that third level as well, the one we call "earthly," and in this way became a human being like us in this world. Still, there was the difference that this level like the others was infinite and uncreated, while in angels and in us the levels are finite and created.

What happened was that although the Divinity that had filled all space without being bound by space (see §§69–72) also penetrated to the most remote elements of nature, before taking on a human nature the divine inflow into the earthly level was indirect, through the angelic heavens. After taking on the human nature it was direct from Divinity itself. This is why all the world's churches before his Coming were representative of spiritual and heavenly realities, while after his Coming they became spiritual and heavenly on the earthly level and representational worship was done away with. This is also the reason why the sun of the angelic heaven (which as already noted [§93] is the first emanation of his divine love and wisdom) shone out with greater radiance and brilliance after he took on a human nature than before. This is also the meaning of the following words in Isaiah: "In that day the light of the moon will be like the light of the sun, and the light of the sun will be sevenfold, like the light of seven days" (Isaiah 30:25 *[30:26]*). This is about the state of heaven and the church after the Lord's coming into the world. There is also Revelation 1:16, "the face of the Human-born One looked like the sun shining at full strength"; and such other passages as Isaiah 60:20; 2 Samuel 23:3, 4; and Matthew 17:1, 2. We might compare our indirect enlightenment through the angelic heaven, which obtained before the Lord's Coming, with the moon's light, which is indirect sunlight. Since this became a direct enlightenment after the Lord's Coming, it says in [the passage just cited from] Isaiah that the light of the moon will be like the light of the sun; and it says in David, "Righteous people will blossom in his day, and peace in abundance until the moon is no more" (Psalms 72:7). This too is about the Lord.

The reason the Lord from eternity, or Jehovah, took on this third **234** level by assuming a human nature in the world is that he could not enter this world except through a nature like our own. The coming could not have been accomplished, then, except by conception from his own Divinity and birth by a virgin. This enabled him to take off a nature that was intrinsically dead, and yet receptive of Divinity, and take on a divine nature. This is the meaning of the Lord's two states in the world, called a state of emptying out and a state of transformation, which I have dealt with in *Teachings for the New Jerusalem on the Lord.*

I have said these things about the three-step ladder of vertical levels in **235** generalizations; but since as stated in the preceding section these levels are characteristic of the largest and smallest things, I cannot say anything about them in detail at this point. I can say only that there are levels like this in everything that has to do with love and therefore in everything that has to do with wisdom, and that as a result there are levels like this in everything that has to do with usefulness. However, in the Lord they are all infinite, while in angels and in us they are finite. How these levels exist in love, wisdom, and use, though, can be described and unfolded only at some length.

236 *These three vertical levels exist in each of us from birth and can be opened in sequence. As they are opened, we are in the Lord and the Lord is in us.* The existence of three vertical levels in us has not been widely recognized before. This is because vertical levels themselves have not been identified, and as long as these levels have been unrecognized, the only levels people could know about are the gradual ones. When these are the only levels people know about, they can believe that our love and wisdom increase only gradually.

It needs to be realized, though, that we all have these three vertical or distinct levels in us from our birth, one above or within the other, and that each vertical or distinct level has horizontal or gradual levels by which it increases incrementally. This is because there are both kinds of level in everything, no matter how large or small, as explained above in §§222–229. Neither kind of level can exist apart from the other.

237 As noted in §232 above, these three vertical levels are called earthly, spiritual, and heavenly. When we are born, we come first into the earthly level, which gradually develops within us in keeping with the things we learn and the intelligence we gain through this learning, all the way to that summit of intelligence called rationality. This by itself, though, does not open the second level, the one called spiritual. This level is opened by a love for being useful that comes from our intelligence; but the love for being useful is a spiritual one, a love for our neighbor.

In the same way, this level can develop by incremental steps all the way to its summit; and it does so by our discovering what is true and good, or by spiritual truths. Even so, these do not open that third level that is called heavenly. This is opened by a heavenly love for being useful that is a love for the Lord; and love for the Lord is nothing but applying the precepts of the Word to our lives, these precepts being essentially to abstain from evil things because they are hellish and demonic and to do good things because they are heavenly and divine. This is how the three levels are opened in us sequentially.

238 As long as we are living in this world, we have no knowledge of any opening of levels within us. This is because our attention is focused on the earthly level, which is the most remote. We are thinking, intending, and talking and acting on that basis; and the spiritual level, which is deeper, does not communicate with the earthly level directly, but only by correspondence. Communication by correspondence is imperceptible.

However, as soon as we put off the earthly level, which happens when we die, we come into awareness of whatever level has been opened within us in the world, of the spiritual level if that level has been opened, of the heavenly level if that level has been opened. If we become conscious on the spiritual level after death, then we no longer think, intend, or talk or act in an earthly way, but spiritually. If we become conscious on the heavenly level, then we think, intend, and talk and act on that level. Further, since communication among the three levels occurs only by correspondence, the differences in level of love, wisdom, and useful function are so definite that there is no communication between them by direct contact.

We can see from this that we do have three vertical levels and that these can be opened in sequence.

Because there are within us these three levels of love and wisdom and **239** therefore of usefulness, it follows that there are three levels of volition and discernment and consequent closure, and therefore of concentration within us on usefulness, since volition is the vessel of love, discernment the vessel of wisdom, and closure the usefulness that results from them. We can see from this that there is within each of us an earthly, a spiritual, and a heavenly volition and discernment, potentially from birth, and effectively when they are opened.

In short, the human mind, consisting of volition and discernment, has three levels from creation and birth, so we have an earthly mind, a spiritual mind, and a heavenly mind. Consequently, we can be raised into angelic wisdom and possess it even while we are living in this world. Still, we become conscious of it only after death, if we become angels; and then we say inexpressible things, things incomprehensible to an earthly-minded person.

I was acquainted with a moderately educated man in the world and saw him and talked with him in heaven after his death. I sensed very clearly that he was talking like an angel and that what he was saying was beyond the grasp of earthly-minded people. The reason was that in the world he had applied the precepts of the Word to his life and had worshiped the Lord; so the Lord had raised him into the third level of love and wisdom.

It is important to know about this raising up of the human mind, since understanding what follows depends on it.

There are two abilities within us, gifts from the Lord, that distin- **240** guish us from animals. One ability is that we can discern what is true and what is good. This ability is called "rationality," and is an ability of our discernment. The other ability is that we can do what is true and what is good. This ability is called "freedom," and is an ability of our volition. Because of our rationality, we can think what we want to think, either in favor of God or against God, in favor of our neighbor or against our neighbor. We can also intend and do what we are thinking, or when we see something evil and are afraid of the penalty, can use our freedom to refrain from doing it. It is because of these two abilities that we are human and are distinguished from animals.

These two abilities are gifts from the Lord within us. They come from him constantly and are never taken away, for if they were taken away, that would be the end of our humanity. The Lord lives in each of us, in the good and the evil alike, in these two abilities. They are the Lord's dwelling in the human race, which is why everyone, whether good or evil, lives forever. However, the Lord's dwelling within us is more intimate as we use these abilities to open the higher levels. By opening them, we come into consciousness of higher levels of love and wisdom and so come closer to the Lord. It makes sense, then, that as these levels are opened, we are in the Lord and the Lord is in us.

241   I have noted above [§§212, 213] that the three vertical levels are like a purpose, a means, and a result, and that the sequence of love, wisdom, and usefulness follows this sequence. I need at this point, then, to say a little about love as the purpose, wisdom as the means, and usefulness as the result.

People who pay attention to their reason when that reason is in the light can see that our love is the purpose of everything we do, since it is what we love that we think about, decide upon, and do, so it is what we have as our purpose. Our reason can also show us that wisdom is the means, since the love that is our purpose gathers in our discernment the means it needs to reach its goal. So it listens to its wisdom, and these resources constitute the means through which it works. We can see without further explanation that usefulness is the result.

Love, though, is not the same in one individual as in another, so wisdom is not the same in one individual as in another, and neither is usefulness. Since these three are matched in kind (as explained in §§189–194 above), the quality of our love determines the quality of our wisdom, and of our usefulness. I say "wisdom," but this means whatever is characteristic of our discernment.

242   *Spiritual light flows in within us through three levels, but not spiritual warmth except to the extent that we abstain from evils as sins and turn to the Lord.* What I have presented thus far indicates that light and warmth emanate from the sun of heaven, that sun, described in part 2, that is the first emanation of divine love and wisdom. The light emanates from his wisdom and the warmth from his love. Further, the light is the vessel of wisdom and the warmth is the vessel of love; and the more we are engaged in wisdom, the more we come into that divine light, and the more we are engaged in love, the more we come into that divine warmth.

We can also tell from what has been presented that there are three levels of light and three levels of warmth, or three levels of wisdom and three levels of love, and that these levels are formed within us in such a way that we are open to divine love and wisdom and therefore to the Lord.

The present task, then, is to show that while spiritual light flows in through these three levels in us, spiritual warmth does not—except to the extent that we abstain from evils as sins and turn to the Lord; or what amounts to the same thing, to show that we can accept wisdom all the way to the third level, but not love—unless we abstain from evils as sins and turn to the Lord; or (what again amounts to the same thing) to show that our discernment can be raised up into wisdom, but our volition cannot be raised up [into love]—except to the extent that we abstain from evils as sins.

It has become abundantly clear to me from my experiences in the spiritual world that our discernment can be raised up into heaven's light, or into angelic wisdom, but that our volition cannot be raised up into heaven's warmth or angelic love unless we abstain from evils as sins and turn to the Lord. I have often seen and sensed that very ordinary spirits who knew only that God exists and that the Lord was born as a human—hardly anything else—understood the mysteries of angelic wisdom completely, almost the way angels do. Nor were they the only ones. Even many members of the demonic mob understood. They understood while they were listening, that is, but not in their private thinking. When they were listening, light flowed into them from above; but in their private thinking the only light that could get in was the light that agreed with their warmth or love. So even after they had heard these mysteries and grasped them, when they turned their hearing away they retained nothing. In fact, the members of the Devil's mob spat it out and denied it categorically. The reason was that the fire of their love and its light, being mindless, brought down a darkness that snuffed out the heavenly light that was flowing in from above.

243

It is the same in this world. Anyone who has any sense at all and has not become inwardly convinced of false principles on the grounds of intellectual pride, on hearing people talk about higher things or on reading

244

about them understands, retains them, and eventually affirms them if there is any desire for learning. This holds true for evil and good people alike. Even evil people who at heart deny the divine gifts of the church can understand, discuss, and preach higher things, and can defend them in scholarly writing. However, when they are left on their own to think about them, their thinking is based on their hellish self-centeredness, and they deny them. We can see from this that our discernment can be in spiritual light even though our volition may not be in spiritual warmth.

It also follows from this that our discernment does not lead our volition, or that wisdom does not give rise to love. It merely teaches and shows the way. It teaches how we should live and shows us the way we should follow. It also follows from this that our volition leads our discernment and gets it to work in unison with itself. The love that is the substance of our volition gives the name of "wisdom" to whatever in our discernment it finds harmonious.

I will be showing below that on its own, apart from discernment, our volition accomplishes nothing [§409]. Everything it does, it does in conjunction with our discernment. However, our volition gains the cooperation of our discernment by flowing into it, and not the other way around.

245 Now I need to describe how light flows into the three levels that make up the human mind. From our birth, the forms that are receptive of warmth and light or love and wisdom (which as already noted [§223] are in a threefold pattern or on three levels) are translucent and let spiritual light pass through, the way clear glass lets physical light through. This is why we can be raised up all the way to the third level in respect to our wisdom. These forms are not opened, though, until spiritual warmth, or the love of wisdom, is united to the spiritual light. It is through this union that the translucent forms are opened level by level.

This is like the light and warmth of the world's sun and plant life on earth. The winter light is just as bright as summer light, but it does not open anything in seeds or trees. However, when the warmth of spring is united to that light then things open. The resemblance stems from the fact that spiritual light is analogous to physical light and spiritual warmth is analogous to physical warmth.

246 The only way to gain that spiritual warmth is by abstaining from evils as sins and then turning to the Lord, since as long as we are caught up in evil pursuits we are caught up in a love for them. We are enmeshed in our cravings for them; and that love for what is evil, that craving, is a form of love that is opposed to spiritual love and desire. Further, the only way to get rid of that love or craving is by abstaining from evils as sins; and since we cannot do that on our own, but only by the Lord's agency, we need to turn to him. When we do abstain from our evils by the Lord's agency, then, our love for evil and its warmth are put aside and a love for what is good, with its warmth, is brought in in its place, enabling a higher level to be opened. The Lord actually flows in from above and opens it and unites the love or spiritual warmth with wisdom or spiritual light. As a result of this union we begin to blossom spiritually like a tree in springtime.

We are differentiated from animals by the inflow of spiritual light **247** into all three levels of our minds; and beyond what animals can do, we can think analytically; we can see things that are true not only on the earthly level but on the spiritual level as well; and when we see them, we can acknowledge them and so be reformed and regenerated. Our ability to accept spiritual light is what we call rationality, already discussed [§240]. It is a gift from the Lord to each one of us, and one that is not taken away, since if it were taken away, we could not be reformed. It is because of this ability called rationality that we not only can think but can say what we are thinking, which animals cannot do. Then because of that second ability called freedom, also discussed above, we can do what we have thought intellectually.

Since I dealt with these two abilities that we claim—rationality and freedom—in §240, there is no need to say more about them here.

If that higher level, the spiritual level, is not opened in us, we become focused **248** *on the physical world and our sense impressions.* I have just explained that there are three levels of the human mind called earthly, spiritual, and heavenly; that these levels can be opened in us in sequence; that the earthly level is opened first; and that afterward, if we abstain from evils as sins and turn to the Lord, the spiritual level is opened, and ultimately the heavenly level. Since the sequential opening of these levels depends on how we live, it follows that the two higher levels may also not be opened, in which case we stay on the earthly level, which is the most remote.

It is recognized in the world that we have an earthly self and a spiritual self, or an outer and an inner self. It is not recognized that the earthly self becomes spiritual by the opening of a higher level within, and that this opening is accomplished by a spiritual life, a life in accord with divine precepts, and that unless we live by these precepts, we remain centered on the physical world.

249   There are three kinds of earthly-minded people. One kind is made up of individuals who have no knowledge of divine precepts, a second of people who know that such precepts exist but give no thought to living by them, and a third of people who trivialize and deny them. As for the first kind, the ones who have no knowledge of divine precepts, they cannot help remaining earthly-minded because there is no way for them to teach themselves. We all learn about divine precepts from others, who know about them from their religion. We do not gain them by direct revelation (see *Teachings for the New Jerusalem on Sacred Scripture* 114–118).

People of the second kind, the ones who know that divine precepts exist but give no thought to living by them, also remain earthly-minded and are not concerned with anything except what is worldly and physical. After death they become employees and servants of the spiritual-minded, performing for them the functions for which they are fitted. This is because an earthly-minded individual is an employee or servant, while a spiritual-minded one is an employer or householder.

People of the third kind, the ones who trivialize and deny divine precepts, not only remain earthly-minded but even become sense-centered to the extent that they trivialize and deny divine precepts. Sense-centered people are the lowest of the earthly-minded, unable to raise their thoughts above deceptive physical appearances. After death, they are in hell.

250   Since people in this world do not know what a spiritual-minded person is and what an earthly-minded person is, and since many call someone "spiritual" who is merely earthly-minded, and vice versa, I need to say the following things clearly.

1. What an earthly-minded person is and what a spiritual-minded person is.
2. What an earthly-minded person is like whose spiritual level has been opened.
3. What an earthly-minded person is like whose spiritual level has not been opened but is not yet closed.
4. What an earthly-minded person is like whose spiritual level has been completely closed.
5. Lastly, the difference between the life of a wholly earthly-minded person and the life of an animal.

251   1. *What an earthly-minded person is and what a spiritual-minded person is.* We are not human because of our faces and bodies but because of our abilities to discern and intend, so "earthly-minded person" and "spiritual-minded person" refer to our discernment and volition, which can be either earthly or spiritual. When we are earthly-minded, we are like an earthly world in respect to our discernment and volition and can even be called a world or microcosm. When we are spiritual-minded, we are like a spiritual world in respect to our discernment and volition, and can even be called a spiritual world or a heaven.

We can see from this that earthly-minded people, being a kind of image of the earthly world, love whatever has to do with the earthly world, while spiritual-minded people, being a kind of image of the spiritual world, love whatever has to do with that world or heaven. Spiritual-minded people do love the earthly world, it is true, but only the way householders love their servants, who enable them to be of service. In fact, the earthly-minded people become spiritual in a way through their service. This happens when an earthly-minded person feels the joy of service from a spiritual source. This kind of earthly-minded person is called "earthly-spiritual."

Spiritual-minded people love spiritual truths, not only loving to know and understand them but intending them as well; while earthly-minded people love to talk about these truths and carry them out as well. Putting truths into action is being of service. This ranking comes from the way the spiritual world and the earthly world go together, since anything that surfaces and exists in the earthly world has its cause in the spiritual world.

We can tell from this that spiritual-minded people are completely distinct from earthly-minded people, and that the only communication between them is the kind that occurs between a cause and its effect.

2. *What an earthly-minded person is like whose spiritual level has been opened.* This you can see from what has already been said [§251]; but I need to add that an earthly-minded person is a complete person when the spiritual level has been opened within. Once that happens, we are actually in the company of angels in heaven at the same time that we are in the company of people on earth, living under the watchful care of the Lord in both realms. Spiritual-minded people derive their imperatives from the Lord through the Word and carry them out by means of their earthly selves.

Earthly-minded individuals whose spiritual level has been opened do not realize that they are thinking and acting from their spiritual selves. They seem to themselves to be acting on their own, though in fact it is not on their own but from the Lord. Earthly-minded people whose spiritual level has been opened do not realize that they are in heaven because

252

of their spiritual selves, either, even though their spiritual selves are surrounded by heaven's angels. Sometimes such people are even visible to angels, but since they are drawn back to their earthly selves, they vanish in a little while.

Earthly people whose spiritual level has been opened do not realize that their spiritual minds are filled with thousands of hidden treasures of wisdom and with thousands of love's joys as gifts from the Lord. They do not realize that they will begin to participate in this wisdom and joy after they die, when they become angels. The reason earthly-minded people are not aware of all this is that communication between our earthly and our spiritual selves takes place by correspondences, and communication by correspondences is perceived in our discernment only as seeing truths in the light, and in our volition only as being helpful because we enjoy it.

253 3. *What an earthly-minded person is like whose spiritual level has not been opened but is not yet closed.* The spiritual level is not opened in us but is still not closed when we are leading a reasonably thoughtful life but do not know very much real truth. This is because that level is opened by a union of love and wisdom, or of warmth and light. Love alone, or spiritual warmth alone, will not do it, and neither will wisdom alone or spiritual light alone. It takes both together. So if we do not know the real truths that constitute wisdom or light, love cannot manage to open that level. All it can do is keep it able to be opened, which is what "not being closed" means. The same holds true for plant life. Warmth alone will not make seeds sprout or trees leaf out. Warmth together with light is what does it.

We need to realize that everything true is a matter of spiritual light and that everything good is a matter of spiritual warmth, and that what is good opens the spiritual level by means of things true, since goodness does what is helpful by means of truths. Helpful acts are the good that love does, deriving their essence from the union of what is good and what is true.

What happens after death to people whose spiritual level is not opened but still not closed is that since they are still earthly-minded and not spiritual-minded, they are in the lowest parts of heaven, where they sometimes have a hard time of it. Alternatively, they may be around the edges of a somewhat higher heaven, where they live in a kind of twilight. This is because (as already noted [§186]) in heaven and in each distinct community the light decreases from the center to the circumference, with the people who are especially engaged with divine truths in the middle and the people only slightly engaged in truths at the borders. People are only slightly engaged with truths if all they have learned from their religion is that God exists, that the Lord suffered for their sake, and that charity and faith are the essential qualities of the church, without making any effort to find out what faith is and what charity is. Yet essentially, faith is truth, and truth is complex, while charity is every duty we fulfill because of the Lord. We do things because of the Lord when we abstain from evils as sins.

This is just what I have already said [§§168, 197]. The purpose is the whole substance of the means, and the purpose through the means is the whole substance of the result. The purpose is thoughtful action, or some good, the means is faith, or something true, and the results are good deeds or acts of service. We can see from this that nothing from charity can be instilled into our deeds except to the extent that our charity is united to those truths that we attribute to faith. They are the means by which charity enters into works and gives them their quality.

4. *What an earthly-minded person is like whose spiritual level has been* **254** *completely closed.* The spiritual level is closed in people who are focused on evil in their lives, especially if they are engaged in distortion because of their evils. It is rather like the way our little nerve fibers contract at the slightest touch of anything unsuitable, as does every muscular motor fiber and every muscle and the whole body, at the touch of something hard or cold. This is how the substances or forms of the spiritual level within us react to things that are evil and to the distortions that result— they are unsuitable. The spiritual level, being in the form of heaven, is open only to things that are good and to the truths that result from what is good. These are congenial to it, while evils and the falsities they give rise to are unsuitable.

This level contracts, and closes by contracting, especially in people who are caught up in a love of being in control for selfish reasons in this world, since this love is the opposite of a love for the Lord. It is also closed, though not as firmly, in people who because of their love for this world are caught up in a mindless craving to acquire the assets of others. The reason these loves close off the spiritual level is that they are the sources of our evils.

The contraction or closure of this level is like a coil twisting back on itself, which is why this level deflects heaven's light once it has been closed. This yields darkness in place of heaven's light. Accordingly, the truth that is found in heaven's light becomes sickening.

For these people, it is not just [the spiritual] level itself that is closed. It is also the higher area of the earthly level, the area called "rational."

Eventually, then, only the lowest area of the earthly level stays open, the area we call "sensory." This is right next to the world and to our outward physical senses, which thereafter constitute the basis of our thinking, talking, and rationalizing. In the spiritual world, earthly-minded people who have become sense-centered because of their evils and consequent distortions do not look human in heaven's light. They look grotesque, with flattened noses. The reason they have these concave noses is that the nose corresponds to a perception of what is true. They cannot bear a single ray of heaven's light, either. The only light in their caves is like the light of embers or smoldering charcoal. We can see from this who the people are whose spiritual level has been closed, and what they are like.

255   5. *The difference between the life of an earthly-minded person and the life of an animal.* I need to deal with this difference more specifically later, in discussing life. At this point I need to say only that we humans differ in having three levels of mind or three levels of discernment and volition, and that these levels can be opened in sequence. Since they are translucent, we can be raised in discernment into heaven's light and see things that are not only civically and morally true but spiritually true as well. Once we have seen many such truths, we can on that basis draw a series of true conclusions, and keep perfecting our discernment in this way forever.

Animals, though, do not have the two higher levels, only the earthly levels, and apart from the higher levels the earthly levels have no ability to think about any civic, moral, or spiritual issue. Further, since these earthly levels cannot be opened and therefore raised into higher light, animals cannot think in sequential order. They can think only in a simultaneous pattern, and that is not really thinking. It is simply acting on the basis of the knowledge that answers to their love; and since they cannot think analytically or survey their lower thought from any higher vantage point, they cannot talk. All they can do is make sounds that suit their love's knowledge.

The only difference between sense-centered people (the lowest of the earthly-minded) and animals is that they can fill their minds with information and think and talk on that basis. They get this from an ability we all possess, our ability to understand what is true if we want to. This ability makes the difference. However, many people have made themselves lower than animals by their abuse of this ability.

256   *In its own right, the earthly level of the human mind is a continuum, but because of its responsiveness to the two higher levels, it seems to have distinct* *levels when it is raised up.* Even though it is hard for people to understand this if they are not yet familiar with vertical levels, it still needs to be disclosed, since it is a matter of angelic wisdom. While earthly-minded people cannot think about this wisdom the way angels do, they can still grasp it mentally if their minds are raised into the level of light that angels enjoy. Our minds can actually be raised that far and enlightened accordingly. However, this enlightenment of our earthly minds does not happen by distinct levels. There is instead a gradual increase, and in keeping with that increase, our minds are enlightened from within, with the light of the two higher levels.

We can understand how this happens by perceiving that for vertical levels, one is above the other, with the earthly level, the terminal one, acting like an inclusive membrane for the two higher levels. As the earthly level is raised toward a higher level, then, the higher activates that outer earthly level from within and enlightens it. The enlightenment is actually happening because of the light of the higher levels from within, but it is received gradually by the earthly level that envelops and surrounds them, with greater clarity and purity as it ascends. That is, the earthly level is enlightened from within, from the light of the higher, distinct levels; but on the earthly level itself, it happens gradually.

We can see from this that as long as we are in this world and are therefore focused on the earthly level, we cannot be raised into wisdom itself, the way it is for angels. We can be raised only into a higher light at the boundary of angels and receive enlightenment from their light, which flows into us from within and illumines us.

I cannot describe this any more clearly. It is better understood through its effects; for if we have some prior knowledge about causes, their effects embody and present them in the light and thereby make them clear.

The following are "effects." (a) Our earthly mind can be raised as far **257** as the light of heaven that surrounds angels, and can therefore sense on the earthly level what angels sense spiritually—that is, it does not sense so fully. Still, our earthly mind cannot be raised all the way into angelic light itself. (b) With our earthly mind raised as far as heaven's light, we can think and even talk with angels; but when this happens, the thought and speech of the angels are flowing into our earthly thought and speech, and not the other way around. This means that angels talk with us in earthly language, in our native tongues. (c) This happens by a flow of the spiritual level into the earthly, and not by any flow of the earthly level into the spiritual. (d) There is no way for our human wisdom, which is earthly as long as we are living in the earthly world, to be raised into angelic wisdom, only into some reflection of it. This is because the raising of the earthly mind is along a continuum, like that of darkness to light, or coarse to fine. Still, if our spiritual level has been opened, we come into consciousness of that wisdom when we die, and we can also come into consciousness of it through the quiescence of our physical senses, and then through an inflow from above into the spiritual elements of our minds. (e) Our earthly mind is made up of both spiritual substances and earthly substances. Our thinking results from the spiritual substances and not from the earthly substances. These latter substances fade away when we die, but the spiritual substances do not. So when we become spirits or angels after death, the same mind is still there in the form it had in the world. (f) The earthly substances of our minds (which fade away after death, as I have just noted) form the skinlike covering of the spiritual bodies we inhabit as spirits and angels. It is by means of this covering, taken from the earthly world, that our spiritual bodies have their stability, the earthly substance being the outermost vessel. This is why there is no angel or spirit who was not born human.

These hidden treasures of angelic wisdom are appended at this point to show the nature of our earthly mind, which will be further discussed later [§§260–263].

258   Each of us is born with the ability to understand truths even at the deepest level where angels of the third heaven live. As our human discernment climbs up on a continuum around the two higher levels, it receives the light of wisdom from those levels in the manner already described in §256. As a result, we can become rational in proportion to its ascent. If it comes up to the third level, it becomes rational from the third level; if it comes up to the second level, it becomes rational from the second level; and if it does not ascend at all, it is rational on the first level. We say that it becomes rational from those levels because the earthly level is the general recipient vessel of their light.

The reason we do not become rational to the highest degree we are capable of is that our love, which is a matter of our intent, cannot be raised up in the same way as our wisdom, which is a matter of our discernment. The love that is a matter of intent is raised only by abstaining from evils as sins and then by those good actions of thoughtfulness that are acts of service, acts that we are then performing from the Lord. So if the love that is a matter of intent is not raised up along with it, then no matter how high the wisdom that is a matter of our discernment has risen, it ultimately falls back to the level of its love. This is why we become rational only on the lowest level if our love is not raised to the spiritual level as well.

We can tell from all this that our rational ability seems to be made up of three levels, one ability from the heavenly level, one from the spiritual level, and one from the earthly level. We can also tell that our rationality, an ability that can be raised, is still with us whether it is raised up or not.

I have stated that everyone is born with this ability, or with rational- **259** ity, but this means everyone whose outward organs have not been damaged by any external events in the womb, or after birth by illness or some head injury, or by the outburst of a senseless love that lowers all restraints. The rational ability cannot be raised up for people like this. The life of their volition and discernment has no boundaries in which it finds definition, that is, boundaries so arranged that the life can accomplish outward deeds coherently. It does act in keeping with outermost boundaries, but not because of them. On the unavailability of rationality in childhood and early youth, see the close of §266 below.

The earthly mind, being the envelope and vessel of the higher levels of the **260** *human mind, is reactive. If the higher levels are not opened, it acts against them; whereas if they are opened, it acts with them.* I explained in the last section that since the earthly mind is on the last level, it surrounds and encloses the spiritual mind and the heavenly mind, which are on higher levels. Now we have reached the point where I need to show that the earthly mind reacts against the higher or inner minds. The reason it reacts is that it does surround, enclose, and contain them. This could not happen without that reaction, since if it did not react, the enclosed inner elements would start to spread and force their way out so that they dissipated. It would be as though the coverings of the human body were not reacting, in which case the viscera within the body would spill out and trickle away; or it would be as though the membranes around the motor fibers of our muscles did not react against the forces of those fibers when they were activated. Not only would the action cease, the whole inner weblike structure would unravel as well.

It is the same with any terminal vertical level. So it is the same with the earthly mind relative to the higher levels, since as I have just said, there are three levels of the human mind, earthly, spiritual, and heavenly, and the earthly mind is on the final level.

The earthly mind's reaction against the spiritual mind is also the reason the earthly mind consists of substances from the earthly world as well as substances from the spiritual world, as noted in §257 above. By their very nature, substances of the earthly world react against substances of the spiritual world, since substances of the earthly world are intrinsically dead and are activated from the outside by substances of the spiritual world. Anything that is dead and is activated from the outside resists by its very nature, and therefore reacts by its very nature.

We can tell from this that the earthly self reacts against the spiritual self, and that there is a conflict. It is all the same whether we refer to the earthly self and the spiritual self or to the earthly mind and the spiritual mind.

261   We can tell from this that if the spiritual mind is closed, the earthly mind is constantly resisting whatever comes from the spiritual mind, fearing that something from that source will flow in that will disturb its states. Everything that flows in through the spiritual mind is from heaven because the spiritual mind is a heaven in form; and everything that flows into the earthly mind is from the world because the earthly mind is a world in form. It follows, then, that when the spiritual mind is closed, the earthly mind resists everything that comes from heaven and will not let it in—except to the extent that it may serve as a means for gaining possession of worldly benefits. When heavenly things serve as means for the purposes of the earthly mind, then even though those means seem to be heavenly, they are still earthly. The purpose gives them their quality, and they actually become like items of information for the earthly self, items in which there is no trace of inner life.

However, since heavenly things cannot be united to earthly ones in this way so that they act as one, they distance themselves; and for people who are purely earthly, heavenly things come to rest outside, at the circumference, around the earthly things that are within. As a result, merely earthly people can discuss and preach heavenly things and can even act them out, even though they are thinking the opposite within. They behave one way when they are alone, and another way in public. But there will be more on this later [§§266, 267].

262   Because of an inborn reflex, the earthly mind or self resists what comes from the spiritual mind or self when that mind loves itself and the world above all else. Then it finds delight in all kinds of evil—in adultery, cheating, vindictiveness, blasphemy, and the like; and it also recognizes only nature as the creatress of the universe. It uses its rational ability to find proofs of all this, and once it has these proofs, it distorts or stifles or diverts whatever of the church and heaven is good and true. Eventually it either escapes such things, or rejects them, or hates them. It does this in spirit, and does it also physically whenever it dares to speak with others from its spirit without fear of losing reputation, for the sake of respectability and profit.

When people are like this, then their spiritual mind closes more and more tightly. It is primarily the justifications of evil by falsity that close it, which is why confirmed evil and falsity cannot be rooted out after death. They can be rooted out only in this world, by repentance.

When the spiritual mind is open, though, the state of the earthly mind is entirely different. Then the earthly mind is inclined to obey the spiritual mind and to be subservient. The spiritual mind acts on the earthly mind from above or from within; and it moves aside the things there that are reactive and adapts to its purposes the things that are cooperative. So it gradually eliminates any overpowering resistance.

263

We need to realize that action and reaction are involved in everything in the universe, no matter how large or small, whether alive or lifeless. This yields a balance throughout, which is canceled when action overcomes reaction or vice versa. It is the same for the earthly mind and the spiritual mind. When the earthly mind is acting on the basis of the delights it loves and the fascinations of its thinking (which are intrinsically evil and false), then the reaction of the earthly mind moves aside whatever comes from the spiritual mind and blocks the doors against its entry. As a result, any action is controlled by whatever agrees with the reaction. This is the nature of the action and reaction of the earthly mind, which is the opposite of the action and reaction of the spiritual mind; and this is what causes the closing of the spiritual mind or the reversing of the spiral.

However, if the spiritual mind is open, then the action and reaction of the earthly mind are reversed. The spiritual mind is acting from above or within, and as it does so it is working through whatever in the earthly mind is amenable, whether it comes from within or from the outside. Then it reverses the spiral characteristic of the action and reaction of the earthly mind. This mind has been in opposition to the purposes of the spiritual mind from birth, deriving this by heredity from our parents, as is well known.

This is the nature of that change of state called reformation and regeneration. The state of the earthly mind before its reformation might be compared to a spiral twisted or twisting downward, while after its reformation it might be compared to a spiral twisted or twisting upward. So before our reformation, we are looking down toward hell, while after our reformation we are looking up toward heaven.

264 *The origin of evil is in the abuse of the abilities proper to us called rationality and freedom.* By rationality, I mean the ability to discern what is true and therefore what is false, and to discern what is good and therefore what is evil. By freedom, I mean the ability freely to think, intend, and do such things.

The following conclusions can be drawn from what has already been said, and will be further supported below. We all possess these two abilities from creation and therefore from birth—they are given us by the Lord. They are not taken away from us. They are the source of the appearance that we think and speak and intend and act with what seems to be autonomy. The Lord dwells in these abilities within each of us, and it is from this union that we live to eternity. We can be reformed and regenerated because of these abilities, and not apart from them; and it is by them that we are distinguished from animals.

265 The origin of evil in the abuse of these abilities will be presented in the following sequence.

1. Evil people, like good people, enjoy these two abilities.
2. Evil people misuse them to validate things that are evil and false, while good people use them to validate things that are good and true.
3. The evil and false things that we have validated stay with us, becoming part of our love and therefore of our life.
4. Things that have become part of our love and life are passed on to our offspring.
5. All evil characteristics, whether inherited or acquired, reside in the earthly mind.

266 1. *Evil people, like good people, enjoy these two abilities.* I explained in the preceding section that as far as understanding things is concerned, the earthly mind can be raised all the way to the light that surrounds angels of the third heaven, seeing what is true, acknowledging it, and then talking about it. We can see from this that since the earthly mind can be raised up in this fashion, evil people and good people alike enjoy the ability we call rationality; and since the earthly mind can be raised up that far, it follows that both evil people and good people can think and talk about such matters.

As for their ability to intend and do such things even though they do not actually intend and do them, this is witnessed by both reason and experience. Reason asks whether people are incapable of intending and doing what they think. However, the fact that we do not intend and do particular things is because we do not want to intend and do them. The ability to intend and do is the freedom that the Lord gives everyone. The reason people do not intend and do what is good when they can is found in a love for evil that finds it distasteful. Still, we can resist this, and many people do.

This has been verified for me several times by experience in the spiritual world. I have listened to evil spirits, people who were demons inwardly and who had in the world rejected the truths of heaven and the church. When their desire for learning was aroused (a desire we all enjoy from childhood on) by the glamor that surrounds every love like the radiance of a flame, then they grasped mysteries of angelic wisdom just as clearly as good spirits who were inwardly angels. The demonic spirits even claimed that they were capable of intending them and acting in keeping with them, but that they did not want to. When they were told that they would want to if they were to abstain from evils as sins, they said that they could do that, too, but that they did not want to. I could see from this that evil and good people alike have the ability we call freedom. Anyone who reflects will see that this is true. The reason we are able to want to do things is that the Lord, the source of that ability, is constantly making it possible; for as already noted [§264], the Lord dwells in these two abilities in everyone. The Lord is therefore in that ability, or in the power we have of wanting.

As for the ability to discern that we call rationality, this is not given us until our earthly mind comes of age. Until then, it is like a seed in unripe fruit that cannot break open underground and sprout. This ability is not found in the people mentioned above in §259, either.

2. *Evil people misuse these abilities to validate things that are evil and false, while good people use them to validate things that are good and true.* **267** The mental ability we call rationality and the volitional ability we call freedom afford us the possibility of validating anything we please. As earthly-minded people, we can raise our discernment to a higher light as far as we want to; but if we are bent on evil and the distortions it causes, we raise it no higher than the upper levels of the earthly mind, rarely to the region of the spiritual mind. This is because we are caught up in the pleasures of our earthly mind's love. If we do rise above that level, the

pleasures of its love die away. If we rise even higher and see true things that are contrary to the pleasures of our life or the basic premises of the intellect that we claim as our own, then we either distort them or ignore them, dismissing them as worthless, or we hold them in our memory so that they may be of use as tools to our life's love or our pride in our own intelligence.

It is obvious from the abundance of heresies in Christendom (each one validated by its adherents) that earthly-minded people can validate whatever they please. Can anyone miss the fact that all kinds of evil and false notions can be validated? We can "prove" (and inwardly, evil people do "prove") that God does not exist and that nature is all there is, having created itself; that religion is only a device for holding the minds of the simple in bondage; that our own prudence accomplishes everything; and that divine providence does nothing but maintain the universe in the pattern in which it was created; and even, according to Machiavelli and his followers, that there is nothing wrong with murder, adultery, theft, deception, and revenge.

Earthly-minded people can justify a host of things like this, can fill books with "proofs"; and once they have been justified, we see these false notions in their own illusory light, and true ideas are in such darkness that they are virtually invisible, like ghosts in the night. In brief, take the falsest notion you can think of, frame it as a proposition, and tell someone clever to prove it, and you will find it "proved" to the absolute stifling of any true light. But then step back from those proofs and take a second look at the same proposition from your own rationality, and you will see how grotesquely false it is.

This shows that we are able to misuse the two abilities the Lord instills in us to validate all kinds of evil and false notions. No animal can do this because animals do not enjoy these abilities. So unlike us, animals are born into the complete pattern of their lives, with all the knowledge necessary for their earthly love.

268 3. *The evil and false things that we have validated stay with us, becoming part of our love and therefore of our life.* "Proofs" of what is evil and false are simply motions away from what is good and true; and as they are multiplied, they become rejections, since what is evil distances and rejects what is good, and what is false does the same to what is true. As a result, proofs of what is evil and false amount to closures of heaven because everything good and true flows in from the Lord through heaven. Once heaven is closed, we are in hell, in some community there where congenial forms of evil and falsity hold sway, with no possibility of getting out.

I have been allowed to talk with people who had justified for themselves the false principles of their religion centuries ago, and I saw that they were still centered in the same principles they had adopted in the world. This is because everything we justify internally becomes part of our love and our life. It becomes part of our love because it becomes part of our intentions and our discernment, and intention and discernment constitute our life. When it becomes part of our life, it becomes part not only of our whole mind but of our whole body as well. So we can see that once we have justified ourselves in our evil and false principles, that is what we are from head to toe; and once we are wholly of this nature, there is no kind of inversion or reversal of direction that will bring us back into the opposite state and thereby drag us out of hell.

This, together with what has been said earlier in this section, shows where evil comes from.

4. *Things that have become part of our love and life are passed on to our offspring.* It is generally acknowledged that we are born into evil and that we get this as an inheritance from our parents. Some people believe that it is not from our parents, but through them from Adam; but this is a mistake. It comes from the father, from whom we get the soul that is clothed with a body in the mother. The semen that comes from the father is the first vessel of life; but it is the kind of vessel it was in the father. It is actually in the form of his love, and everyone's love is the same in its largest and its smallest forms. There is within it a striving toward the human form, a form into which it gradually develops. It follows, then, that the evils we call hereditary come from our fathers and are therefore handed down from our grandfathers and earlier ancestors to their offspring in sequence.

Experience tells us this, too. There is a likeness of disposition in peoples that comes from their first ancestor, a greater likeness within extended families, and a still greater likeness within individual households. The similarity is so clear that we recognize lineages not only by their dispositions but by their faces as well. There will be more about the way evil love is born into us from our parents later on, when I discuss the way the mind (that is, our volition and discernment) corresponds to the body and its members and organs. At this point I cite only a few things in order to show that evils are handed down from our parents in sequence and that they grow, piling up one generation after another, until we are nothing but evil at birth. The viciousness of evil increases in proportion to the closing of the spiritual mind, with the earthly mind closing to anything from above as well. This is remedied in our descendants only by

269

their abstaining from evils as sins, with the Lord's help. There is no other way to open the spiritual mind and thereby bring the earthly mind back into a corresponding form.

270   5. *All evil characteristics and their consequent distortions, whether inherited or acquired, reside in the earthly mind.* The reason evils and their consequent distortions reside in the earthly mind is that in form, or in image, this mind is an earthly world. The spiritual mind, though, is in form or in image a heaven, and there is no way for evil to find a welcome in heaven. So from birth, this latter mind is not open, only potentially so. The earthly mind derives its form in part from substances of the earthly world, but the spiritual mind derives its form solely from substances of the spiritual world. This latter mind is kept in its wholeness by the Lord so that we can become human. We are actually born animal, but become human.

The earthly mind, with everything in it, turns in spirals from right to left, while the spiritual mind turns in spirals from left to right. So the two minds are turning in opposite directions—a sign that evil is resident in the earthly mind and that on its own, it resists the spiritual mind. Further, turning from right to left is turning downward, toward hell, and turning from left to right moves upward, toward heaven. I have been shown this by the experience that evil spirits cannot turn their bodies from left to right, only from right to left, while good spirits find it hard to turn from right to left and easy to turn from left to right. Their turning follows the flow of the deeper levels of their minds.

271   *Evil and false things are absolutely opposed to good and true things because evil and false things are demonic and hellish, while good and true things are divine and heavenly.* On first hearing, everyone will admit that evil and good are opposites, and that the distortions of evil are opposite to the truth of what is good. However, the whole feeling and consequent sense of people who are engaged in evil pursuits is that evil is good. Evil gratifies their senses, especially sight and hearing, and therefore it also gratifies their thoughts and consequently their perceptions. Because of this, while they do recognize that evil and good are opposites, as long as they are engaged in evil they call evil good and good evil because of their delight.

For instance, if we use our freedom wrongly to think and do evil, we call it freedom; and the opposite, which is thinking what is intrinsically good, we call slavery. Yet this latter is true freedom, and the former is slavery. Again, people who love adultery call adultery freedom, and they call it slavery to be restrained from adultery. They find delight in lasciviousness and discomfort in chastity. People who love power for selfish reasons feel a living delight in that love, a delight that surpasses any other kind of delight. So they call everything associated with that love good and everything that conflicts with it bad, when in fact the opposite is true.

It is the same with every other evil; so even though everyone does admit that evil and good are opposites, people who are engaged in evil pursuits have an opposite picture of this opposition. Only people who are engaged in good pursuits have a fair picture. While involved in evil, no one can see what is good, but people who are involved in something good can see what is evil. It is as though evil were down below in a cave, and good up above on a mountain.

Since most people do not know what evil is and how absolutely opposed it is to good, and since it is important to know this, I need to make this clear in the following sequence. `272`

1. An earthly mind engaged in things evil and therefore false is a form and an image of hell.
2. An earthly mind that is a form and image of hell has three descending levels.
3. The three levels of an earthly mind that is a form and image of hell are the opposites of the three levels of a spiritual mind that is a form and image of heaven.
4. An earthly mind that is a hell is absolutely opposed to a spiritual mind that is a heaven.

1. *An earthly mind engaged in things evil and false is a form and an image of hell.* I cannot describe at this point what an earthly mind is like in its substantive form within us, what it is like in the form derived from the substances of the two worlds woven together in our brains, where that mind primarily dwells. A general picture of this form will be offered later, where I will be dealing with the correspondence of the mind and the body. At this point, I need only say something about the states of that form and the changes of state that give rise to perceptions, thoughts, aims, intentions, and what is associated with them, since it is in regard to these that an earthly mind engaged in evil and false pursuits is a form and an image of hell. This form establishes a substantive form as a ground—changes of state cannot occur apart from a substantive form as their ground, just as there can be no sight without an eye and no hearing without an ear. `273`

As for the form or image by which the earthly mind reflects hell, that form and image is like this. The dominant love, together with its urges, being the general state of this mind, acts the part of a devil in hell; and the distorted thoughts that arise from that dominant love are like that devil's gang. Nothing more nor less than this is meant in the Word by "the Devil and its cohorts."

The situation is much the same, since the dominant love in hell is a love of power for selfish reasons. That is what is referred to as "the Devil" there; and attractions to what is false, with the thoughts that arise from that love, are referred to as "the Devil's gang." It is the same in each of hell's communities, with differences like individual variations on a single theme.

An earthly mind that is engaged in evil and therefore false pursuits has a similar form; so after death, earthly-minded people of this kind come into a community of hell that resembles themselves. They then behave in unison with that hell in every respect. They are actually coming into their own form, that is, into the state of their own minds.

There is also another love, called satan, secondary to the earlier love called the Devil. This is the love of owning the assets of other people, using fair means or foul. Malice, deviousness, and deceit are its gang.

People who are in this hell are called satans collectively, while people in the former hell are called devils collectively. In fact, the ones who do not act in secret do not reject the title. This is why the hells as a whole are called "the Devil" and "Satan."

The reason the two hells are broadly distinguished by these two loves is that all the heavens are distinguished by two loves into two realms, a heavenly one and a spiritual one. The demonic hell is an inverse parallel to the heavenly realm and the satanic hell an inverse parallel to the spiritual one. (On heaven's division into two realms, a heavenly one and a spiritual one, see *Heaven and Hell* 26–28 *[20–28]*.)

The reason this kind of earthly mind is a hell in form is that every spiritual form is the same in its largest and smallest manifestations. This is why every angel is a heaven in smaller form, as has also been explained in *Heaven and Hell*, in §§51–58. It also follows from this that every individual or spirit who is a devil or satan is a hell in smaller form.

274   2. *An earthly mind that is a form and image of hell has three descending levels.* In §§222–229 above, it was explained that there are two kinds of levels, called vertical and horizontal, in the largest and smallest instances of everything. This holds true as well of the earthly mind in its largest and smallest forms. At this point, we are talking about vertical levels.

By virtue of its two abilities, called rationality and freedom, the earthly mind is in a state that allows it to rise up by three levels or descend by three levels. It rises up as a result of good and true actions, and it descends as a result of evil and false actions. Further, when it rises up, the lower levels that tend toward hell are closed off, and when it descends the higher levels that tend toward heaven are closed off. This is because they resist each other.

The three higher and lower levels are neither open nor closed in us when we are first born. This is because at that time we are ignorant of what is good and true and of what is evil and false. However, as we engage ourselves in these things, the levels are opened and closed in one direction or the other.

When they are opened toward hell, then the highest or central place is given to our dominant love, which is a matter of our volition. A second or intermediary place is given to distorted thinking, which is a matter of the discernment derived from that love. The lowest place is given to the realization of our love by means of our thinking, or of our volition by means of our discernment.

All this is like the vertical levels already discussed, which in their sequence are like a purpose, its means, and its result, or like first, intermediate, and final ends.

The downward course of these levels is toward the body; so as they move lower, things become coarser, focused on what is material and bodily.

If truths from the Word are recruited on the second level for its formation, then these truths are distorted because of the first level, which is a love for what is evil. They become servants, slaves. We can tell from this what truths of the church and the Word are like in people who are engaged in a love for what is evil or whose earthly minds are hell in form—that is, since they are serving a devil as its means, these truths are being profaned. The love for evil that takes control in a hellish earthly mind is its devil, as already noted [§273].

3. *The three levels of an earthly mind that is a form and image of hell are* **275** *the opposites of the three levels of a spiritual mind that is a form and image of heaven.* I have already explained [§§130, 248, 270] that there are three levels of mind called earthly, spiritual, and heavenly, and that a human mind made up of these levels looks and turns toward heaven. We can therefore see that when an earthly mind is looking downward and turning toward hell, it is likewise made up of three levels, with each of its levels the opposite of a level of the mind that is a heaven.

This has been made quite clear to me by things I have seen in the spiritual world. I have seen that there are three heavens marked off by three vertical levels and three hells also marked off by three vertical levels, or levels of depth, with the hells opposite to the heavens in every detail. Further, the lowest hell is the opposite of the highest heaven, the intermediate hell the opposite of the intermediate heaven, and the highest hell the opposite of the lowest heaven. It is the same with an earthly mind that is a hell in form. Spiritual forms are in fact consistent in their largest and smallest instances.

The reason the heavens and the hells are in this kind of opposition is that their loves are opposed in this fashion. Love for the Lord and a consequent love for their neighbor constitute the inmost level in the heavens, while love for themselves and love for the world constitute the inmost level in the hells. Wisdom and intelligence from their loves constitute the intermediate level in the heavens, while stupidity and madness from their loves (which put on the appearance of wisdom and intelligence) constitute the intermediate level in the hells. It is the final effects of these two levels, though, either coming to rest in the memory as knowledge or finding definition in the body in actions, that constitute the final level in the heavens; while the realizations of the two levels that become either knowledge or actions constitute the most superficial level in the hells.

The following experience showed me how good and true elements of heaven are changed into evil and false things and therefore into their opposites in the hells. I heard that a divine truth was flowing down from heaven into hell, and heard that on the way down it was transformed step by step into something false, so that when it reached the lowest hell it had turned into its exact opposite. I could see from this that depending on their level, the hells are in opposition to the heavens as far as anything good and true is concerned, and that things become evil and false by flowing into forms that are turned backward. It is recognized, that is, that our perception and sense of anything that flows in depend on the recipient forms and their states.

I was also shown by the following experience that things are turned into their opposites. I was given a view of the hells in their position relative to the heavens, and the people there seemed to be upside down, heads below and feet above. I was told, though, that they seem to themselves to be standing upright. We might compare them to people in the southern hemisphere.

We can tell from this experiential evidence that the three levels of an earthly mind that is a form and image of hell are the opposites of the three levels of an earthly mind that is a form and image of heaven.

4. *An earthly mind that is a hell is absolutely opposed to a spiritual mind that is a heaven.* When loves are opposite, then all perceptive functions are opposite. It is from love, which constitutes our essential life, that everything else flows, like streams from their spring. In the earthly mind, things that are not from that source separate themselves from things that are. What comes from the dominant love is in the center, and everything else is at the sides. If these latter elements are truths of the church drawn from the Word, they are pushed even farther away and eventually are exiled. Then the individual, or the earthly mind, feels evil as good and sees falsity as truth, and vice versa. This is why it believes that malice is wisdom, insanity is intelligence, deviousness is prudence, and evil arts are skillfulness. Then too, it completely trivializes the divine and heavenly things that are proper to the church and its worship and puts supreme value on bodily concerns and the world. By doing this it inverts the state of its life, assigning matters of the head to the soles of the feet and walking all over them, and promoting matters of the soles of the feet to the head. When we do this, we move from life to death. (We may call someone "alive" whose mind is a heaven, and someone "dead" whose mind is a hell.)

276

Everything in the three levels of the earthly mind is enclosed in the works that are done by our physical actions. The information about levels conveyed in this part may serve to disclose this hidden principle, namely that everything proper to our minds, to our volition and discernment, is enclosed in our actions or deeds, much like the things we can and cannot see in a seed, a piece of fruit, or an egg. The actions or deeds themselves may seem to be nothing but what shows on the surface, but there are countless elements within them. There are the energies of the motor fibers of the whole body that are cooperating; and there are all those actions of the mind that are rousing and directing those energies, actions on three levels, as already explained [§§200–201]. Further, since all the actions of the mind are involved, so are all the actions of volition, all the desires of our love, that make up the first level. So are all the actions of our discernment, all the thoughts that shape our perception, which make up the second level. All the contents of our memory, all the images of our thinking that are closest to our speech, are also drawn from this source; they

277

constitute the third level. It is from these, focused into actions, that our deeds arise, deeds in whose outward form the antecedents that actually dwell within are not visible.

On the final level as the composite, vessel, and foundation of the prior ones, see §§209–216 above, and on the vertical levels finding their full realization in their final form, see §§217–221.

278 There is a reason that our physical acts look so simple and plain to the eye, like the outer forms of seeds, fruits, and eggs and like almond nuts in their kernels, when in fact they contain within themselves all the prior elements that have given rise to them. The reason is that every final form is a covering that serves to mark it off from its antecedents. Then too, every level is enveloped with a membrane that serves to mark it off from another. As a result, elements of the first level are unrecognizable to the second level, and elements of this are unrecognizable to the third level. For example, the love of our volition, which is the first level of our mind, is discernible in the wisdom of our discernment, which is the second level of our mind, only by a kind of delight in thinking about something. That first level (the love of our volition, as already noted [§277]) is discernible in the knowledge of our memory, which is the third level, only as a kind of pleasure found in being knowledgeable and in talking.

The obvious conclusion from this is that a deed that is a physical act encloses all these elements, even though it seems as simple as can be in its outward form.

279 In support of this is the fact that the angels who are with us are aware in detail of the actions of our minds within our deeds. Spiritual angels perceive what is enclosed from our discernment, and heavenly angels what is enclosed from our volition. This may seem like a paradox, but it is true. It does need to be realized, though, that the mental elements involved in a contemplated or present deed are in the center, with the rest surrounding in proportion to their relevance.

Angels say that they perceive what someone is like from a single deed, though the image of someone's love will vary depending on the way it finds definition in desires and therefore in thoughts. In brief, every one of the acts or deeds of a spiritual person is like a delicious, nourishing, and beautiful fruit to angels, a fruit that yields flavor, nourishment, and pleasure when it is sliced and eaten.

On angels' having this kind of perception of our actions and deeds, see §220 above.

280 It is the same with our speech. Angels recognize our love from the sound of our speech, our wisdom from the way the sound is articulated, and our knowledge from the meaning of the words. They also tell me that these three elements are in every word, because a word is like a realization that has the sound, the articulation, and the meaning within it. Angels of the third heaven have told me that they sense from any word a speaker says in a sentence the general state of that individual's mind, and some specific states as well.

I have explained at some length in *Teachings for the New Jerusalem on Sacred Scripture* that in the individual words of Scripture there is something spiritual that expresses divine wisdom and something heavenly that expresses divine love, and that angels are aware of these when someone is reading the Word devoutly.

This leads to the conclusion that the deeds of people whose earthly **281** minds are going down to hell by three levels contain everything they have that is evil and therefore false, and that the deeds of people whose earthly minds are moving up into heaven contain everything they have that is good and true, and also that angels perceive both simply from what we say and do. This is why it says in the Word that we are to be judged according to our works and that we will have to give an account of our words.

Angelic Wisdom
About
Divine Love

Part 4

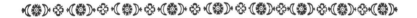

*T*HE *Lord from eternity, who is Jehovah, created the universe and every-*
thing in it not from nothing but from himself. It is known worldwide
and acknowledged through an inner perception by everyone who is wise
that there is one God who is the creator of the universe. Further, the Word
informs us that the God who created the universe is called "Jehovah,"
from "being," because God alone *is.* In *Teachings for the New Jerusalem on
the Lord* there is ample evidence from the Word that the Lord from eternity is that Jehovah.

Jehovah is called the Lord from eternity because Jehovah took on a
human nature in order to save us from hell. At that time too he com-
manded his disciples to call him "Lord." So in the New Testament,
Jehovah is called "the Lord," as we can tell from [the citation of the
verse] "You shall love *Jehovah your God* with all your heart and all your
soul" (Deuteronomy 6:5) [as] "You shall love *the Lord your God* with all
your heart and with all your soul" in the New Testament (Matthew 22:35
[22:37]). We find the same in other Old Testament passages cited in the
Gospels.

People who think rationally and clearly see that the universe was not 283
created from nothing because they see that nothing can arise from nothing. Nothing is simply nothing, and to make something out of nothing

is self-contradictory. Anything that is self-contradictory is in conflict with the light of truth that comes from divine wisdom, and if something is not from divine wisdom, it is not from divine omnipotence either.

Everyone who thinks rationally and clearly also sees that everything has been created out of a substance that is substance in and of itself. This is the essential being from which everything that exists can arise. Since only God is substance in and of itself and is therefore essential being, it follows that there is no other source of the arising of things.

Many people do see this, since reason enables them to. However, they do not dare argue it for fear that they might arrive at the thought that the created universe is God because it is from God—either that, or the thought that nature is self-generated, which would mean that its own core is what we call "God." As a result, even though many people have seen that the only source of the arising of everything is God and God's essential being, they have not dared move beyond the first suggestion of this. If they did, their minds might get ensnared in a so-called Gordian knot with no possibility of escape. The reason they could not disentangle their minds is that they were thinking about God and God's creation of the universe in temporal and spatial terms, terms proper to the physical world, and no one can understand God and the creation of the universe by starting from the physical world. Anyone whose mind enjoys some inner light, though, can understand the physical world and its creation by starting from God, because God is not in time and space.

On Divinity not being in space, see §§7–10 above; on Divinity filling all space in the universe nonspatially, see §§69–72, and on Divinity being in all time nontemporally, see §§72–76 [73–76]. We will see later that even though God did create the universe and everything in it out of himself, still there is not the slightest thing in the created universe that is God. There will be other things as well that will shed an appropriate light on the subject.

284   In part 1 of the present work, I discussed God as divine love and wisdom and as life, and as that substance and form that constitute the one and only reality. In part 2, I dealt with the spiritual sun and its world and with the physical sun and its world, showing that the universe and everything in it was created by God by means of these two suns. Part 3 was about the levels that apply to absolutely everything that has been created. Now in this fourth part, I will be dealing with God's creation of the universe. The reason for presenting all this material is that angels have been expressing their grief to the Lord about seeing nothing but darkness when they look into our world, seeing among us no knowledge about God, heaven, and the creation of nature, knowledge that could serve them as a basis for wisdom.

The Lord from eternity, or Jehovah, could not have created the universe and everything in it except as a person. If people have an earthly, physical con- **285** cept of the Divine-Human One, they are utterly incapable of understanding how a human God could create the universe and everything in it. They think to themselves, "How can a human God wander from place to place through the universe creating things?" or "How can God speak the word from one place, and things be created as soon as the word is spoken?" Things like this come to mind when people say that God is a person if people are thinking about the Divine-Human One the same way they do about earthly people, and when their thought about God is based on nature and its attributes, time and space. On the other hand, if their thought about God is not based on earthly people, not based on nature and its space and time, they grasp clearly that the universe could not have been created unless God were a person.

Focus your thought on the angelic concept of God, of a human God, and as far as you can, eliminate any concept of space, and you will be close to the truth in your thinking.

Some scholars have actually grasped the fact that spirits and angels are not in space because they conceive of spirit as being apart from space. Spirit is like thought. Even though our thought is within us, it enables us to be present somewhere else, no matter how far away. This is the state of spirits and angels, who are people even in respect to their bodies. They seem to be wherever their thought is because in the spiritual world place and distance are apparent only, and are in complete accord with what people are thinking about with interest.

We can tell from this that the God who is visible as a sun far above the spiritual world, who cannot be given any appearance of space, is not to be thought of in spatial terms. In that case, we can understand that the universe was not created out of nothing but out of God, and that God's human body is not to be thought of as large or small or of some particular height because these are matters of space. This means that God is the same from first to last, in the largest and smallest things. It means also that this Person is at the heart of everything created, but nonspatially so.

On Divinity as being the same in the largest and smallest things, see §§77–82 above; and on Divinity as filling all spaces nonspatially, see

§§69–72. Since Divinity is not within space, it is not on the same continuum as the inmost aspect of nature.

286   As for God's inability to create the universe and everything in it except as a person, this is something a discerning individual can grasp very clearly on the following basis. Inwardly, we cannot deny that love and wisdom, mercy and forgiveness exist in God. God, as the source of what is good and true, is their essence. Since we cannot deny this, we cannot deny that God is a person, since none of these things can exist apart from a person. The person is their subject, and to separate them from their subject is to say that they do not exist.

Think of wisdom, and visualize it as outside a person. Is it anything? Can you conceive of it as something ethereal or flamelike? No, unless perhaps you think of it as within these things; and if it is within them, it must be wisdom in a form like ours. It must be in every aspect of that form. Nothing can be lacking if wisdom is to be within it.

In brief, the form of wisdom is human, and because a person is a form of wisdom, a person is also a form of love, mercy, forgiveness—of whatever is good and true, because these act in complete unison with wisdom.

On the fact that love and wisdom cannot occur except in some form, see above, §§40–43.

287   We can also tell that love and wisdom are human by looking at heaven's angels, who are people in full beauty to the extent that they are caught up in love, and therefore in wisdom, from the Lord. The same conclusion follows from what it says in the Word about Adam's being created in the image and likeness of God (Genesis 1:26), because he was created in the form of love and wisdom.

All earthly individuals are born in the human form as to their physical bodies. This is because our spirit, which is also called our soul, is a person; and it is a person because it is receptive of love and wisdom from the Lord. To the extent that our spirit or soul actually accepts love and wisdom, we become human after the death of these material bodies that we are carrying around. To the extent that we do not accept love and wisdom we become grotesque creatures, retaining some trace of humanity because of our ability to accept them.

288   Since God is a person, the whole angelic heaven, taken as a single unit, presents itself as a single person. It is divided into regions and districts according to our human members, organs, and viscera. There are heavenly communities that make up the district of the brain and all its components, of all the facial parts, and of all our physical internal organs; and these districts are distinguished from each other exactly the way they are in us. In fact, angels know what district of the [heavenly] person they live in.

Heaven as a whole has this appearance because God is a person; and God is heaven because the angels who constitute heaven are recipients of love and wisdom from the Lord, and recipients are images.

I have explained at the close of a series of chapters in *Secrets of Heaven* that heaven is in the human form in all respects.

This shows us the senselessness of concepts people have when they **289** think about God in nonhuman terms and about divine attributes as not being in a human God. Separated from person, these concepts are nothing but theoretical constructs.

On God as the essential person, from whom we are human by virtue of our acceptance of love and wisdom, see §§11–13 above. I stress this here for the sake of what follows, to make it clear that the universe was created by God because God is a person.

The Lord from eternity, or Jehovah, brought forth the sun of the spiritual **290** *world out of himself, and created the universe and all its contents from it.* Part 2 of the present work dealt with the sun of the spiritual world, and the following points were made there. In the spiritual world, divine love and wisdom look like a sun (§§83–88). Spiritual warmth and spiritual light emanate from that sun (§§89–92). That sun is not God. Rather, it is an emanation from the divine love and wisdom of the Divine-Human One. The same is true of warmth and light from that sun (§§93–98). The sun of the spiritual world is seen at a middle elevation, as far from angels as the physical world's sun is from us (§§103–107). The east in the spiritual world is where the Lord is seen as the sun, and the other directions follow from that (§§119–124 *[119–123]*, 125–128 *[124–128]*). Angels always face the Lord as the sun (§§129–134, 135–139). The Lord created the universe and everything in it by means of that sun that is the first emanation of divine love and wisdom (§§151–156). The physical world's sun is nothing but fire and is therefore dead; and since nature has its origin in that sun, it is dead. Further, the physical world's sun was created so that the work of creation could be finished off and completed (§§157–162). There would be no creation if it were not for this pair of suns, one living and one dead (§§163–166).

One of the things explained in part 2, then, was this: that sun is not **291** the Lord. Rather, it is an emanation from the Lord's divine love and wisdom. It is called an emanation because that sun is brought forth from the divine love and divine wisdom that in and of themselves are substance and form; and Divinity emanates by means of it.

However, our reason by its nature will not consent to anything unless it sees the reason behind it, unless it sees how it has happened. In the present instance, reason needs to grasp how the spiritual world's sun was brought forth, inasmuch as it is not the Lord but an emanation from the Lord, so something must be said about this as well. I have had many conversations with angels about this. They have told me that they grasp it clearly in their spiritual light, but that it is almost impossible for them to present it to us in our earthly light because there is such a difference between the two kinds of light, and therefore between their thoughts and ours.

They did say, though, that it is like the aura of feelings and consequent thoughts that surrounds every angel, through which angels' presence is established for people both nearby and at a distance. This surrounding aura is not the actual angel, but it is derived from every part of the angel's body. Coherent substances flow from it like a river, and the emanations envelop them. These substances bordering angels' bodies, substances constantly energized by the two fountains of their life, the heart and the lungs, stir the atmospheres into their activities, and in this way establish a sense of the angel's virtual presence among others. This means that there is not a separate aura of feelings and consequent thoughts that go forth in connected fashion, even though that is what we call it, because the feelings are simply states of the forms of the mind within.

The angels went on to say that all angels have this kind of aura around them because the Lord does, and that the aura around the Lord is similarly derived from him. This aura is their sun, or the sun of the spiritual world.

292   I have fairly often been allowed to perceive that there is this kind of aura around an angel or spirit and that there is a general aura around groups in community. I have also been allowed to see this aura in various guises, sometimes in heaven looking like a faint flame and in hell like a harsh flame, sometimes in heaven looking like a delicate and bright cloud and in hell like a dense black cloud. I have also been allowed to sense these auras as different kinds of aroma and stench. This has convinced me that everyone in heaven and everyone in hell is surrounded by an aura made up of substances distilled and separated from his or her body.

293   I have also noticed that an aura flows out not only from angels and spirits but also from absolutely everything you see in that world—from trees and their fruits there, for example, from shrubs and their blossoms, from plants and grasses, even from soils and their particles. I could therefore see that this is a universal characteristic of things both living and lifeless, that everything is surrounded by something resembling what lies within it and that this is constantly breathing forth.

The experience of numerous scholars informs us that something like this happens in the physical world. For example, an outgoing wave is constantly flowing from individuals and from every animal, also from trees, fruits, shrubs, and flowers, and even from metals and stones. The physical world gets this from the spiritual world, and the spiritual world gets it from Divinity.

Since the elements that make up the sun of the spiritual world are **294** from the Lord and are not the Lord, they are not intrinsic life but are devoid of intrinsic life. In the same way, the elements that flow out from angels and from us and form surrounding auras are not the angels or the people. They are derived from them but are devoid of their life. They are part of the angel or person only in the fact that they are in harmony with them because they are derived from those forms of their bodies that are forms of the life within them.

This is a mystery that angels can see in thought and express in speech with their spiritual concepts, while we cannot do the same with our earthly concepts. This is because a thousand spiritual concepts go to make up one earthly one, and we cannot resolve a single earthly concept into any spiritual one, let alone into several. The reason for this is that they differ as to the vertical levels discussed in part 3.

The following experience taught me what kind of difference there **295** is between angels' thoughts and our thoughts. They were told to think about something spiritually and then to tell me what they had been thinking. Once they had done this and tried to tell me, they could not, and they explained that they could not articulate it. The same thing held true for both their spiritual speech and their spiritual writing. There was not a single word of spiritual speech that resembled a word of earthly speech, no element of spiritual writing that resembled earthly writing except the letters, and each of these contained a complete meaning.

Remarkably enough, though, they told me that they seemed to themselves to be thinking and talking and writing in their spiritual state the same way we do in our earthly state even though there is no similarity whatever. I could see from this that what is earthly and what is spiritual differ as to vertical level, and that they communicate with each other only through correspondences.

296 *There are three things in the Lord that are the Lord—a divine element of love, a divine element of wisdom, and a divine element of service. These three things are made visible outside the sun of the spiritual world—the divine element of love through its warmth, the divine element of wisdom through its light, and the divine element of service through the atmospheres that enclose it.* On the emanation of warmth and light from the spiritual world's sun—warmth from the Lord's divine love and light from the Lord's divine wisdom—see §§98–92 [93–98], 99–102, and 146–150. I now need to note that the third thing that emanates from the sun there is an atmosphere that serves as the vessel of warmth and light, and that it emanates from that divine aspect of the Lord that is called "service."

297 Anyone who thinks with some enlightenment can see that love has service as its goal, that love tends toward service, and that love brings about service through wisdom. In fact, love cannot accomplish anything useful by itself, only by means of wisdom. After all, what is love unless there is something that is loved? That "something" is service. Service is what is loved; and since it is brought forth by means of wisdom, it follows that service is the vessel of love and wisdom.

I explained in §§209–216 above (as well as elsewhere) that these three, love, wisdom, and service, follow in sequence by vertical levels, and that the final level is the composite, vessel, and foundation of the preceding levels. It therefore stands to reason that these three elements— elements of divine love, divine wisdom, and divine service—are in the Lord, and in essence are the Lord.

298 I will be explaining at ample length below [§§319–335] that if you look at both the inner and the outer aspects of humans, we are a form suited to all kinds of service, and that all the useful functions in the created universe have their equivalents in these kinds of service. At this point I need only mention it in order to call attention to the fact that God as a person is the very form suited to all kinds of service, the one in whom all useful functions in the created universe find their source. This means that in terms of its useful functions, the created universe is an image of God.

By "useful functions," I mean those processes that were created by the Divine-Human One, or the Lord, as part of the design. I do not mean activities that derive from our own self-concern. That concern is hell, and its activities violate the design.

Bear in mind, then, that these three elements—love, wisdom, and service—are in the Lord and are the Lord. Bear in mind also that the Lord is everywhere, is in fact omnipresent. Then consider that the Lord cannot make himself manifest to any angel or to us as he really is and as he is in his sun. This is why he makes himself manifest by means of things that can be accepted, doing so as to love in the form of warmth, as to wisdom in the form of light, and as to service in the form of an atmosphere.

The reason the Lord manifests himself as to service in the form of an atmosphere is that an atmosphere serves as a vessel for warmth and light the way service serves as a vessel for love and wisdom. The warmth and light that radiate from Divinity as the sun cannot radiate in nothing, in a vacuum, but need some vessel as their medium. We call this vessel the atmosphere that surrounds the sun, takes it in its embrace, and carries it to the heaven where angels are and from there to the world where we are. This is how the Lord's presence is made manifest everywhere.

I explained in §§173–178 and 179–183 above that there are atmospheres in the spiritual world just as there are in the physical world; and I noted that the atmospheres of the spiritual world are spiritual, and that those of the physical world are physical. Given the origin of the spiritual atmosphere most closely surrounding the spiritual sun, then, it stands to reason that in all respects it is, in essence, of the same quality as the sun is in its essence.

With their spiritual concepts, which are nonspatial, angels assert the truth of this by saying that there is only one single substance underlying everything and that the spiritual world's sun is that substance. Further, since Divinity is not in space and since it is the same in the largest and smallest things, the same holds true for that sun that is the first emanation of the Divine-Human One. They further assert that the one substance, the sun, radiating by its atmospheres, gives rise to the variety of everything in the created universe, in accord with both the gradual or horizontal levels and the distinct or vertical ones.

Angels have told me that there is no way to understand such things unless space is banished from our concepts; that if space is not banished, superficial appearances will inevitably give rise to illusions. We are not susceptible to them, though, if we hold in mind the fact that God is the absolute reality underlying everything.

Further, in the light of angelic concepts, which are nonspatial, it is perfectly clear that in the created universe there is nothing living except the Divine-Human One—the Lord—alone, that nothing moves except by life from God, and that nothing exists except by means of the sun from God. So it is true that in God we live and move and have our being.

302   *The atmospheres—three in number in each world, spiritual and physical—in their final forms terminate in the kinds of material substance characteristic of our earth.* In §§173–176 *[173–178]* of part 3, I explained that there are three atmospheres in each world, the spiritual and the physical, distinguished from each other by vertical levels and diminishing as they move downward by horizontal levels. Since the atmospheres do diminish as they move lower, it follows that they are constantly becoming denser and less active, ultimately so dense and inactive that they are no longer atmospheres but inert substances, and in a physical world they become stable, like the substances on earth that we call "matter."

There are three consequences of this origin of material substances. First, material substances also have three levels. Second, they are kept in interconnection by the enveloping atmospheres. Third, they are suited in their forms to the production of all kinds of useful activity.

303   No one who thinks that there are constant intermediate steps between what is first and what is final, and that nothing can come into being except from some antecedent, and ultimately from what is first, can fail to agree that the material substances on earth have been brought forth by the sun by means of its atmospheres. What is first is the spiritual world's sun, and what is first relative to that sun is the Divine-Human One, or the Lord.

Since the atmospheres are those relatively early things by which the sun makes itself present in outermost things, and since those relatively early things are constantly diminishing as they work and extend themselves all the way to their limits, it follows that when their action and expansion come to rest at their limits, they become the kinds of material substance that we find on earth, retaining from the atmospheres that gave rise to them a tendency and effort to produce useful functions.

People who propose a creation of the universe and everything in it with no constant intermediate steps from what is first cannot help but formulate theories that are fragmentary and disconnected from actual causes. When these theories are explored by a mind that probes the matter more deeply, they look not like houses but like a pile of rubble.

304   Because of this common origin of everything in the created universe, its smaller components have a similar characteristic. That is, they go from their beginning to their limits, limits that are in a relatively quiet

state, in order to come to rest and persist. In the human body, this is how the fibers develop from their first forms until they become tendons, and the fibers together with their smaller vessels develop from their beginnings until they become cartilage and bone, where they become stable and durable.

Because there is this kind of process from beginnings to limits for our human fibers and vessels, there is a similar procession of the states of these fibers and vessels, their states being sensations, thoughts, and feelings. These too go through a sequence from their beginnings, where they are in the light, to their limits, where they are in darkness; or from their beginnings, where they are in warmth, to their limits, where they are not. Since they have this kind of progression, there is a similar progression for love and everything involved in it and for wisdom and everything involved in it. In short, this kind of progression is characteristic of everything in the created universe. This is just what I said in §§222–229 above, that there are levels of both kinds in everything that has been created, no matter how large or small.

The reason there are both kinds of level in even the smallest things is that the spiritual sun is the sole substance that gives rise to everything, according to the spiritual concepts of angels (§300).

There is nothing of absolute Divinity in the material substances that make **305** *up earth, but they are still derived from absolute Divinity.* On the basis of the origin of earth as described in the preceding section, we may conclude that there is no trace of absolute Divinity in the earth's material substances; they are completely devoid of absolute Divinity. There are, as already stated [§§184, 189], boundaries and limits of the atmospheres, whose warmth lapses into cold, light into darkness, and activity into torpor. Still, by being connected with their source, the substance of the spiritual sun, they retain something that is in that sun from Divinity. As noted above in §§291–298 *[291–294]*, this was the aura that envelops the Divine-Human One, the Lord. The material substances of earth arise from this aura by extension from the sun, by means of the atmospheres.

There is no other way to describe the origin of earth from the spiri- **306** tual sun by means of the atmospheres using words that issue from earthly concepts. It can be described differently using words derived from spiritual concepts, though, because these are nonspatial; and since they are nonspatial, they do not fit into any words of an earthly language.

See above (§295) on the fact that spiritual thought, speech, and writing are so different from earthly thought, speech, and writing that they have nothing in common, and communicate only by means of correspondences. It will have to do, then, that we understand the origin of earth to some extent physically.

307 *All useful functions, which are the goals of creation, are in forms, and they get these forms from the material substances characteristic of earth.* All the things I have been talking about so far—the sun, the atmospheres, and the earth—are simply means toward goals, and the goals of creation are what are brought forth from earth by the Lord as the sun, through the atmospheres. These goals are called useful functions, and they include everything involved in the plant kingdom, everything involved in the animal kingdom, and ultimately the human race and the angelic heaven that comes from it.

These are called useful functions because they are receptive of divine love and wisdom and because they focus on God the Creator as their source and thereby unite him with his master work in such a way that they continue to exist through him in the same way they arose. I say "they focus on God the Creator as their source and unite him with his master work," but this is talking in terms of the way things seem. It actually means that God the Creator works it out so that these useful functions seem to focus on and unite themselves to him on their own initiative. I will describe later [§§310–317] how they focus on and thereby unite themselves to him.

I have already dealt with these subjects to some extent in appropriate places; in §§47–51, for example, divine love and wisdom cannot fail to be and to be manifested in others that it has created; in §§54–60 *[55–60]*, everything in the created universe is a vessel of divine love and wisdom; and in §§65–68, the useful functions of every created thing tend upward to us step by step, and through us to God the creator, their source.

308 Can anyone fail to see quite clearly that the goals of creation are useful functions? Simply bear in mind that nothing can arise from God the Creator—nothing can be created, therefore—that is not useful. If it is to be useful, it must be for the sake of others. Even if it is for its own sake, it is still for others, because we are useful to ourselves in order to be fit to be useful to others. Anyone who keeps this in mind can also keep in mind the thought that functions that are truly useful cannot arise from us but must be in us from one who brings forth nothing but what is useful—the Lord.

Since the subject is the forms of useful functions, I need to discuss them in the following sequence.

1. Earth has an active tendency to bring forth useful functions in particular forms, or forms of useful functions.
2. In all such forms there is some image of the creation of the universe.
3. In all such forms there is some human image.
4. In all such forms there is some image of what is infinite and eternal.

1. *Earth has an active tendency to bring forth useful functions in particular forms, or forms of useful functions.* The presence of this tendency in the earth is a corollary of its origin, since the material substances that make up the earth are boundaries and limits of the atmospheres that come from the spiritual sun as useful functions (see above, §§305 and 306). Further, since the material substances that make up the earth are from this source, and since their compounds are constantly held together by the surrounding pressure of the atmospheres, it follows that this gives them a constant active tendency to bring forth forms of useful functions. They derive their very ability to bring these forth from their origin as the boundaries of the atmospheres, with which they are therefore in harmony.

I said that this tendency and quality are in the earth, but by this I mean that they are characteristic of the material substances that make up the earth, whether in the earth itself or exhaled by the earth as atmospheres. It is generally recognized that the atmospheres are full of such tendencies.

The presence of this tendency and quality in earth's material substances shows quite clearly in the fact that all kinds of seed are opened to their cores by warmth, are impregnated by substances so subtle that they can only be from a spiritual source, and in this way have the potential of uniting themselves to their function, which is multiplication. After this, they unite with matter of a physical origin to bring forth forms of useful functions, and then, so to speak, bring them forth from the womb so that they emerge into the light, which enables them to sprout and grow.

From then on, this tendency is constantly working from the earth through the roots all the way to the boundaries, and from the boundaries back to the beginning where the function itself dwells in its source. This is how useful functions are transformed into forms, and how as forms

309

310

develop from their beginnings to their limits and back from their limits to their beginnings, they derive from their function, which is like their soul, a usefulness of each and every component. I am saying that the useful function is like the soul because its form is like its body.

It also follows that there is a still deeper tendency, a tendency to bring forth processes that support the development of the animal kingdom, since all kinds of animal are nourished by plants. It also follows that there is a very deep element in this tendency, a tendency to be of use to the human race. These conclusions follow from the following premises: (a) There are boundaries, and all antecedent things are gathered together in proper sequence within these boundaries, as explained in any number of places above. (b) Each kind of level is found in the largest and smallest instances of everything, as explained in §§222–229 above. The same holds true for their tendency. (c) All useful functions are brought forth by the Lord from outermost things, so there must be an active tendency toward useful functions in outermost things.

311   Still, all these tendencies are not alive. They are tendencies of the energies of the ultimate expressions of life, energies that ultimately have within them, because of the life they come from, a striving to return to their origin by the means at hand. In their final forms, the atmospheres are energies of this sort, energies by which the material substances characteristic of earth are prompted to take form and are maintained in forms both inwardly and outwardly. I am not at leisure to explain this in greater detail, since that would be a major undertaking.

312   The first productive thing earth does when it is still fresh and in all its simplicity is to bring forth seeds. Earth's first tendency could not be anything else.

313   2. *In all such forms there is some image of creation.* There are three kinds of forms of functions: forms of the functions of the mineral kingdom, forms of the functions of the plant kingdom, and forms of the functions of the animal kingdom. The forms of the functions of the mineral kingdom are beyond description because they are not open to our sight. The first forms are the material substances that make up the earth at their most minute. The second forms are compounds of these, which are infinitely varied. The third forms come from decayed vegetation and from dead animals, and from the gaseous vapors they are constantly giving forth, which combine with the earth to form its soil.

These three levels of the forms of the mineral kingdom offer an image of creation in that as they are activated by the sun through its atmospheres and their warmth and light, they do bring forth useful functions in particular forms, functions that are goals of creation. This image of creation in their tendencies (described in §310 above) lies deeply hidden.

We can see how the forms of functions in the plant kingdom offer an image of creation in the way they develop from their beginnings to their limits and from their limits to their beginnings. Their beginnings are seeds, and their limits are their stalks clothed with bark. Through the bark, which is the limit of the stalk, they develop toward seeds, which are their beginnings, as already noted. The stalks clothed with bark echo the planet clothed with soils that give rise to the creation and formation of all its useful functions. There is ample evidence that plant growth takes place through the bark and cortical layers, working through the stalks and branches as extensions of the coverings of the roots into the beginnings of fruits, and in the same way through the fruits into seeds. An image of creation in the forms of functions is offered in the development of their formation from beginnings to limits and from limits to beginnings, as well as in the fact that throughout their development there is the goal of producing fruits and seeds that are useful.

We can see from what I have just been saying that the process of creation of the universe goes from its very beginning, the Lord clothed with the sun, to its limit, which is the soil, and from this, through its functions, back to its very beginning, the Lord. We can see also that the goals of the whole creation are useful functions.

We need to realize that the warmth, light, and atmospheres of the physical world contribute absolutely nothing to this image of creation. This image is entirely the work of the warmth, light, and atmospheres of the spiritual world's sun. These bring the image with them and instill it into the forms of the functions of the plant kingdom. All that the warmth, light, and atmospheres of the physical world do is open the seeds, keep their productivity increasing, and provide the matter that gives them solidity.

They do not accomplish this with energies from their own sun, though, which are nothing in their own right. They accomplish it with energies from the spiritual sun that is constantly prompting them to do so. They contribute absolutely nothing to the process of giving the forms an image of creation. The image of creation is spiritual; but in order for it to be visible and to function usefully in a physical world, in order for it to be solid and durable, it needs to be "materialized," or filled in with this world's matter.

There is a similar image of creation in the forms of the functions of the animal kingdom. For example, a body is formed from the seed

314

315

316

deposited in the womb or egg, a body that is its final form; and when this matures, it produces new seeds. The sequence is like the sequence of forms of functions in the plant kingdom. The seeds are the initial elements; the womb or egg is like the soil; the state before birth is like the state of the seed in the earth while it is making its roots; the state after birth until reproduction is like the sprouting of a tree until its fruit-bearing state.

We can see from this parallelism that there is a likeness of creation in the animal forms just as there is in plant forms. Specifically, there is a sequence from beginnings to limits and from limits to beginnings.

There is a similar image of creation in the details of our own nature, since the sequence of love through wisdom into useful functions is similar, and so therefore is the sequence of intent through discernment into act, and of charity through faith into works. Intent and discernment, charity and faith, are the first and originating elements, while acts and deeds are the final ones. There is a return from these latter, through the delights of being useful, to the first elements, which as noted are intent and discernment, or charity and faith. We can see clearly that the return is by way of the delights we find in being useful from the pleasure we sense in acts and deeds that come from some love. The delights of acts and deeds are the delights we attribute to being useful.

There is a similar sequence from beginnings to limits and from limits to beginnings in the purely organic forms of our desires and thoughts. There are in our brains the star-shaped forms called gray matter, with fibers stretching from them into the medullary matter and through the neck into the body. There they go to their limits, and from these limits they return to their beginnings. The return of the fibers to their beginnings is by way of the blood vessels.

There is a similar sequence of all our desires and thoughts, which are shifts and changes of the states of their forms and substances. The fibers that stretch out from their forms or substances are analogous to the atmospheres that come from the spiritual sun and are vessels of warmth and light. The physical acts are like the things produced from the earth by means of the atmospheres, with the delights of their useful functions returning to their source.

It is scarcely possible, though, to gain a full mental grasp of the nature of their sequence and of the way it embodies an image of creation, since the thousands upon thousands of energies at work in an action seem to be a single event. Further, the delights of useful functions do not give rise to concepts in our thought, but simply affect us without being clearly perceived.

On these matters, see what has already been presented about the way the functions of everything created tend upward by vertical levels to us, and through us to God the creator, their source (§§65–68), and how the goal of creation—that everything should return to the Creator and that there should be a union—becomes manifest in outermost forms (§§167–172).

These matters will be seen in clearer light, though, in the next part [§§371–431], when I discuss the correspondence of volition and discernment with the heart and lungs.

3. I explained above, in §§61–64, that *in all such forms there is some human image.* It will be made clear in the next section that all useful functions from beginnings to limits and from limits to beginnings have a relationship and a responsiveness to everything in humans, so that we are a kind of image of the universe and conversely the universe, from a functional point of view, is in our image. **317**

4. *In all such forms there is some image of what is infinite and eternal.* We can see an image of the infinite in these forms from the tendency and potentiality of filling the space of the whole world and even of many worlds, without end. A single seed brings forth a tree, shrub, or plant that takes up its own space. From each tree, shrub, or plant, there come seeds, in some cases thousands of them. Assuming these to be planted and to have sprouted, they take up their spaces; and if from each of their seeds new generations arise again and again, after a few years the whole world is full. If the propagation continues, any number of worlds is filled, and so on to infinity. Figure on a thousand seeds coming from one, and then multiply a thousand by a thousand ten or twenty or a hundred times, and you will see. **318**

There is a similar image of eternity in these processes. Seeds reproduce year after year, and the reproductions never cease. They have not paused from the creation of the world to the present, and they will not stop forever.

These two facts are obvious indications and eloquent signs that everything in the universe was created by an infinite and eternal God.

In addition to these images of what is infinite and eternal, there is another image in variety. There can never be a substance, state, or thing in the created universe that is exactly the same as any other. Not in the atmospheres, not on earth, not in the forms that arise from them, and therefore not in any of the things that fill the universe can anything identical ever be brought forth. We can see this very clearly in the variety of all human faces. There is not one identical to another in all the world, and never can be to eternity. This means that there is no human spirit like another, since the face bears the stamp of the spirit.

319   *From a functional point of view, everything in the created universe is in our image; and this testifies that God is human.* The ancients called the individual person a microcosm because each of us reflects the macrocosm, that is, the universe in its entirety. Nowadays, though, people do not know why the ancients gave us this name. Nothing of the universe or the macrocosm is visible in us except that we are nourished by its animal and plant kingdoms and are physically alive, that we are kept alive by its warmth, see by its light, and hear and breathe by its atmospheres. These things, though, do not make us a microcosm the way the universe and everything in it is a macrocosm.

Rather, the ancients learned to call us a microcosm or little universe from the knowledge of correspondences that the earliest people enjoyed and from their communication with angels of heaven. Heaven's angels actually know from what they see around themselves that if we focus on functions, we can see an image of a person in everything in the universe.

320   We are a microcosm or little universe because the created universe has a human image if it is seen in terms of functions. However, this notion remains outside the scope of the thinking we do on the basis of the universe as we see it in this physical world and outside the scope of the knowledge that derives from that thinking. This means that the only way this thought can be established is by an angel who is in the spiritual world or by someone who has been granted entry into that world to see what is there. Since this has been granted to me, I can unveil this mystery from what I have seen there.

321   We need to realize that to all outward appearances, the spiritual world is just like the physical world. You can see lands there, mountains, hills, valleys, plains, fields, lakes, rivers, and springs like the ones in our earthly world; everything, then, that belongs to the mineral kingdom. You can see parks as well, gardens, groves, and woods, with all kinds of trees and shrubs with their fruits and seeds, smaller plants, flowers, herbs, and grasses; everything, then, that belongs to the plant kingdom. You can see all kinds of animals, birds, and fish—everything that belongs to the animal kingdom. The people there are angels and spirits.

This is prefaced to let it be known that the whole spiritual world is just like the whole physical world, the sole difference being that things there are not static and stable the way they are in a physical world because there is nothing of nature there. Everything is spiritual.

There is very solid ground for believing that there is a human image to the universe of the other world in the fact that everything listed in §321 is happening concretely around angels and around angelic communities. It is as though these things were being brought forth or created by them. They persist around them without fading away. You can tell that they are apparently brought forth or created by the angels because when an angel goes away or when a community relocates, these things are no longer visible. Then too, when other angels arrive to take their place, the appearance of everything around them changes. The trees and fruits of the parks change, the blossoms and seeds of the flower beds change, the herbs and grasses of the fields change, and so do the kinds of animals and birds.

322

The reason things occur and change like this is that everything occurs in response to the angels' feelings and consequent thoughts. They are responsive entities, and because the things that respond are integral aspects of that to which they respond, they are their visual images.

The actual image is not visible when the focus is on the forms of anything, but it is visible when the focus is on their functions. I have been allowed to see that when angels' eyes have been opened by the Lord so that they see these things as they answer to functions, the angels recognize and see themselves in their surroundings.

Since the things that occur around angels in response to their feelings and thoughts resemble a kind of universe in being lands, plants, and animals, and since they amount to an image that represents the angels, we can see why the ancients called us a microcosm.

323

There is ample support for the truth of this in *Secrets of Heaven* and also in the book *Heaven and Hell,* as well as throughout the preceding pages where I have dealt with correspondence [§§52, 83, 87]. I explained there that there is nothing in the created universe that does not answer to something in us, not only to our feelings and consequent thoughts, but also to our physical organs and viscera—not in respect to their substances, but in respect to their functions.

324

This is why when the Word talks about the church and its people, there is such frequent mention of trees like the olive and the vine and the cedar, of gardens and groves and woods, and of the beasts of the field, the fowl of the air, and the fish of the sea. They are mentioned because they correspond and are united by corresponding, as noted. So too, when we are reading things like this in the Word, angels are not conscious of them but of the church in their stead, or of the church's people in regard to their state.

325 Since there is a human image to everything in the universe, Adam's wisdom and intelligence are described by the Garden of Eden, where there were trees of every kind, as well as rivers, precious stones, and gold, along with the animals that he named. All of these meant things that were within him and that made him what we call "human."

Quite similar things are said of Assyria in Ezekiel 31:3–9, meaning the church as far as its intelligence is concerned, and about Tyre in Ezekiel 28:12 and 23 *[13]*, meaning the church in regard to its firsthand knowledge of what is good and true.

326 We can tell from all this, then, that if we focus on functions, there is a human image to everything in the universe. We can also tell that this testifies to the fact that God is human, because the things just listed do not come into being around angelic people from themselves, but from the Lord through them. They actually arise from the flow of divine love and wisdom into the angels, who are recipients, and are brought forth to their sight the way the universe is created. So people there know that God is human and that the created universe, functionally viewed, is an image of God.

327 *All of the Lord's creations are useful functions; and they are useful functions in the sequence, on the level, and in the specific way that they relate to humanity and through humanity to the Lord, their source.* I have already made the following points on this subject. Nothing can arise from God the Creator that is not useful (§308). The useful functions of everything created tend upward, step by step, from the lowest to us, and through us to God the Creator, their source (§§65–68). The goal of creation—that everything should return to the Creator and that there should be a union—becomes manifest in outermost forms (§§167–172). They are useful to the extent that they focus on their Creator (§307). Divinity cannot fail to exist in and be manifested in others that it has created (§§47–51). Everything in the universe is a vessel according to its usefulness, and this depends on its level (§38 *[58, 66]*). Seen in terms of its functions, the universe is an image of God (§39 *[169, 298]*). There are many other relevant statements as well. These witness to the truth that all the Lord's creations are useful functions, and that they are useful functions in the sequence, on the level, and in the specific way that they relate to humanity, and through humanity to the Lord, their source. It remains now to say something more detailed about useful functions.

By this "human" to whom useful functions relate, I mean not only **328** an individual but also groups of people and smaller and larger communities such as republics and monarchies and empires and even that largest community that comprises the whole world, since all of these are human. So too in the heavens the whole angelic heaven is like a single individual in the Lord's sight, and so is each individual community of heaven. This is why each individual angel is human. On this subject, see *Heaven and Hell* 68–103 *[68–102]*. This shows what is meant by "human" in the following pages.

We can tell what a useful function is from the goal of the creation of **329** the universe. The goal of the creation of the universe is to bring about an angelic heaven; and since an angelic heaven is the goal, so is humanity or the human race, since that is where heaven comes from. It follows, then, that everything that has been created is an intermediate goal, and that the functions are useful in the sequence, on the level, and in the specific way that they relate to humanity, and through humanity to the Lord.

Since the goal of creation is a heaven from the human race (and **330** therefore the human race itself), the intermediate goals are everything else that has been created. Because these do relate to us, they focus on these three aspects of us: our bodies, our rational functioning, and, for the sake of our union with the Lord, our spiritual functioning. We cannot be united to the Lord unless we are spiritual; we cannot be spiritual unless we are rational; and we cannot be rational unless we are physically whole. These aspects are like a house, with the body as its foundation, the structure of the house as our rational functioning, and the contents of the house as our spiritual functioning. Living in the house is union with the Lord.

This enables us to see the sequence, level, and focus of the relationship to us of the useful functions that are intermediate goals of creation. That is, they are for the support of our bodies, for the development of our rational ability, and for our acceptance of what is spiritual from the Lord.

Useful functions for the support of our bodies have to do with its nourishment, clothing, shelter, recreation and pleasure, protection, and the **331** preservation of its state. The useful things created for physical nourishment are all the members of the plant kingdom that we eat and drink, such as fruits, grapes, seeds, vegetables, and grains. Then there are all the members of the animal kingdom that we eat, such as steers, cows, calves, deer, sheep, kids, goats, lambs, and the milk they give, as well as many kinds of bird and fish.

The useful things created for clothing our bodies also come in abundance from these two kingdoms, as do those for our shelter and for our recreation and pleasure, for our protection, and for the preservation of our state. I will not enumerate these because they are familiar, so listing them would only take up space.

There are of course many things that we do not find useful, but these extras do not prevent usefulness. In fact, they enable useful functions to continue. Then there are abuses of functions; but again, the abuse of a function does not eliminate the useful function, just as the falsification of something true does not destroy the truth except for the people who are doing the falsifying.

332 *Useful functions for the development of our rational ability* are all the ones that teach us what I have just been talking about. These are called academic disciplines and fields of study having to do with nature, economics, politics, and morals, things that we get from parents and teachers, from books, from our dealings with each other, or from ourselves through our inner reflection about these subjects. These develop our rational ability to the extent that they are higher-level functions, and they become secure to the extent that we apply them to our lives.

There is not room to list these useful functions both because there are so many of them and because their relationship to the common good varies.

333 *Useful functions for our acceptance of what is spiritual from the Lord* are all the elements of our religion and its worship, everything, then, that teaches us to recognize and understand God and to recognize and understand what is good and what is true—that therefore teaches us eternal life. These, like academic disciplines, we get from parents, teachers, sermons, and books, and especially by devoting ourselves to living by them. In the Christian world, this comes through teaching and preaching from the Word, and through the Word, from the Lord.

We can describe the range of these functions much as we describe physical functions—in terms of nourishment, for example, clothing, shelter, recreation and pleasure, and protection of our state, as long as we apply them to the soul. We may compare nourishment to the good that love does, clothing to the truth that wisdom provides, dwelling to heaven, recreation and pleasure to life's happiness and heavenly joy, protection to [safety from] the attacks of evil, and preservation of our state to eternal life.

The Lord grants all these gifts upon our acknowledgment that everything physical also comes from the Lord and that we are simply like servants or stewards given responsibility for the Lord's goods.

It is abundantly clear that these are for our use and that they are gifts freely given if we look at the state of angels in the heavens. They have **334** bodies, rational abilities, and spiritual receptivity just as we on earth do. They are nourished for free, because they are given their food daily. They are clothed for free, because they are given their clothing. They are housed for free, because they are given their homes. They have no anxiety about any of these things; and to the extent that they are spiritually rational, they enjoy pleasure, protection, and preservation of their state.

The difference is that angels see that these things come from the Lord because they are created in response to the angels' state of love and wisdom, as explained above in §322, while we do not see this because things recur according to the calendar and happen not according to our states of love and wisdom but according to our efforts.

Even though we say that functions are useful because they relate to **335** the Lord through us, we cannot say that they are from us for the sake of the Lord. They are from the Lord for our sake because all useful functions are infinitely united in the Lord, and none of them are in us except as gifts from the Lord. We can actually do nothing good on our own, only from the Lord, and the good we do is what we are calling useful functions. The essence of spiritual love is to do good to others for their sake and not for our own. This is infinitely more so in regard to the essence of divine love. It is like the love of parents for their children. They do good for them out of love, for the children's sake, not for their own sake. We can see this clearly in the love mothers have for their little ones.

People believe that because the Lord is to be revered, worshiped, and praised the Lord loves reverence, worship, and praise for his own sake. In fact, he loves them for our sake, because they bring us into a state where something divine can flow in and be felt. This is because by these activities we are removing that focus on self that prevents the inflow and acceptance. The focus on self that is self-love hardens and closes our heart. It is removed by our realization that in our own right we are nothing but evil and that nothing but what is good comes from the Lord. This yields the softening of heart and humility from which reverence and worship flow.

It follows from this that the purpose of the useful functions the Lord provides for himself through us is that he may bless us out of his love; and since this is what he loves to do, our receiving it is the joy of his love.

No one should believe that the Lord is with people who simply worship him. He makes his home with people who do his commandments—that is, his useful functions—and not with the others. See also what it says about this in §§47, 48, and 49 above.

336   *Evil functions were not created by the Lord. Rather, they came into being along with hell.* All good things that find expression in act are called functions, and all evil things that find expression in act are also called functions. The latter, though, are called evil functions, while the former are called good functions. Since everything good is from the Lord and everything evil from hell, it follows that only good functions have been created by the Lord, and that all the evil ones have come from hell.

The particular functions I am talking about in this section are all the things we see on earth, like all kinds of animal and all kinds of plant. In both instances, the ones that are good for us are from the Lord and the ones that do us harm are from hell. By the same token, "useful functions from the Lord" means all the things that help develop our rational ability and that enable us to be receptive of spiritual gifts from the Lord; while "evil functions" means everything that destroys our rational ability and makes it impossible for us to become spiritual.

The reason harmful things are called "useful functions" is that they are useful to evil people for their evildoing, and also because they serve to soak up malice and therefore lead to remedies. I use "useful functions" in this dual sense, and do the same with "love," speaking of "a good love" and "an evil love." Whatever love brings forth it calls useful.

337   I will use the following sequence to show that good functions are from the Lord and that evil functions are from hell.

1. Which things in our world I mean by "evil functions."
2. Everything that is an evil function exists in hell, and everything that is a good function exists in heaven.
3. There is a constant inflow from the spiritual world into the earthly world.
4. The inflow from hell activates things that are evil functions, in places where there are things that answer to them.

5. The lowest spiritual level, separated from what is higher, is what does this.

6. There are two forms in which activation by inflow occurs, the plant form and the animal form.

7. Each form gets the ability and the means of propagating its own kind.

1. *Which things in our world I mean by "evil functions."* "Evil functions" in our world means everything harmful in both kingdoms, the animal and the plant, and harmful things in the mineral kingdom as well. There is no room to list all the harmful things in these kingdoms, for this would be simply to pile up names; and piling up names with no indication of what kind of harm each species inflicts would bring none of the usefulness this work intends. I may simply name a few by way of information. **338**

In the animal kingdom, there are poisonous snakes, scorpions, crocodiles, lizards, owls, mice, locusts, frogs, and spiders, and also flies, wasps, moths, lice, and mites. In short, there is everything that consumes grains, leaves, fruits, and seeds, our food and our drink, and inflicts harm on animals and people. In the plant kingdom there are many herbs that are harmful, poisonous, and lethal, as well as plants and shrubs of the same sort. In the mineral kingdom there are all the toxic substances.

We can see from these few examples what I mean by "evil functions" in this world of ours. "Evil functions" are all the things that conflict with the good functions discussed in the previous section.

2. *Everything that is an evil function exists in hell, and everything that is a good function exists in heaven.* Before we can see that all evil functions that occur on our earth come not from the Lord but from hell, some kind of preface about heaven and hell is needed. Unless this is understood, evil functions may be credited to the Lord just like good ones and thought to be together with them from creation, or they may be credited to nature and thought to originate in its sun. People cannot be rescued from these two errors unless they know that nothing whatever happens in the physical world that does not find its cause and therefore its origin in the spiritual world and that what is good comes from the Lord and what is evil comes from the Devil, that is, from hell. "The spiritual world" means both heaven and hell. **339**

In heaven, you can see all the good functions described in the preceding section. In hell, on the other hand, you can see all the evil functions just listed in §338—wild animals of every kind like snakes, scorpions, lizards, crocodiles, tigers, wolves, foxes, boars, night birds, owls, bats, mice, rats, frogs, locusts, spiders, and many kinds of harmful insect. You can also see toxic and dangerous things of all kinds, and poisons in both plants and soils—in a word, everything that does injury and that kills people. In the hells, things like this are just as vividly visible as they are on and in the earth.

I say that they are visible there, but they do not exist there the same way they do on earth. They are pure reflections of the cravings that spew from the evils of [demonic spirits'] loves, presenting themselves to others in these forms. Because there are things like this in the hells, foul stenches pour out as well, smells of carrion, feces, urine, and decay that demonic spirits relish, the way animals relish things that contain toxins.

It stands to reason, then, that things like this in the earthly world do not find their source in the Lord, created from the beginning, and that their origin is not from nature through its sun, but that they are from hell. It is abundantly clear that their origin is not from nature, through its sun, from the fact that what is spiritual flows into what is earthly and not vice versa. It is clear that they are not from the Lord from the fact that hell is not from him, so neither is anything in hell that reflects their evils.

340   3. *There is a constant inflow from the spiritual world into the physical world.* Unless people realize that there is a spiritual world and that it is as distinct from the physical world as an antecedent circumstance is from its consequence or a cause from what it causes, they cannot know anything about this inflow. This is why people who have written about the origin of plants and animals have found it necessary to trace them back to nature. If they do trace them back to God, they say that God gifted nature with the ability to bring forth plants and animals in the beginning. They do not realize that nature is not "gifted" with any power. In its own right, it is dead and contributes no more to bringing things forth than a tool contributes to the work of an artisan—if it is to accomplish anything, it needs constantly to be activated. It is spiritual reality, reality that finds its origin in the sun where the Lord is and that goes to the limits of nature, that produces the forms of plants and animals and causes the miracles that we see in both, filling them in with earthly substances so that the forms are stable and enduring.

It is acknowledged, then, that there is a spiritual world, that what is spiritual comes from a sun where the Lord is who is its source, and that this spiritual reality stirs nature into action the way something living stirs something lifeless. It is acknowledged further that there are things in that spiritual world that resemble things in our physical world. We can therefore see that plants and animals have come into being solely from the Lord through that world and that they constantly keep coming into being through it. This means that there is a constant inflow from the spiritual world into the physical one. There will be ample support for this in the next section.

The production of harmful things on earth through an inflow from hell happens by the same law of tolerance that applies to the very evils that flow from hell into people. I will discuss this law in *Angelic Wisdom about Divine Providence.*

4. *The inflow from hell activates things that are evil functions, in places where there are things that answer to them.* The things that answer to evil functions (that is, harmful plants and animals) are characteristic of corpses, decay, feces and manure, spoilage, and urine. As a result, the plants and little creatures like these, the ones just listed, turn up in places where these substances are found. There are more such species in the tropics, where we find snakes, basilisks, crocodiles, scorpions, mice, and the like.

341

Everyone knows that swamps, marshes, manure piles, and rotten soils teem with creatures like these and that vicious insects fill the air like clouds, and vicious bugs infest the earth like armies and devour plants down to their very roots. I noticed once in my own garden that in the space of a cubit almost all the dust turned into tiny winged creatures, because when I stirred it with my stick they rose up in clouds.

We can see simply from experience that carrion and decay are congenial and close kin to these vicious and useless little creatures. It is particularly clear when we consider the reason, namely that there are foul stenches like these in the hells, where such little creatures are also found. That is why hells are named after their odors, some called morgues, some manure piles, some urinals, and so on. They are all covered, though, so that their exhaust fumes do not escape, for when they are opened a little (which happens when newly arriving demons are let in), it induces vomiting and headaches; while the ones that are also toxic cause a loss of consciousness. The dust itself in hell is like this, so it is known there as "the dust of doom."

We can see from this that these vicious creatures are found where foul substances like this occur because they suit each other.

I need now to deal with the question of whether creatures like this come from eggs brought through the air or in rain or by the devious paths

342

of water, or whether they come from the actual fluids and odors. Experience overall does not support the notion that the vicious little creatures and insects I have been talking about come out of eggs, either borne to their site or hidden in the ground since creation. That is, worms turn up in tiny seeds, in nuts, in pieces of wood, and in stones; they come from leaves; lice and maggots turn up on plants and in plants that are congenial to them. Then there are the flies that show up in houses, fields, and forests in summer where there is no corresponding supply of egglike matter. There are the ones that destroy meadows and lawns, and that fill and infest the air in warm climates, besides the invisible ones that swim and fly in stagnant water, sour wine, and disease-laden air. These experiences support the people who say that the odors, stenches, and vapors themselves, coming from the plants, soil, and ponds, also provide the beginnings of such creatures.

The fact that they multiply by eggs or by a discharge once they have begun does not rule out their spontaneous generation, since every little creature gets organs of generation and propagation along with its other viscera, as discussed below in §347.

There is further support in a previously unknown experience, namely that things like this occur in the hells as well.

343   The hells just mentioned have not only a communication but even a union with similar phenomena on earth. This follows from the fact that the hells are not distant from us but are around us and even in us when we are evil. They are therefore in direct contact with earth. We are surrounded by angels of heaven or by spirits of hell in regard to our desires and consequent thoughts and as to the deeds that result from them both, deeds that are either good or evil functions. Since the same kind of things we have on earth exists in the heavens and the hells as well, it follows that the inflow from that source produces such things directly when conditions are right. Everything visible in the spiritual world, whether in heaven or in hell, reflects passions and desires because everything there arises in response to them. As a result, when passions and desires that are intrinsically spiritual find circumstances that are congenial or responsive, there is something spiritual there that provides a soul and something physical that provides a body. There is in everything spiritual an inherent tendency to clothe itself with a body.

The reason the hells are around and are therefore in direct contact with the earth is that the spiritual world is not in space, but is found wherever there is a responsive feeling.

In the spiritual world, I once heard two presidents of the British [Royal] Society, Sir Sloane and Sir Folkes, discussing the origin of seeds and eggs and their propagations on earth. The first attributed all this to nature, saying that from creation they were gifted with a power and energy for propagation by means of the sun's warmth. The second said that this force was continually coming from God the Creator into nature. To resolve the disagreement, Sir Sloane was shown a lovely bird and told to examine it closely to see whether it was at all different from similar birds on earth. He held it in his hand and examined it carefully and said that there was no difference. He knew that it was simply the feeling of a particular angel that was being portrayed outwardly as a bird and that it would vanish or go out of existence along with that feeling, which then happened.

344

This experience convinced Sir Sloane that nature contributed nothing whatever to the propagation of plants and animals. It is simply what flows into nature from the spiritual world. He said that if that particular bird had been filled in with appropriate earthly matter down to the last detail and so had become stable, it would have been a lasting bird just like our earthly birds, and that the same held true for things that came from hell.

He went on to say that if he had known what he now knew about the spiritual world, he would not have attributed anything to nature except the service it provides to spiritual reality from God, for giving stability to the forces that are constantly flowing into nature.

5. *The lowest spiritual level, separated from what is higher, is what does this.* I explained the following things in part 3. What is spiritual flows from its sun all the way down to the borders of nature by three steps, and these steps are called heavenly, spiritual, and earthly. They are within us from creation and therefore are inherent in us from birth. They are opened in proportion to our lives. If the heavenly level is opened, which is the highest and central one, then we become heavenly. If the spiritual level is opened, which is the intermediate one, then we become spiritual. If only the earthly level, the lowest and most remote, is opened, then we become earthly; and if we become nothing but earthly, we love only what has to do with our bodies and the world. To the extent that this is the case, we do not love things that are heavenly and spiritual and we do not turn toward God; and to that extent we become evil.

345

We can see from this that the lowest spiritual level, called "the spiritual-earthly level," can be separated from what lies above it and that it is so separated in the people who constitute hell. This lowest spiritual level cannot be separated from what lies above it either in animals or in soils and turn toward hell. This can happen only in humans.

It therefore follows that when the lowest spiritual level is separated from what lies above it the way it is for people in hell, this is what creates those evil functions on earth that I have just been discussing.

As for the claim that the harmful things on earth can be traced back to us and therefore to hell, this is supported by conditions in the land of Canaan described in the Word. When the Israelites lived by the Commandments, the land provided them with food as well as flocks and herds, while when they lived contrary to the Commandments it became barren and cursed, so to speak, bringing forth thorns and briars instead of grain. Their flocks and herds miscarried and wild beasts invaded. We can draw the same conclusion from the locusts, frogs, and lice in Egypt.

346   6. *There are two forms in which activation by inflow occurs, the plant form and the animal form.* It is common knowledge that our earth brings forth only two basic forms, since there are two kingdoms of nature called the animal kingdom and the plant kingdom. All the members of each kingdom have many things in common. In the animal kingdom, for example, all its members have organs of sense as well as organs of motion, members, and viscera that are animated by their brains, hearts, and lungs. As for the plant kingdom, all its members put down roots into the ground and form stems, branches, leaves, flowers, fruits, and seeds. If we look at the way both the animal and the plant kingdoms are brought forth in these forms, the beginning is by a spiritual inflow and a working from heaven's sun, where the Lord is, and not from any inflow and working of nature from its sun. This serves only to stabilize them, as already noted [§§339–340].

All the greater and lesser animals start from something spiritual on the lowest level, the one called "earthly." Only we humans come from all the levels, from the three that are called heavenly, spiritual, and earthly. Since each vertical or distinct step declines gradually from perfection to imperfection the way light declines into darkness, so do animals. The perfect ones are elephants, camels, horses, mules, cattle, sheep, goats, and the other members of flocks and herds. The less perfect are the winged ones, and the imperfect are fish and shellfish. Since they are the lowest of this level, it is as though they were in darkness, while the others are in light.

Still, since these all get their life only from the lowest spiritual level, the one called earthly, the only direction they can look is toward the earth and their food and, for propagation, their kindred. For all of them, their soul is an earthly desire and urge.

The same holds true for members of the plant kingdom. There are complete, less complete, and incomplete ones. The complete ones are fruit trees, the less complete are vines and shrubs, and the incomplete are grains. However, plants derive a usefulness from the spiritual reality that is their source, and animals derive passionate and impulsive natures from the spiritual reality that is their source, as already noted [§§313–316].

[7.] *Whenever it occurs, each form gets the means of propagating its own kind.* I explained in §§313–318 above that there is some image of creation, some human image—even some image of what is infinite and eternal—in all the things that the earth brings forth, which as noted belong either to the plant or to the animal kingdom. I also noted that this image of the infinite and eternal shines forth in their capacity for infinite and eternal proliferation. This is why they all get means of propagation, members of the animal kingdom by seeds in eggs or the womb or by a discharge, and members of the plant kingdom by seeds in the ground. We can tell from this that even though the incomplete and harmful animals and plants begin from a direct inflow from hell, from then on they are propagated by the means of seeds, eggs, or grafts. The one source, that is, does not rule out the other.

347

An example may illustrate the fact that both good and evil functions have a spiritual origin, namely the sun where the Lord is. I heard that some good and true gifts had been let down by the Lord through the heavens to hell, and that as they were accepted step by step, all the way to the lowest level of hell, they were turned into the evil and false things that were opposite to the good and true gifts. The reason this happened was that the recipient subjects turn everything that flows in into things that agree with their own forms, just as the pure light of the sun becomes offensive colors or blackness in objects whose inner substances are in the sort of form that stifles light and extinguishes it, and just as swamps, manure piles, and corpses turn the sun's warmth into stenches.

348

We can tell from this that even evil functions come from the spiritual sun, but [they are] good functions turned into evil ones in hell. This shows that the Lord has not created and does not create anything but good functions, while hell brings forth the evil ones.

What we can see in the created universe bears witness to the fact that nature has brought forth nothing and brings forth nothing. Divinity brings forth everything from itself, and does so through the spiritual world. Many people

349

in our world take events at face value and say that the sun produces the things that we can see in our meadows, fields, gardens, and forests by its warmth and light, that the sun hatches grubs from eggs by its warmth and makes the beasts of the earth and the birds in the sky reproduce, and even that it brings us to life. People can talk this way if they are simply talking in terms of appearances but are not really ascribing these powers to nature. They are not actually thinking about it. It is like people talking about the sun, saying that it rises and sets and makes days and years, that it is now at one height or another. They are likewise talking in terms of appearances, and they can do so, without thinking about the sun as stationary and the earth as revolving.

People who prove to themselves that the sun does produce the things we see on earth by its warmth and light end up giving nature credit for everything, even the creation of the universe. They become materialists and ultimately atheists. They can later say that God created nature and endowed it with the ability to do all this, but they say this out of fear of harm to their reputation. All the while, by "God the Creator" they really mean nature—for some of them, its inmost essence—and completely trivialize the divine qualities that the church teaches.

350　Still, we must forgive some people who attribute what they see to nature, and this for two reasons. First, they have had no knowledge of heaven's sun, where the Lord is, or about the inflow from it. They have had no knowledge of the spiritual world and its state or of its presence with us. As a result, they could think of spiritual reality only as a purer form of earthly reality, so that angels were either in the ether or in the stars, the Devil either was an evil person or, if he were actually to come into existence, would be in the air or in the depths, and that our own souls after death were either at the center of the earth or in a mysterious "elsewhere" until judgment day, along with other notions of the same sort that give rise to delusions born of their ignorance of the spiritual world and its sun.

The second reason for forgiving them is that they have had no way to know how Divinity produces all the things we see on our earth where there are so many things both good and evil. They have been afraid of drawing their conclusion, to keep from attributing evil to God or giving birth to a materialistic concept of God, equating God with nature, and therefore confusing them.

These are two reasons for forgiving people who believe that nature brings forth the things we can see by a power instilled at creation. However, we should not forgive people who make atheists of themselves by "proving" this role of nature, because they could "prove" the same role for Divinity. Ignorance does excuse, true, but it does not cancel deliberate proof of what is false, since this falsity is intimately connected to evil and therefore to hell. As a result, people who opt decisively for nature to the point that they divorce Divinity from it attach no weight to sin, since all sin is against the Divinity they have divorced and thus rejected. If people in spirit attach no weight to sin, then after death, when they become spirits, they rush as captives of hell into the unspeakable consequences of their cravings, cravings whose reins have been loosened.

People who believe that Divinity is at work in the details of nature can prove the role of Divinity for themselves by a host of things they observe in nature—just as fully as and even more fully than people who decide in favor of nature. People who decide for Divinity pay attention to the miracles they see in the way both plants and animals reproduce. In the reproduction of plants, they see that a root goes forth from a tiny seed cast into the ground, with a stem from the root and then twigs, leaves, flowers, fruit, all the way to new seeds. It is exactly as though the seed knew the sequence or the process for its own renovation. What rational person could believe that the sun, which is nothing but fire, knows this, or that it can endow plants with the ability to accomplish this with its warmth and light, that it can work these miracles in plants with the intent to perform some useful function? Anyone whose rational abilities are lifted up, on seeing and pondering such things, can only think that they come from One who has infinite wisdom, from God.

People who acknowledge Divinity see this and think this way. People who do not acknowledge Divinity, though, do not see this or think this way because they do not want to. So they lower their rational abilities down to the sensory level that gets all its concepts from the light that envelops our physical senses. They then "prove" their fallacies by saying, "Can't you *see* the sun making this happen by its warmth and light? What is anything that you cannot see? Is it anything at all?"

People who decide in favor of Divinity pay attention to the miracles they see in the way animals reproduce. At this point I may mention only what happens in eggs. Hidden within the egg is the chick "in seed" or in potential, with everything it needs for coming to hatching and for the whole sequence after hatching until it becomes a bird, a flying creature in the image of its parents. If people pay close attention to the nature of the form involved and think deeply about it, they cannot fail to be stunned. They see, for example, that in the smallest creatures as in the largest, in the invisible ones as in the visible, there are sensory organs for sight,

351

smell, taste, and touch; there are organs of motion called muscles—these creatures actually fly and walk; and they have organs around their hearts and lungs that are activated by their brains. We have been informed by people who have written about their anatomy that even lowly insects enjoy these gifts: see especially Swammerdam's *Book of Nature.*

People who attribute everything to nature do see these things, but they simply think that they happen and say that nature makes them happen; and they say this because they have diverted their minds from thinking about Divinity. If people have diverted their minds from thinking about Divinity, then when they see the miracles in nature they cannot think rationally, let alone spiritually. They think in terms of sensation and matter, and in so doing think about nature from within nature and not from above it. This is just what people in hell do. The sole difference between them and animals is that they have rational capacity; that is, they could understand and think differently if they wanted to.

352　　If people turn from thinking about Divinity when they see nature's miracles and therefore become sense-centered, they do not take into account the fact that their eyesight is so crude that they see a host of tiny insects as a single cloud. Yet each one of those insects is designed for sensing and for moving, which means it is equipped with fibers and vessels, with tiny hearts, windpipes, viscera, and brains. These are woven together out of the most delicate substances in nature, and the ways they are woven are responsive to a particular life that activates their smallest elements quite precisely.

If we consider the fact that our eyesight is so crude that a host of such creatures, each one with all its countless complexities, looks to us like a little cloud, and then realize that in spite of this, people who are sense-centered think and judge on the basis of this sight, we can see how coarsened their minds are, and therefore how benighted they are in spiritual matters.

353　　Any people who want to can decide in favor of Divinity on the basis of what they can see in nature, and people do so decide who base their thinking about God on life. They do this, for example, when they see the birds of the air. Each species knows its foods and where to find them, recognizes its kindred by sound and sight, and knows which of them are friends and which are hostile. They join in marriage and know how to mate and how to build their nests skillfully. They lay their eggs there and incubate them, knowing how long the incubation should last; and when the time has come they hatch their chicks, love them most tenderly, shelter them under their wings, gather food and nourish them, all this until the chicks come of age and can do the same, having their own families and thus ensuring the continuance of their kind.

Anyone who wants to think about the divine inflow through the spiritual world into the physical world can see it in these events. Anyone who wants to can say at heart, "Knowledge like this cannot be flowing into them from the sun, through its light rays. The sun, which provides nature with its origin and essence, is pure fire, so its light rays are absolutely lifeless." We can therefore come to the conclusion that things like this come from an inflow of divine wisdom into the very boundaries of nature.

Anyone who looks at larvas can decide in favor of Divinity on the basis of observation of nature. Larvas are moved by the pleasure of some impulse to exchange their earthly state for one that is a parable of heaven. So they crawl off to particular places where they put themselves into a kind of womb in order to be reborn. There they become chrysalises, mature pupas, caterpillars, nymphs, and eventually butterflies. At the close of this transformation they are equipped with beautiful wings according to their species, fly in the air as though it were their heaven, play in it cheerfully, form marriages, lay eggs, and provide themselves with descendants. All the while they are nourishing themselves on sweet, soft food from flowers. **354**

Does anyone who is deciding for Divinity on the basis of observation of nature fail to see a kind of reflection of our earthly state in the caterpillars and of our heavenly state in the butterflies? Yet people who are deciding for nature, since they emphatically reject any "heavenly state," say that these are simply earthly instincts.

Anyone can decide for Divinity on the basis of observations of nature by looking at what we know about bees. Bees know how to collect wax from plants and flowers and how to extract honey, how to build cells like little homes and arrange them in a form like a city, with open spaces for entrance and exit. They scent at a distance the flowers and plants from which they collect wax for their dwellings and honey for their food. Laden with them they fly back to their own territory, to their own hive. In this way, they provide themselves with food and shelter for the coming winter just as though they saw it coming. They appoint a female leader as queen to be the source of their progeny and they build a kind of hall above her, surrounding her with servants; and when the time of birth has arrived, she goes from cell to cell with her retinue of servants and lays her eggs, with the attendant crew sealing the cells to protect them from the air. This provides them with a new generation. **355**

Later, when this generation has reached the age when it can do the same, it is driven out of its home, and once it has been driven out it first gathers itself and then forms a swarm so that its company will not be dispersed, and flies off in search of a home. About autumn, too, the useless drones are taken out and shorn of their wings so that they cannot return and use up food to which they contribute nothing. There is much more, which enables us to conclude that it is for the useful function they perform for the human race and from an inflow from the spiritual world that they have a form of government like ours on earth and even like angels' in heaven. Can anyone furnished with rationality fail to see that things like this do not come from the physical world? What does the sun, the source of nature, have in common with a government that rivals and reflects heavenly government?

On the basis of all this and of other miracles among simple animals, people who acknowledge and worship nature decide for nature, while people who acknowledge and worship God decide for Divinity on the very same basis. That is, a spiritual-minded person sees spiritual forces in these events, and an earthly-minded person sees physical forces in these events. We see [reflections of] our own nature.

As for me, things like this have been testimonies to a spiritual inflow into nature, of the spiritual world into the physical world, an inflow, therefore, from the Lord's divine wisdom. Ask yourself seriously whether you could even think analytically about any form of government, any civil law, any moral virtue, or any spiritual truth unless Divinity were flowing in with its wisdom through the spiritual world. In my own case, I never could and I still cannot. I have actually been constantly watching this inflow perceptibly, tangibly, for nineteen years, so I am saying this on the basis of evidence.

356 Can anything earthly have useful functioning as a goal and arrange functions in sequences and forms? Only someone wise can do this, and only God, who has infinite wisdom, can arrange and form the universe in this way. Who else—or what else—can foresee and make available all the things that serve for our food and clothing, food from the fruits of the earth and from animals, and clothing from both as well?

It ranks among the miracles that the humble insects called silkworms provide splendid, beautiful, silken clothing for both women and men, from queens and kings to maids and servants, and that the humble insects called bees provide wax for the candles that lend their brilliance to temples and courts. These and many other facts are clear evidence that the Lord produces everything that happens in nature from himself through the spiritual world.

I need to add that I have seen people in the spiritual world who, on the basis of their observations of the world, had decided in favor of nature to the point of becoming atheists. In spiritual light, their intelligence seemed to be open downward and closed upward because in thought they were looking down to the earth and not up to heaven. The upper surface of their sensory functioning, which is the lowest level of intelligence, seemed to have a kind of covering on it. For some people, it flashed with hellfire, for some it was black as soot, and for some it was leaden and corpselike. Beware of decisions in favor of nature, then. Decide for Divinity: there is no lack of material.

357

ANGELIC WISDOM
ABOUT
DIVINE LOVE

PART 5

❖(❋)❖❖((❋))❖❖((❋))❖❖((❋))❖❖((❋))❖❖((❋))❖❖((❋))❖❖((❋))❖❖((❋))❖❖((❋))❖

THE Lord has created and formed within us two vessels and dwellings for **358** *himself called volition and discernment. Volition is for his divine love and discernment for his divine wisdom.* I have already discussed the divine love and wisdom of God the Creator, who is the Lord from eternity, and I have discussed the creation of the universe. Now I need to say something about our own creation.

We read that we were created in the image of God and according to his likeness (Genesis 1:26). In this passage "the image of God" means divine wisdom and "the likeness of God" means divine love, since wisdom is nothing more than the image of love. Love actually presents itself to view and to recognition in wisdom, and since that is where we see and recognize it, wisdom is its image. Then too, love is the reality of life and wisdom is its consequent manifestation. This "image and likeness" of God is strikingly visible in angels. Love shining from within is in their faces and wisdom in their beauty, with beauty as the form of their love. I have seen this, and I have come to know it.

We could not be images of God according to his likeness unless he **359** were within us and were our life from our very center. God's presence within us and God's being our life from our very center follow from what I explained in §§4–6 above, namely that God alone is life and that we and angels are life-receivers from him.

157

The Word tells us that God is in us and makes his home with us; and because the Word tells us this, preachers are fond of telling us to prepare ourselves to let God come into our lives so that he may be in our hearts and that our hearts may be his dwelling. The devout say the same in their prayers. Some [preachers] talk and preach more explicitly about the Holy Spirit, who they believe is within them when they are filled with holy zeal as the source of their thought, speech, and preaching. I have explained in §§51–53 of *Teachings for the New Jerusalem on the Lord* that the Holy Spirit is the Lord and not some God who is a separate individual. The Lord actually says, "In that day you will know that you are in me and I in you" (John 14:21 *[14:20]*), and he says similar things in John 15:24 *[15:4]* and 17:23.

360 Since the Lord is divine love and wisdom, then, and these two are he himself in essence, if he is to live within us and give us life he must have created and formed his own vessels and dwellings within us, one for love and one for wisdom. These vessels and dwellings within us are called volition and discernment, volition being the vessel and dwelling of love, and discernment being the vessel and dwelling of wisdom.

We will see below that these two belong to the Lord within us and that these two are the source of all our life.

361 It is both known and unknown in the world that we all have volition and discernment and that they can be distinguished from each other the way love and wisdom can. We know this from common sense, but not from our considered thinking and even less from written works. Judging the matter simply on common sense, would anyone *not* realize that the volition and discernment within us are distinguishable? Everyone grasps this on first hearing. We can say to someone, "That individual means well but does not understand things well," or "That individual understands things well but does not mean well. I like people who understand and mean well but not people who understand well and mean harm." When people start thinking about volition and discernment, though, they do not regard them as two distinguishable functions but mix them together. This is because their thinking is in touch with their physical sight. They understand even less about the distinct difference between volition and discernment when they start writing, which is because then their thinking is in touch with the sensory level that is our own human possession. This is why some people can think and talk well but still not write well, as is frequently the case with the female sex. The same holds in many other cases.

Does anyone fail to realize, simply on the basis of common sense, that people who live good lives are saved and people who live evil lives are damned? That people who live well come to be with angels and see, hear, and talk there like people? Or that the people who have a conscience are the ones who do what is fair because it is fair and what is right because it is right? If people step back from common sense, though, and give the matter serious thought, they do not know what conscience is or that the soul can see, hear, and talk the way we can or that a good way to live is anything more than giving to the poor. Then if you start writing on the basis of this thinking, you support these opinions with superficial and deceptive observations and with words that are all sound and no substance. This is why many of the scholars who have given much thought to this—and even more, the ones who have written about it—have undermined, obscured, and even destroyed their common sense. This is also why simple people see what is good and true more clearly than people who believe they are wiser.

This common sense comes from an inflow from heaven and descends through thought all the way to sight; but thought separated from common sense fades into fantasy based on sight and on self-importance.

You may test the truth of this. Say something true to people who have common sense and they will see it; tell them that we exist and move and live from God and in God and they will see it; tell them that God is living within us in our love and wisdom and they will see it; say even that volition is the dwelling of love, and discernment the dwelling of wisdom, and explain it a little and they will see it; say that God is love itself and wisdom itself and they will see it; ask them what conscience is and they will tell you. But say these same things to scholars who have not been thinking on the basis of common sense but on principles derived either from preconceptions or from what they observe in the world, and they will not see.

Then figure out who are the wiser.

Volition and discernment, the vessels of love and wisdom, are in the whole **362** *brain and every part of it and therefore in the whole body and every part of it.* This will be explained in the following sequence.

1. Love and wisdom, and the volition and discernment that come from them, constitute our very life.
2. Our life is found in its primary forms in our brains and in secondary forms in our bodies.

3. The quality of a life in its primary forms determines its quality overall and in every part.

4. By means of its primary forms, life is in the whole from every part
and in every part from the whole.

5. The quality of the love determines the quality of the wisdom and
therefore the quality of the person.

363   1. *Love and wisdom, and the volition and discernment that come from
them, constitute our very life.* Hardly anyone knows what life is. When
people think about it, it seems like something ethereal, something with
no specific image. It seems like this because people do not know that
only God is life and that his life is divine love and wisdom. We can see
from this that the life in us is nothing else and that there is life in us to
the extent that we accept it.

We know that warmth and light radiate from the sun and that everything in the universe is a recipient, growing warm and bright in proportion to its receptivity. The same holds true as well for the sun where the
Lord is, whose radiating warmth is love and whose radiating light is wisdom, as explained in part 2. It is from these two emanations from the
Lord as the sun, then, that life comes.

We can tell that life is love and wisdom from the Lord from the fact
that we grow sluggish as love ebbs away from us and dull as wisdom ebbs
away; and if they leave us completely, we are snuffed out.

There are many forms of love that have been given their own names
because they are derivatives, such as desires, cravings, appetites, and their
gratifications and delights. There are many forms of wisdom, too, like
perception, reflection, memory, thought, and focus on a subject. Further, there are many forms that come from both love and wisdom, such
as agreement, decision, and resolve to act, among others. All of these
belong to both [love and wisdom], but they are assigned their names on
the basis of what is dominant and nearer to hand.

Finally, our senses are derived from these two, our sight, hearing,
smell, taste, and touch, with their own pleasures and satisfactions. The
appearance is that our eye is seeing, but our discernment is seeing
through our eye, which is why we ascribe sight to our discernment. The
appearance is that our ear is hearing, but our discernment is hearing
through our ear. This is why we speak of the attentiveness and listening
that are actually functions of discernment as "hearing." The appearance
is that our nostrils smell and that our tongue tastes, but discernment is
smelling with its perceptiveness and is tasting as well; so we refer to

perceptiveness as smelling and tasting, and so on. The wellsprings of all these functions are love and wisdom; we can therefore tell that these two constitute our life.

Everyone sees that discernment is the vessel of wisdom, but not many see that volition is the vessel of love. This is because our volition does nothing by itself, but acts through our discernment. It first branches off into a desire and vanishes in doing so, and a desire is noticeable only through a kind of unconscious pleasure in thinking, talking, and acting. We can still see that love is the source because we all intend what we love and do not intend what we do not love.

2. *Our life is found in its primary forms in our brains and in secondary forms in our bodies.* "In its primary forms" means in its beginnings, and "in secondary forms" means in the things that are produced and formed from these beginnings. "Life in its primary forms" means volition and discernment. It is these two functions that occur in their primary forms in our brains and in their derivative forms in our bodies.

We can tell that the primary forms or beginnings are in the brain for a number of reasons. (a) Simply from the feeling we have when we are focusing our minds and thinking, our sense that we are thinking with our brain. We turn our sight inward, so to speak, and furrow the brow with a sense that this concentration is happening inside, especially behind the forehead and a little above it. (b) From the way we are formed in the womb, where the brain or head is formed first and remains larger than the body for some time. (c) The head is above and the body below, and the orderly arrangement is for the higher to activate the lower and not the other way around. (d) If the brains are damaged in the womb by some wound, by disease, or by lack of concentration, thinking becomes uncertain, and sometimes the mind becomes deranged. (e) All the outer senses of the body—sight, hearing, smell, taste, and the all-inclusive sense of touch—as well as speech, are in the front part of the head called the face; and they are in direct touch with the brain through fibers and get their active and sensitive life from it. (f) This is why we can see people's feelings of love in a kind of image in their face and their thoughts of wisdom in a kind of light in their eyes. (g) Anatomy informs us that all the fibers go down from the brains through the neck into the body, and that none go up from the body through the neck into the brain. Where the fibers have their primary forms and beginnings is where life is in its primary forms and beginnings. Can anyone maintain a denial that the origin of life is where the fibers originate? (h) Ask anyone with common sense where thinking happens, or where one thinks, and the answer you

364

365

will get is "In one's head." But then ask someone who has located the seat of the soul in some little gland or in the heart or somewhere else where desire and its consequent thought begin, whether it is in the brain, and the answer you will get is either "No" or "I don't know." You may find the reason for this uncertainty in §361 above.

366   3. *The quality of a life in its primary forms determines its quality overall and in every part.* For the reader to understand this, I need to say just where these primary forms are in the brains and how they branch off.

We can see from anatomy just where these primary forms are in the brain. This tells us that there are two brains and that these have extensions from the head into the spine. It tells us that the brains consist of two substances called the cortical substance and the medullary substance, with the cortical substance consisting of countless little glandlike things and the medullary substance of countless fiberlike things. Since the little glands are at the heads of the little fibers, then, they are also their primary forms. The fibers begin there and they radiate outward, gradually gathering into nerves; and once they have gathered or formed nerves they go down to the sensory organs in the face and the motor organs in the body and form them. Check with anyone versed in the knowledge of anatomy and you will find this to be true.

This cortical or glandular substance constitutes the surface of the brain and the surface of the corpora striata that make up the medulla oblongata, to link with the cerebellum and through the cerebellum to the spinal cord. Wherever the medullary or fibrous substance is found, however, it begins and goes from the cortical substance. This is the source of the nerves that all the parts of the body come from. This fact is learned from dissection.

If people know this from the science of anatomy or from people versed in that science, they can see that the primary forms of life are nowhere but where the beginnings of the fibers are, and that the fibers cannot radiate from themselves but from the primary forms. The primary forms or beginnings that look like little glands are almost beyond counting. We can compare their abundance to the number of stars in the universe, and the abundance of fibers that come from them to the number of rays that radiate from the stars and bear their warmth and light to the planets.

We may also compare the abundance of these little glands to the abundance of angelic communities in the heavens. These too are beyond counting and are similarly arranged, so I have been told; and the abundance of little fibers radiating from these little glands can be compared to the spiritual good and true activities that flow down like rays in much the same way.

This is why the individual human being is like a universe and like a heaven in miniature, as I have stated and explained throughout what precedes [§§19, 186, 203, 231]. We can tell from this that the quality of life in its primary forms determines its quality in secondary forms, or that the quality of life in its beginnings in the brain determines its quality in the things in the body that originate there.

4. *By means of its primary forms, life is in the whole from every part and in every part from the whole.* This is because in terms of its origin, the whole—brain and body together—consists of nothing but the fibers that come from these primary forms in the brains. They have no other source, as we can see from the things just presented in §366. So the whole comes from each part. The reason that life in each part comes through the primary forms from the whole is that the whole provides each part with the share that it needs and thereby makes it a part of the whole. In brief, the whole arises from the parts and the parts are sustained by the whole. We can see from many things in the body that there is this kind of mutual sharing, and through it, a union.

It is much the same in the body as it is in a state, republic, or monarchy. The commonwealth arises from the people who are its parts, and the parts or individuals are sustained by the commonwealth. It is the same in everything that is in some form, especially humans.

5. *The quality of the love determines the quality of the wisdom and therefore the quality of the person.* This is because the quality of love and wisdom determines the quality of volition and discernment, volition being the vessel of love and discernment the vessel of wisdom, as already explained [§§358–361]; and these two constitute us as humans and give us our quality.

Love is highly complex, so complex that its various forms are without limit. This we can tell from the human race on earth and in the heavens. There is not a single individual or angel so like another that there is no difference. Love is what makes the difference, each individual being her or his own love. People think that wisdom is what differentiates, but wisdom comes from love. It is love's form, for love is the underlying reality of life and wisdom is the manifestation of life from this underlying reality.

The world believes that intelligence is what makes us human, but people believe this because our discernment can be raised up into heaven's light, as already explained [§§242–243, 255–256, 258], and it can seem

367

368

as though we were wise. However, any discernment that goes too far, that is, discernment that is not wisdom of love, appears as though it were ours. This makes us seem like intelligent people, but that is only an appearance. The discernment that goes too far is actually a love for knowing and being wise and not at the same time a love for applying our knowledge and wisdom to life. So in this world it either ebbs away over time or waits around temporarily on the edges, outside the contents of memory. After death, then, it is separated from us, and nothing is left but what agrees with the real love of our spirit.

Since love does constitute our life and therefore ourselves, all the communities of heaven and all the angels of those communities are arranged according to the passions that come from their loves. No community and no angel within a community is located by any gift of discernment apart from his or her love. The same holds for the hells and their communities, but that depends on loves that are opposite to heavenly loves.

We can tell from this that the quality of the love determines the quality of the wisdom, and that these determine the quality of the person.

369   It is generally recognized that our quality is determined by the quality of our primary love, but this is applied only to our minds and spirits, not to our bodies, which means that it is not applied to the whole person. However, an abundance of experience in the spiritual world has taught me that from head to toe, from the primary elements in our heads to the very limits of our bodies, our nature is determined by our primary love. All the people in that world are forms of their love, angels forms of heavenly love and demons forms of hellish love. These latter have misshapen faces and bodies, while the former have lovely faces and bodies. Further, when their love is attacked, their faces change; and if it is attacked severely, they disappear completely. This is a distinctive feature of the spiritual world. It happens because their bodies are completely at one with their minds.

We can see why from what has already been said, namely that everything in the body is secondary. That is, it is woven from fibers that come from specific origins that are vessels of love and wisdom; and when the origins have a particular nature, the secondary elements cannot be different. As a result, wherever the origins reach out, the secondary elements follow. They cannot be separated.

This is why people who lift their minds to the Lord are completely lifted to the Lord, and why people who plunge their minds into hell are wholly plunged there. So the whole person comes either into heaven or into hell, depending on the love of her or his life.

It is a matter of angelic wisdom that the human mind is a person because the Lord is a person, and that the body is a covering of the mind that senses and acts. So they are one single being, not two.

We do need to note that while the essential forms of the members, organs, and viscera of the body are basically woven from fibers that begin from primary origins in our brains, still they are stabilized by the kinds of material substance that we find on earth, and from solid substances in the air and the ether. This happens by means of the blood. So if all the parts of the body are to maintain their proper form and hold up in their proper functions, we need to be nourished by material food and constantly reassembled. **370**

There is a correspondence between volition and the heart and between discernment and the lungs. This will be presented in the following series. **371**

1. Everything in the mind goes back to volition and discernment, and everything in the body goes back to the heart and the lungs.
2. There is a correspondence of volition and discernment with the heart and the lungs and a consequent correspondence of everything in our minds with everything in our bodies.
3. Volition corresponds to the heart.
4. Discernment corresponds to the lungs.
5. This relationship enables us to discover many secrets about our volition and discernment and also about love and wisdom.
6. Our mind is our spirit, and the spirit is a person, with the body being a covering through which the mind or spirit senses and acts in its world.
7. The union of the human spirit and body is accomplished through the correspondence of volition and discernment with the heart and lungs, and disunion is caused by a lack of correspondence.

1. *Everything in the mind goes back to volition and discernment, and everything in the body goes back to the heart and the lungs.* "Mind" means simply volition and discernment, which embrace everything that moves us and everything we think. This means that it embraces everything that belongs to our feeling and thinking. The things that move us belong to our volition, and the things we think about belong to our discernment. **372**

We recognize that everything we think belongs to our discernment because discernment is the basis of our thinking. It is not so clear to us, however, that everything that moves us belongs to our volition. This is because when we are thinking, we do not pay attention to our feeling but only to what we are thinking. It is like our listening to someone talk and paying no attention to the tone quality but only to the discourse itself. Yet the feeling within our thinking is like the tone quality within our speech, so that we can tell how people are feeling from their tone of voice and can tell what they are thinking from what they say.

The reason feelings belong to volition is that every feeling is an aspect of love, and as already noted [§§358–361], volition is the vessel of love.

People who do not know that feelings belong to volition confuse feeling with thinking. They actually say that feeling is the same as thinking even though they are not the same but simply act in unison. We can see this confusion in casual speech when someone says "I think I'll do that" meaning "I intend to do that." The fact that they are two things also shows up in casual speech when someone says "I'd like to think about that." When someone does "think about that," there is volition's feeling within discernment's thought just the way there is tone quality within speech, as noted.

It is generally recognized that everything in the body depends on the heart and the lungs; but it is not generally recognized that there is a correspondence of the heart and the lungs with volition and discernment. This matter, then, needs to be dealt with later [§§374–393].

373 Since volition and discernment are vessels of love and wisdom, they are two organic forms, or organized forms made out of the purest substances. They need to be like this in order to be vessels. The fact that their organization is not visible to the eye offers no objection because their organization is finer than eyesight, even when amplified by a microscope. Tiny insects are finer than eyesight, too, insects containing sensory and motor organs, since they feel and crawl and fly. Careful observers of their anatomy have discovered with their microscopes that insects also have brains, hearts, windpipes, and viscera. If these insects are invisible to our eyesight—to say nothing of the tiny inner organs they are made of—and we do not deny that they are organized down to the last detail, how can anyone say that the two vessels of love and wisdom called volition and discernment are not organized forms? How can love and wisdom, which are life from the Lord, act on some nonagent or on something that has no substantial presence? How else could thought have a residence? Or could someone talk on the basis of thoughts that had no residence? Is the brain where thinking happens not a complete whole, with every single component organized? We can actually see its organized forms with the naked eye, seeing the vessels of volition and discernment in their primary forms quite clearly in the cortical substance, where they look like very small glands (see above, §366).

Please do not think about these matters in terms of a vacuum. A vacuum is nothing, and nothing happens in nothing or comes from nothing. On the concept of a vacuum, see §82 above.

2. *There is a correspondence of volition and discernment with the heart and the lungs and a consequent correspondence of everything in our minds with everything in our bodies.* This is something new, since it has not yet been recognized because people have not known what anything spiritual was or how it differed from what is physical. As a result, they have not known what correspondence is, correspondence being a relationship between spiritual and physical things, and the means of their union.

While I am saying that people have not yet recognized what anything spiritual is or how it corresponds to what is physical, which has left them ignorant of what correspondence is, still they could have known both of these facts. Is anyone unaware that feelings and thoughts are spiritual and that therefore everything that has to do with feelings and thoughts is spiritual? Is anyone unaware that action and speech are physical, and that therefore everything that has to do with action and speech is physical? Is anyone unaware that feelings and thoughts, which are spiritual, impel us to speak and act? Is there anyone who could not learn from this how spiritual and physical things correspond? Is it not thought that impels the tongue to speak and desire combined with thought that impels the body to act? These are two distinguishable activities. I can think and not speak, and I can intend and not act. Further, we know that the body does not think and intend, but that thinking flows into speech and intention into action.

Then too, do not feelings radiate from the face and show their impress there? Everyone recognizes this. Seen in its own right, is not feeling spiritual, while the changes of the face that we call expressions are physical? Can anyone fail to conclude, then, that there is a responsiveness, and therefore that there is a correspondence of everything in the mind with everything in the body? Further, since everything in the mind goes back to feeling and thought (or to volition and discernment, which amounts to the same thing), while everything in the body goes back to the heart and the lungs, can anyone fail to conclude that there is a correspondence of volition with the heart and of discernment with the lungs?

The reason things like this have gone unrecognized, even though they could have been recognized, is that we have become so superficial that we are unwilling to give credence to anything but what is physical. This gratifies our love and therefore gratifies our discernment; so we are uncomfortable raising our thoughts above the physical level toward anything spiritual separated from what is physical. As a result, our physical love and its gratification prevents us from thinking of the spiritual as anything but a purer version of the physical, and of correspondence as anything but a flow along a continuum. In fact, strict materialists cannot conceive of anything separated from what is physical. To them, it is nothing.

Another reason these things have not been seen and therefore recognized is that we have displaced from our field of vision all the matters of religion that we refer to as "spiritual" by the dogma, prevalent throughout Christendom, that theological matters, "spiritual" matters, as defined by the councils and by some primates of the church, are to be believed blindly because (so they say) they transcend understanding. This has led some people to believe that anything spiritual is like a bird that flies beyond the air into the ether, beyond the reach of our eyesight. In fact, though, it is like a bird of paradise flying so close to our eyes that its lovely feathers brush the pupils, willing to be seen. "Our eyesight" means our intellectual sight.

375   The correspondence of volition and discernment with heart and lungs cannot be simply proven—that is, not by rational arguments—but it can be proven by effects. It is much the same as it is with the causes of events. Although we can see them rationally, we see them clearly only through their effects. The causes are in the effects and present themselves to view there. Only then is the mind sure about causes. I will discuss the effects of this correspondence later [§§378–384].

However, to prevent anyone from getting detoured into preconceived theoretical concepts of the soul in the discussion of these correspondences, some of the material presented in the preceding section may be reread: for example, §§363–364, on love and wisdom, and therefore volition and discernment, constituting our essential life; §365, on our life occurring in its fundamental forms in our brains, and secondarily in our bodies; §366, on the quality of our life in its fundamental forms determining its quality throughout and in every part; §367, on the fact that through these fundamental forms there is life in the whole from every part and life in every part from the whole; §368, on the quality of the love determining the quality of the wisdom, and therefore the quality of the person.

In support of this I may include here a portrayal of the correspon- **376** dence of volition and discernment with the heart and the lungs that I saw in the company of angels in heaven. By a fascinating flowing, spiral movement, beyond words to express, the angels formed an image of a heart and an image of lungs, including all the deeper tissues within them; and they followed the flow of heaven, since heaven tends toward forms like this because of the inflow of love and wisdom from the Lord. In this way they portrayed the union of the heart and the lungs and at the same time their correspondence with volition's love and discernment's wisdom. They call this correspondence and union a "heavenly marriage," and they say that it is the same throughout the body and in its individual members, organs, and viscera, with whatever is in them from the heart and the lungs. Further, anywhere that the heart and the lungs are not active, each in its turn, there can be no motion of life prompted by some voluntary principle and no sensation of life prompted by some cognitive principle.

I am about to discuss the correspondence of the heart and the lungs **377** with volition and discernment. Upon this rests the correspondence of everything in the body, called the members of the body as a whole, the sensory organs, and the body's viscera. Further, the correspondence of physical things with spiritual ones has not been recognized even though it was fully demonstrated in two works, one of which is *Heaven and Hell* and the other of which is on the spiritual meaning of the Word in Genesis and Exodus, titled *Secrets of Heaven*. For all these reasons, I should like now to point out the sections of these two works where I have written explanations of correspondence.

In *Heaven and Hell*, there is material on the correspondence of everything in heaven with everything in us, §§87–102; and on the correspondence of everything in heaven with everything on earth, §§103–115.

In the work on the spiritual meaning of the Word in Genesis and Exodus, titled *Secrets of Heaven*, there is material on the correspondence of the face and its expressions with the feelings of the mind: §§1568, 2988, 2989, 3631, 4796, 4797, 4880 *[4800]*, 5195 *[5165]*, 5168, 5695, 9306; on the correspondence of the body in its motions and actions with matters of discernment and volition: §§2988, 3632, 4215; on the correspondence of the senses in general: §§4318–4330; on the correspondence of the eyes and their sight: §§4403–4420; on the correspondence of the nostrils and smell: §§4624–4634; on the correspondence of the ears and hearing: §§4652–4634 *[4652–4659]*; on the correspondence of the tongue and taste: §§4791–4805; on the correspondence of the hands, arms, legs, and feet: §§4931–4953; on the correspondence of the groin and the reproductive organs: §§5050–5062; on the correspondence of the inner viscera of the body, particularly the stomach, thymus, the cisterna, the chyle and its ducts and the mesentery: §§5171–5180, 5189 *[5181]*; on the correspondence of the spleen: §9698; on the correspondence of the peritoneum, kidneys, and bladder: §§5377–5396 *[5377–5391]*; on the correspondence of the liver and the ducts of the liver, of the bladder, and of the pancreas: §§5183–5185; on the correspondence of the intestines: §§5392–5395, 5379; on the correspondence of the bones: §§5560–5564; on the correspondence of the skin: §§5552–5573; on the correspondence of heaven with a person: §§911, 1900, 1982 *[2162]*, 2996, 2998, 3624–3649, 3741–3745, 3884, 4091 *[4041]*, 4279 *[4280]*, 4423 *[4323]*, 4524, 4525, 6013, 6057, 9279, 9632; on the fact that everything in the physical world and its three kingdoms corresponds to something you can see in the spiritual world: §§1632, 1881, 2758, 2890–2893 *[2990–2993]*, 2897–3043 *[2987–3003]*, 3213–3227, 3483, 3624–3649, 4044, 4053, 4156, 4366 *[4936]*, 4939, 5116, 5377, 5428, 4477 *[5477]*, 8211, 9280; that everything you see in heaven is a correspondence: §§1521; 1532, 1619–1625, 1807, 1808, 1971, 1974, 1977, 1980, 1981, 2299, 2601, 3213–3226, 3348, 3350, 3457 *[3475]*, 3485, 3748 *[3747]*, 9481, 9570, 9576, 9577. The correspondence of the literal meaning of the Word with its spiritual meaning is dealt with throughout, and is also treated in *Teachings for the New Jerusalem on Sacred Scripture* 5–26 and 27–69.

378   3. *Volition corresponds to the heart.* As I mentioned above [§375], this cannot be shown in a clearer and more precise way than by examining the effects of volition. It can be shown in some detail by the fact that all the feelings that arise from love induce changes in the motions of the heart. We can tell this from the arterial pulse that acts synchronously with the heart. It has countless changes and motions in response to feelings that arise from love. The only ones we can detect with the finger are that it may beat slower or faster, boldly or gently, soft or hard, regularly or irregularly, and so on. So it varies from happiness to sorrow, from peace of mind to rage, from courage to fearfulness, from fevers to chills, and so on.

Since the motions of the heart (called systole and diastole) do vary in this way depending on the feelings that arise from someone's love, many of the ancients and some moderns have ascribed feelings to the heart and named it as the home of the feelings. So in common language we have come to speak of a magnanimous heart or a timid one, a happy or a sorrowful heart, a soft or a hard heart, a great or a mean heart, a whole or a broken heart, a heart of flesh or one of stone, of being heavy, soft, or gentle at heart, of putting our heart into a task, of giving our whole heart, giving a new heart, resting at heart, taking to heart, of not laying something to heart, of hardening the heart, of being a friend at heart. We have the words concord and discord and envy and many others that have to do with love and its feelings.

The Word says similar things because it was composed in correspondences. It makes no difference whether you say love or volition, since volition is the vessel of love, as already noted [§§358–361].

It is generally recognized that there is a vital warmth in humans and in all animals, but people do not know where it comes from. People discuss it on the basis of conjecture, so if they do not know anything about the way matter is responsive to spirit, they identify the warmth of the sun as its source, some focusing on the activity of particles and some on life itself. However, since these last do not know what life is, they are just substituting one word for another. **379**

However, once people realize that there is a relationship of responsiveness between love and its feelings on the one hand and the heart and its derivative vessels on the other, they can know that love is the source of our vital warmth. Love radiates as warmth from the spiritual sun where the Lord is and is felt as warmth by angels. This spiritual warmth, which essentially is love, is what flows into the heart and its blood by correspondence and instills both its warmth and its life. We know that we are warmed and virtually kindled by our love, depending on its intensity, and that we become sluggish and cold as that intensity decreases. We feel and see this, feeling it in a warmth throughout our bodies and seeing it as our faces flush. In contrast, we feel its loss as a physical chill and see it as faces turn pale.

Since love is our life, the heart is the beginning and ending of our life; and since love is our life and the soul brings its life through the body in the blood, the blood is called the soul in the Word (see Genesis 9:4 and Leviticus 17:14). I will be explaining later [§383] what "soul" means in its various senses.

It is because of the correspondence of the heart and blood with love and its feelings, too, that blood is red. There are all kinds of colors in the **380** spiritual world, with red and white as the primary ones and the rest deriving their characteristics from these and from their opposites, which are a dark, fiery hue and black. Red corresponds to love there, and white to wisdom.

The reason red corresponds to love is that its source is the sun's fire; and the reason white corresponds to wisdom is that its source is the sun's light. Further, since love corresponds to the heart, blood needs to be red and to point to its source.

This is why the light is flamelike and angels wear reddish-purple in heavens where love for the Lord predominates, while the light is clear and angels wear white linen in heavens where wisdom predominates.

381   The heavens are divided into two realms, one called "heavenly" and the other called "spiritual." In the heavenly realm, love for the Lord reigns supreme, while in the spiritual realm, wisdom from that love reigns. The realm where love reigns is called the heart region of heaven, and the realm where wisdom reigns is called the lung region of heaven.

We need to realize that the whole angelic heaven, all in all, reflects a single person and looks like a single person to the Lord. Consequently, the heart forms one realm and the lungs another. There is actually a general cardiac and pulmonary motion throughout heaven, and a secondary one in every individual angel. The general cardiac and pulmonary motion is from the Lord alone, because he is the sole source of love and wisdom. These two motions occur in the sun where the Lord is, the sun that comes from the Lord, and from there flows into the angelic heaven and into the universe. Cancel out the notion of space and think about omnipresence and you will be assured that this is true.

On the division of heaven into two realms, one heavenly and one spiritual, see *Heaven and Hell* 26–28 *[20–28]*; and on the whole angelic heaven, taken as a unit, reflecting a single individual, see §§59–87 *[59–86]* of the same work.

382   4. *Discernment corresponds to the lungs.* This follows from what has already been said [§§378–381] about volition's correspondence with the heart. There are, that is, two dominant things in the spiritual person or mind, namely volition and discernment, and there are two dominant things in the physical self or the body, namely heart and lungs. There is a correspondence of everything in the mind with everything in the body, as already noted [§§374–377]. It then follows that if volition corresponds to the heart, discernment corresponds to the lungs.

Everyone can observe internally that discernment corresponds to the lungs on the basis of thought and on the basis of speech. On the basis of thought: we cannot think at all without the concurrence and support of the breath of our lungs. So quiet thought is accompanied by quiet breathing, deep thought by deep breathing. We hold and release our breath, we suppress or intensify our breathing, in response to our thinking—in response, then, to the inflow of some feeling related to what we love, breathing slowly, rapidly, eagerly, gently, or intently. In fact, if we suppress our breathing completely, the only way we can think is in the spirit, by its breathing, which is not clearly noticeable.

On the basis of speech: not even the shortest word comes from the mouth without the support of our lungs. The sound that is articulated into words comes entirely from the lungs through the trachea and epiglottis. So depending on the inflation of this bellows and the opening of its passageways, speech is either amplified into shouting or, by their contraction, muted; and if the passage is completely blocked, speech and thought both cease.

Since our discernment corresponds to our lungs, and our thinking therefore to their breathing, "soul" and "spirit" in the Word mean discernment, as in "you shall love the Lord your God with your whole heart and your whole soul" (Matthew 22:35 *[22:37]*), or "God will give a new heart and a new spirit" (Ezekiel 36:26; Psalms 51:12, 13 *[51:10]*). I have already explained [§§378–381] that the heart means the love of our volition, so soul and spirit mean the wisdom of our discernment. **383**

You may see in *Teachings for the New Jerusalem on the Lord* 50–51 that the spirit of God, also called the Holy Spirit, means divine wisdom and therefore divine truth, the means of our enlightenment.

This is why "the Lord breathed on the disciples and said, 'Receive the Holy Spirit'" (John 20:22). This is also why it says, "Jehovah God breathed the breath of life into Adam's nostrils, and he became a living soul" (Genesis 2:7), and why God said to the prophet, "Prophesy over the spirit and say to the wind, 'Come, spirit, from the four winds and breathe upon these who have been slain, so that they may live'" (Ezekiel 37:9). There are similar statements elsewhere as well. It is why the Lord is called the spirit of the nostrils and also the breath of life.

Since our breathing comes through our nostrils, they are used to mean perception. An intelligent person is referred to as "keen-scented," and a dense person as "dull-scented." This is also why in Hebrew and in some other languages, "spirit" and "wind" are expressed by the same word. In fact, the word "spirit" is derived from [a root that means] breathing; so when people die we speak of their "breathing their last."

This is also why people believe that a spirit is a wind or something airy, like the breath that issues from our lungs, and believe the same of the soul as well.

We can tell from this that "loving God with the whole heart and with the whole soul" means with all our love and all our discernment, and that "giving a new heart and a new spirit" means a new volition and a new discernment.

It is because the spirit means discernment that it says of Bezalel that "he was filled with the spirit of wisdom, intelligence, and knowledge" (Exodus 31:3) and of Joshua that "he was filled with the spirit of wisdom" (Deuteronomy 34:9), and that Nebuchadnezzar said of Daniel that "a superlative spirit, one of knowledge and intelligence and wisdom was in him" (Daniel 6:5 *[5:11, 12, 14]*), and why it says in Isaiah that "those who are wandering in spirit will know intelligence" (Isaiah 29:24). Similar statements may be found in many other places.

384   Since all the elements of the mind have to do with volition and discernment and all the elements of the body with the heart and lungs, there are two brains in our heads, as distinct from each other as volition and discernment. The cerebellum serves volition primarily, and the cerebrum serves discernment primarily. In the same way, heart and lungs are distinct from everything else in the body. They are marked off by the diaphragm and enclosed in their own membrane, the pleura, forming the region of the body known as the chest.

These two aspects are found united in other parts of the body, the ones called members, organs, and viscera; so they too occur in pairs— arms and hands, legs and feet, eyes, and nostrils, for example. Within the body there are the kidneys, the ureters, and the reproductive glands; and the viscera that are not paired are still divided between right and left. Further, the brain itself is divided into two hemispheres, the heart into two ventricles, and the lungs into two lobes. The right side has to do with the good that results from truth and the left to the truth that results from good; or in other words, the right refers to the good that love can do, which leads to the truth of wisdom, while the left refers to the truth of wisdom that results from the good that love can do. Since the union of what is good and what is true is reciprocal, and since they become a virtual single whole by virtue of that union, these pairs within us act together as a unit in our deeds, motions, and sensations.

385   *5. This relationship enables us to discover many secrets about our volition and discernment and also about love and wisdom.* There is little awareness in this world of the actual nature of volition and love because we cannot love deliberately, and intend from love, the way we can apparently think deliberately. In the same way, we cannot deliberately control the motions of our hearts the way we can control the breathing of our lungs. Given, then, the ignorance in this world of the nature of volition and love and our knowledge of the nature of our heart and lungs (since they are present to the examination of our eyesight and have been examined and described by anatomists, while volition and discernment are not present to the examination of our eyesight), once we know that they correspond and act in unison by means of that correspondence, we can discover many secret things about volition and love that otherwise we could not. We can discover things, for example, about the union of volition with discernment and the reciprocal union of discernment with volition, or about the union of love with wisdom and the reciprocal union of wisdom with love. We can discover how love branches off into feelings, how those feelings are associated with each other, and how they flow into our perceptions and thoughts and ultimately, by means of correspondence, into our physical actions and sensations.

These secrets, and many others, can be discovered and explained by examining the way the heart and the lungs are united, how the blood flows from the heart into the lungs and back from the lungs into the heart, and from there through the arteries into all the members, organs, and viscera of the body.

6. *Our mind is our spirit, and the spirit is a person, with the body being a covering through which the mind or spirit senses and acts in its world.* It is hard for people to accept with any trust the notion that our mind is our spirit and that the spirit is a person if they have thought that the spirit is a wind and that the soul is something ethereal, like the breath breathed out from our lungs. They ask how the spirit can be a person when it is a spirit, or how the soul can be a person when it is a soul. They say the same about God because God is called a spirit.

386

They have gathered these concepts of spirit and soul from the fact that in some languages there is only one word for "spirit" and "wind," so when someone dies, they talk about "the last breath" or "giving up the ghost" and that when someone has suffocated or fainted, life comes back when the spirit or life comes back into the lungs. Since this seems to be nothing but wind and air, they conclude on the basis of their eyes and their physical senses that after death our spirit or soul is not a person.

Various theories have sprouted from this materialistic assessment of the spirit and the soul, resulting in the belief that we are not persons until Judgment Day comes, that until then we are in some undefined place waiting for the reunion [with our bodies]. This is discussed in *Supplements on the Last Judgment [and the Spiritual World]* 32–38.

It is because the human mind is our spirit that angels, who are also spirits, are called "minds."

387   The reason our mind is our spirit and the spirit is a person is that *mind* means everything involved in our volition and discernment, and these are found in their primary forms in our brains and in their derivative forms in our bodies. Consequently, they are everything we have as far as our basic form is concerned. Since this is the case, the mind, or our volition and discernment, activates the body and everything in it at will. Does not the body do whatever the mind thinks and intends? Does not the mind prick up the ear to listen, focus the eye to see, move the lips and tongue to speak, activate the hands and fingers to do what it wants and the feet to walk where it wants to go? Is the body, then, anything but obedience to the mind? Could the body be like this if the mind in its derivative forms were not present in it? Does it make rational sense to believe that the body obediently does what the mind wants as though they were two individuals, one above and the other below, one giving orders and the other submitting? Since this is contrary to all reason, it follows that our life exists in its primary forms in our brains and in derivative forms in our bodies, as explained in §365 above; and that the nature of life in its primary forms determines its nature in the whole body and in every part of it (§366). It follows that through these primary forms life exists from every part in the whole and from the whole in every part (§367).

I have already explained [§§362–370] that everything in the mind goes back to volition and discernment, that volition and discernment are the vessels of love and wisdom from the Lord, and that these two constitute our life.

388   We can also see from what has been said that the human mind is the essential person. The very first outline of the human form, or the essential human form, complete in all detail, comes from its primary forms, extended from the brain through its nerves, as already explained [§366].

This is the form we attain after death, the form we call a spirit or an angel, a form that is an absolutely complete person, but a spiritual one. The material form that was added on the outside in the world is not the human form in its own right, but is derived from that form, added on the outside so that we can function usefully in the physical world. It also provides us with a stable vessel for our spiritual natures, a vessel drawn from the purer substances of this world, that we take with us [after death] in order to carry on and continue our lives.

It is an item of angelic wisdom that the human mind, both in a general way and in every least detail, is in a constant effort toward the human form because God is human.

For a person to be a person, no part that occurs in a complete person **389** can be lacking either from the head or from the body, since there is nothing there that does not belong to and constitute that form. It is actually the form of love and wisdom, which in its own right is divine. It contains all the specific forms of love and wisdom that are infinite in the Divine-Human One but finite in his images—in us, in angels, and in spirits. If any part were missing that occurs in that person, then some specific corresponding form of love and wisdom would be missing, some form through which the Lord can be present with us from our core to our boundaries, providing for lives of service in the created world out of his divine love, through divine wisdom.

7. *The union of the human spirit and body is accomplished through the* **390** *correspondence of volition and discernment with the heart and the lungs, and disunion is caused by a lack of correspondence.* It has not yet been realized that our mind, meaning our volition and discernment, is our spirit, and that the spirit is a person. It has also not yet been realized that our spirit has a pulse and breathing just as the body does. As a result, there has been no way to know that the pulse and breathing of the spirit within us flows into the pulse and breathing of our body and causes them.

If our spirit enjoys a pulse and breathing just as our body does, it follows that there is the same kind of correspondence between the pulse and breathing of our spirit and the pulse and breathing of our body. The mind, as already noted [§§386–389], is our spirit; so when the correspondence between these two activities ceases, there is a separation—death.

Separation or death occurs when the body either by disease or by trauma reaches a state when it can no longer act in concert with its spirit. In this way, the correspondence ceases; and when the correspondence ceases, so does the union. This is not when the breathing alone stops, but when the heartbeat stops, since as long as the heart is working, love is still there with its vital warmth, maintaining life. We can see this in cases of fainting or suffocation as well as in the state of the fetus in the womb.

In brief, our physical life depends on the fact that our physical pulse and breathing are responsive to the pulse and breathing of our spirit; and when this responsiveness ceases, physical life ceases and the spirit departs, to continue its life in the spiritual world. This life is so much like our life in the physical world that we do not realize we have died.

Most people are in the spiritual world within two days after leaving their bodies. I have talked with some individuals after two days.

391 Proof that spirits have a pulse and breathing just as we earthly people do in our bodies can come only from spirits and angels themselves when someone is enabled to talk with them. This has been granted to me; so when I have asked them, they have told me that they are just as much people as we are in this world and that they too have bodies, but spiritual ones. They have told me that they too can feel their hearts beating in their chests and in the arteries in their wrists just the way we people in the physical world do. I have asked a good many about this, and they have all said the same thing.

I have been enabled to learn from my own experience that the human spirit is breathing within the body. Occasionally, angels have been allowed to control the extent of my breathing, to diminish it at will and eventually to restrain it to the point that only the breathing of my spirit was left to me, at which point I could actually sense it. The same thing happened to me when I was shown what it is like to die: see *Heaven and Hell* 449.

Sometimes, too, I have been restricted to nothing but the breathing of my spirit, and then was sensibly aware of its harmony with the general breathing of heaven. On any number of occasions, too, I have been in a state like that of angels and have been lifted up to them in heaven; and at times like these I was in the spirit and out of the body, using my breathing to talk with them just as we do in this world.

These and other firsthand proofs have made it clear to me not only that our spirits are breathing within our bodies, but also that they do so after we leave our bodies behind; and also that the breathing of our spirits is so subtle that we do not sense it. It flows into the obvious breathing of our bodies almost the same way a cause flows into an effect or a thought flows into the lungs and through the lungs into speech.

We can also see, then, that the union of spirit and body in us is brought about by the responsive relationship between the motions of the heart and the lungs of the two.

392 The reason these two motions (that of the heart and that of the lungs) happen so reliably is that the whole angelic heaven is engaged in these two life motions both overall and in individual instances. The reason the whole angelic heaven is engaged in them is that the Lord is instilling them from the sun where he is and which comes from him. This sun causes these two motions at the Lord's behest. Further, since by design all heaven and earth depend on the Lord through that sun, since they are as intimately connected as a work that is linked together from beginning to end, and since the life of love and wisdom comes from him and all the activities in the universe depend on life, we can see that this is their only source. It follows that their variations depend on the way love and wisdom are accepted.

I will be saying more about the correspondence of these motions later [§417], describing what they are like for people who breathe together with heaven and people who breathe together with hell, for example, and what they are like for people whose speech is in touch with heaven but whose thought is in touch with hell—that is, for hypocrites, flatterers, charlatans, and the like.

393

From the correspondence of the heart with volition and the lungs with discernment, we can learn everything that can be known about volition and discernment or love and wisdom—everything, therefore, that can be known about the human soul. A host of people in learned circles have sweated over their research about the soul. However, since they have not known anything about the spiritual world and our state after death, all they have been able to do has been to formulate theories not about the nature of the soul but about how it works in the body. Their only conceivable notion of the nature of the soul was of something supremely pure, something in the ether, with the ether itself as its vehicle. They have not dared publish much about this for fear of attributing something physical to the soul when they knew that the soul was spiritual.

394

Given this concept of the soul as well as the knowledge that the soul is at work in the body producing everything involved in sensation and motion, they have, as I just noted, sweated over their research into the way the soul works in the body. Some have stated that this happens by an inflow, others that it happens by a harmony. However, since this has led to no discoveries satisfactory to a mind that wants to see whether something is true or not, I have been granted the privilege of talking with angels and becoming enlightened on the matter through their wisdom. One item of their wisdom is that the human soul that lives after death is the human spirit and that it is a perfectly formed person. Further, this soul of ours is our volition and discernment, whose soul is love and wisdom from the Lord. It is these two that constitute our life, a life that is from the Lord alone and that is the Lord. To enable us to accept him, he makes us feel as though this life belongs to us; but to prevent us from claiming life as our own possession and thereby undermining our ability to accept him, the Lord teaches us that every element of love that we call good and every element of wisdom that we call true comes from him. Nothing of it comes from us; and since these two are our life, every trace of life that is really alive comes from him.

395   Since in essence the soul is love and wisdom and these two are within us from the Lord, two vessels have been created within us, vessels that are also dwellings for the Lord. One of these is for love and the other is for wisdom. The one for love is called volition, and the one for wisdom is called discernment. Further, since love and wisdom in the Lord are distinguishably one (see §§17–22 above), and since divine love is a property of the Lord's divine wisdom and divine wisdom a property of his divine love (see §§34–39), and since these as well emanate from the Divine-Human One, the Lord—then the two vessels and dwellings within us called volition and discernment have been created by the Lord in such a way as to be distinguishably two but to function as a single unit in everything we do and everything we sense. Volition and discernment cannot be separated in these functions.

However, since we are intended to become vessels and dwellings, our discernment has necessarily been given the ability to be lifted above our own love into some of wisdom's light, which is beyond our own love. This enables us to see and learn how we are to live if we are to attain to heavenly love as well as heavenly light and so enjoy blessedness forever.

Since we have now misused our ability to lift our discernment above our own love, we have destroyed within ourselves the possibility of being the Lord's vessels and dwellings, that is, vessels and dwellings of love and wisdom from the Lord. We have done this by making our volition the dwelling of love for ourselves and love for the world, and our discernment the dwelling of whatever justifies these loves.

This is why these dwellings—our volition and discernment—have become dwellings of hellish love, and by our justification of these loves vessels of that hellish thought that is treasured as wisdom in hell.

396   The reason love for ourselves and love for the world are hellish loves, the reason we could become absorbed in them and thereby destroy our own volition and discernment, is that as created, love for ourselves and love for the world are heavenly loves. They are in fact loves proper to our physical self and of service to our spiritual loves the way foundations are of service to houses. It is love for ourselves and love for the world that prompt us to care about our bodies, to want nourishment, clothing, and housing, to take care of our homes, to look for jobs in order to be useful, to be granted respect due to the worth of our responsibilities so that people heed us, and even to find delight and recreation in worldly pleasures. All of these activities, however, should be for the sake of usefulness. They bring us into a state of serving the Lord and the neighbor. In contrast, when there is no love for serving the Lord and the neighbor, when there is nothing but love for using the world to suit ourselves, then the love becomes hellish instead of heavenly. It makes us focus our minds and spirits on our self-image, which intrinsically is completely evil.

To make sure that we are not in heaven as to our discernment, which is possible, and in hell as to our volition, which would give us a mind divided against itself, after death any elements of discernment that transcend our own love are taken away. The result is that for everyone, volition and discernment eventually act in unison. For people in heaven, their volition loves what is good and their discernment thinks what is true. For people in hell, their volition loves what is evil and their discernment thinks what is false. **397**

The same holds true for us in this world when we are thinking from the spirit. This happens when we are alone, though many people think differently during their physical lives, when they are not alone. The reason for this difference is that they lift their discernment above the self-concern of their volition, or the love of their spirit.

I mention all this to show that volition and discernment are two distinguishable functions, still created to be one function, and that they are constrained to act in unison after death, if not before.

Now, love and wisdom (and therefore our volition and discernment) are that entity that we call the soul, and we need next to explain how the soul's impulses affect the body and make everything in it work. We can learn about this from the responsive relationship between the heart and volition and between the lungs and discernment. For these reasons, the following matters have been disclosed on the basis of that relationship. **398**

1. Love, or volition, is our essential life.
2. Love or volition is constantly striving toward the human form and toward everything the human form comprises.
3. Unless it is married to wisdom or discernment, love or volition cannot accomplish anything through its human form.
4. Love or volition prepares a home or bridal chamber for its spouse-to-be: wisdom or discernment.

5. Love or volition also prepares everything in its human form so that it can act in unison with wisdom or discernment.

6. After the "wedding," the first union is with a desire for knowing, which gives rise to a desire for what is true.

7. The second union is with a desire for discerning, which gives rise to a sense of what is true.

8. The third union is with a desire to see what is true, which gives rise to thought.

9. Through these three unions, love or volition engages in its life of sensing and its life of acting.

10. Love or volition leads wisdom or discernment into every corner of its house.

11. Love or volition does not do anything without its spouse.

12. Love or volition marries wisdom or discernment to itself and arranges things so that wisdom or discernment marries it willingly.

13. Because of the power given it by love or volition, wisdom or discernment can be raised up, can accept things in heaven's light, and can grasp them.

14. Love or volition can be raised up in the same way and can grasp things in heaven's warmth provided it loves its spouse to that degree.

15. Otherwise, love or volition pulls wisdom or discernment back from its height so that they act in unison.

16. If they are raised up together, love or volition is cleansed by wisdom in our discernment.

17. Love or volition is polluted in and by our discernment if they are not raised up together.

18. Love that has been cleansed by wisdom in our discernment becomes spiritual and heavenly.

19. Love that has been polluted in and by our discernment becomes limited to nature and our senses.

20. There still remain that ability to discern that we call rationality and that ability to act that we call freedom.

21. When love is spiritual and heavenly, it is a love for the Lord and for our neighbor; while when it is limited to nature and our senses, it is a love for the world and for ourselves.

22. It is the same for charity and faith and their union as it is for volition and discernment and their union.

399   1. *Love, or volition, is our essential life.* This follows from the responsive relationship between the heart and our volition discussed in §§378–381 above; for our volition acts in our mind the same way our heart acts in our body. Further, just as everything in the body depends on the heart for its origin and for its motion, everything in the mind depends on volition for its origin and its life. By "volition" I mean "love," since volition is the vessel of love and love is the essence of life (see §§1–3 above). The love that is the essence of life, further, comes from the Lord alone.

By looking at the heart and its extension in the body through arteries and veins, we can learn that love or volition is our life. This is because things that correspond to each other act in the same way, the only difference being that one is physical and the other spiritual.

The science of anatomy shows us how the heart acts in the body. It shows us, for example, that everything is alive or responsive to life where the heart is at work through the channels it extends from itself, and that everything is not alive where the heart is not at work through its channels. It shows further that the heart is both the first and last thing that acts in the body. We can tell that it is first by looking at embryos, and that it is last by looking at the dying. We can tell that it acts separately from the lungs by looking at people who have suffocated or fainted. This enables us to see that the life of the mind depends entirely on volition just the way the life that supports the body depends entirely on the heart and that our volition remains alive even when thought ceases, just the way the heart does when breathing ceases. This too we can see in embryos, in the dying, and in people who have suffocated or fainted.

It follows from all this that love or volition is our very life.

2. *Love or volition is constantly striving toward the human form and toward everything the human form comprises.* This we can see from the way the heart corresponds to volition, since we know how everything in the body is formed in the womb. We know that everything is formed there by fibers from the brain and by blood vessels from the heart and the fabric of all our organs and viscera are made from these two materials. This enables us to see that everything within us comes into being from the life of our volition, which is love, from beginnings in our brains, through these fibers, with everything in our bodies coming from the heart through its arteries and veins.

Clearly then, life (which is love and its consequent volition) is constantly striving toward the human form; and since the human form comprises everything that is within us, it follows that love or volition is engaged in a constant effort to form all these things. The reason this

400

effort is toward the human form is that God is a Person and divine love and wisdom is the life of that Person. This is the source of every trace of life.

Everyone can see that if the life that is the essential person were not activating something that intrinsically is not life, nothing that is within us could be formed the way it is. There are thousands upon thousands of things within us that are acting in unison, totally united in their effort toward an image of the life that is their source so that we can become his vessel and dwelling.

We can see from this that love—and from love, our volition, and from volition, our hearts—is constantly striving toward the human form.

401   3. *Unless it is married to wisdom or discernment, love or volition cannot accomplish anything through its human form.* This too we can see from the way the heart corresponds to our volition. The human fetus is alive as to its heart but not as to its lungs. Blood is not yet flowing from the heart into the lungs and enabling them to breathe, but is flowing through an opening into the left ventricle of the heart. As a result, the fetus cannot yet move any part of its body, but rests bound; and it cannot sense anything, with its sensory organs closed.

It is the same with the love or volition. [The fetus] is alive because of it, but in darkness. That is, it lacks sensation and action. As soon as the lungs are opened, though, which happens after birth, it begins to sense and to act and at the same time to intend and to think.

We can tell, then, that unless it is married to wisdom or discernment, love or volition cannot accomplish anything through its human form.

402   4. *Love or volition prepares a home or bridal chamber for its spouse-to-be, wisdom or discernment.* In the created universe and in every detail of it there is a marriage between what is good and what is true. This is because what is good is a matter of love and what is true is a matter of wisdom, and these two exist in the Lord, from whom everything was created.

We can see how this marriage happens in us, reflected in the union of our heart with our lungs, since the heart corresponds to love or what is good and the lungs to wisdom or what is true (as explained in §§378–381 and 382–384 above).

We can see from their union how love or volition pledges itself to wisdom or discernment, and later leads it or enters a kind of marriage with it. It pledges itself by preparing a home or room for wisdom, and it leads it by a marriage that takes place through desires. Then it brings wisdom with it into its house.

The only way to verify this would be to use spiritual language because love and wisdom are spiritual, which means that volition and discernment are spiritual as well. They can be presented in earthly language, but only with a hazy perception, because people do not know what love is or what wisdom is or what desires for what is good are or what desires for wisdom are, namely desires for what is true. However, we can see the nature of the pledging and marriage between love and wisdom (or volition and discernment) through the parallelism that obtains because of their correspondence with the heart and the lungs. Things are the same for the one as for the other, so similar that the only difference is that one is spiritual and the other physical.

We can tell from the heart and the lungs, then, that the heart first forms the lungs and then weds itself to them. It forms the lungs in the fetus and weds them after birth. The heart does this in its own home, called the chest, where they gather. This is separated from the rest of the body through the membrane called the diaphragm and the envelope called the pleura.

It is the same with love and wisdom, or with volition and discernment.

5. *Love or volition also prepares everything in its human form so that it can act in unison with wisdom or discernment.* I am talking about volition and discernment, but it needs to be absolutely clear that volition is the whole person. Actually, volition is found with discernment in primary forms in the brain and in derivative forms in the body, so (as explained in §§365, 366, and 367 above) it is found in the whole body and in every part. We can tell from this that volition is the whole person in respect both to overall form and to the particular form of every part. We can tell also that discernment is its partner just as the lungs are the partner of the heart.

People need to guard against entertaining any notion of volition as something apart from the human form: the two are the same.

We can see from this not only how volition prepares a room for discernment but also how it prepares everything in its home, the whole body, so that it can act in unison with discernment. The preparation is like this. The whole body and all its parts are united to discernment just as they are united to volition; or just as the whole body and all its parts are subject to volition, they are subject to discernment.

403

As for how the whole body and all its parts are prepared for a union with discernment like that with volition, this can be seen only as it is reflected or imaged by the science of anatomy in the body. This shows how everything in the body is so connected that when the lungs breathe, the whole body and every part of it is moved by the lungs' breathing just as by the heart's beating. We learn from anatomy that the heart is united to the lungs by its auricles and that these extend into the recesses of the lungs. We learn also that all the viscera of the whole body are connected to the chest cavity by ligaments—so closely connected that when the lungs breathe, the whole body and everything in it, together and individually, receive an impulse from the breathing. When the lungs swell, then the ribs expand the chest, the pleura dilates, and the diaphragm is stretched; and along with them all the lower parts of the body, which are connected to them by ligaments, receive some impulse from the motion of the lungs. Let me say no more, or people who lack anatomical knowledge will find themselves confused because of their unfamiliarity with the terminology of this discipline. Just ask people who are experienced and skilled in anatomy whether everything in the whole body, from the chest on down, is not so tied together that when the lungs swell during breathing, the whole body and everything in it is stirred into motion in time with the lungs.

This enables us to see what kind of union volition prepares for discernment, union with the whole human form and everything it comprises. Just search out the connections and examine them with the eye of the anatomist, and then look at their coordination with the breathing lungs and with the heart in the light of those connections. Then think "discernment" for "lungs" and "volition" for "heart," and you will see.

404   6. *After the "wedding," the first union is with a desire for knowing, which gives rise to a desire for what is true.* "After the wedding" means our state after birth, beginning with a state of ignorance and continuing through a state of discernment all the way to a state of wisdom. The first state, that of pure ignorance, is not what I mean by the wedding, since our discernment has no thought at that point, only a faint impulse of our love or volition. This state is a prelude to the wedding. It is recognized that there is a desire for knowing in the second state, the one characteristic of our childhood. This is what enables little ones to learn to talk and to read and then gradually to learn the kinds of things that constitute discernment. We cannot doubt that love—which is a matter of volition—is doing this, since unless love or volition were the driving force, it would not happen.

Everyone who reflects rationally on experience realizes that after we are born we all have a desire for knowing and that this is the basis of our learning the kinds of things that lead gradually to the formation, development, and attainment of discernment. We can also see that this gives rise to a desire for what is true, since once we have become discerning because of our desire for knowing, we are motivated not so much by a desire for knowing as by a desire for systematic thinking and drawing conclusions about subjects that we love—economics, perhaps, or civic or moral issues. When this desire rises all the way to spiritual concerns, it becomes a desire for spiritual truth. We can see that the first step or prelude was a desire for knowing from the fact that a desire for what is true is a higher level of the desire for knowing. This is because being moved by truths comes from wanting to know them because of our desire and then absorbing them with passionate delight when we find them.

7. *The second union is with a desire for discerning, which gives rise to a sense of what is true.* Anyone can see this who is willing to explore the matter with some rational insight. Rational insight shows that a desire for what is true and a sense of what is true are two abilities enjoyed by our discernment, abilities that merge into one for some people but not for others. They merge into one for people who want to grasp what is true intelligently, but not for people who want only to know about what is true. We can also see that our engagement in the grasp of truth depends on our desire to understand it. If you take away the desire to understand what is true, there will be no grasp of what is true; while if you grant the desire to understand what is true, there will be a grasp of it proportional to the intensity of the desire. This is because no one of sound reason ever lacks a sense of what is true as long as the desire to understand it is present. I have already explained [§162] that everyone has the ability to discern what is true that we call rationality.

8. *The third union is with a desire to see what is true, which gives rise to thought.* A desire for knowing is one thing; a desire for discerning is another thing; and a desire to see something is something else again. We can also say that a desire for what is true is one thing; a grasp of what is true is another thing; and thinking is something else again. If people have no clear grasp of the workings of the mind, they can see this only dimly; but it is clear for people who can grasp them clearly. The reason people see this only dimly if they cannot grasp the workings of the mind clearly is that these activities are all happening at the same time in the thinking of people who are caught up in a desire for what is true and in a grasp of what is true; and when they happen at the same time, they cannot be

distinguished from each other. We are engaged in conscious thinking when our spirit is thinking in the body. This is the case especially when we are in the company of others. However, when we are engaged in a desire for discerning and come thereby into a grasp of what is true, then we are engaged in the thinking of our spirit. This is meditation, which does indeed reach down into our physical thought, but subtly. It is on a higher level and looks into thought processes based on memory as below it, since it is using them either for decision or for support. The actual desire for what is true, though, is felt only as an impulse of our volition stemming from a kind of pleasure. This resides within reflection like its life, and draws little attention.

We may conclude from all this that these three abilities—the desire for what is true, the grasp of what is true, and thought—follow in sequence from love and are nowhere manifest but in our discernment. When love enters discernment (which happens when the union is realized), then it first gives rise to the desire for what is true, then to the desire to understand what it knows, and finally to a desire to see in physical thought whatever it understands. Thinking is actually nothing but an inner sight. Thinking does happen first because it is a function of our earthly mind; but when it comes to thinking on the basis of a grasp of what is true because of a desire for what is true, that happens last. That kind of thinking is the thinking of wisdom, while the other is thinking on the basis of memory, using the sight of our earthly mind.

All the workings of love or volition outside our discernment are based not on desires for what is true but on desires for what is good.

405 Granted, rational people can understand that these three follow sequentially in our discernment from the love that belongs to our volition, but they still cannot see it clearly enough to believe it with confidence. However, since by virtue of correspondence the love proper to volition acts in concert with the heart and the wisdom proper to discernment acts in concert with the lungs, as already explained, there is no better way to see and show what I have just said about the desire for what is true, the grasp of what is true, and thinking (see §404 above) than by looking at the lungs and their construction; so I need to describe this briefly.

After birth, the heart sends blood into the lungs from its right ventricle, and once it has passed through, it sends it into its left ventricle. This is what opens the lungs. The heart does this by means of the pulmonary arteries and veins. The lungs have bronchia that branch off and ultimately turn into the little sacs where the lungs admit air and thereby breathe. There are also arteries and veins (called "bronchial") around the bronchia and their branches. They start from the azyga or vena cava and the aorta, and they are distinct from the pulmonary arteries and veins. This enables us to see that the blood flows into the lungs by two routes and flows out of them by two routes. This is why the lungs can breathe in a different rhythm from the heart. It is widely recognized that the rhythms of the heart and the rhythms of the lungs are not the same.

Now, since the correspondence of the heart and lungs is with our volition and discernment, as already explained [§§371–393], and since union by correspondence means that the one behaves in the same way as the other, we can see from the blood flow from the heart into the lungs how volition flows into discernment and causes the things mentioned in §404 about our desire for what is true, about our grasp of what is true, and about thought. Correspondence has shown me this and even more on this topic, which I cannot describe briefly.

Since love or volition answers to the heart and wisdom or discernment answers to the lungs, it follows that the blood vessels from the heart to the lungs answer to desires for what is true and that the branches of the lungs' bronchia answer to perceptions and thoughts generated by those desires. If you were to look into the way the lungs are woven from these origins and draw the parallel with the love of our volition and the wisdom of our discernment, you could see a kind of image of what I have said in §404 and come to believe it with confidence.

However, since not many people are familiar with the anatomical data about the heart and the lungs, and since supporting a proposition with unfamiliar material yields confusion, I forbear presenting any further instances of the parallelism.

9. *Through these three unions, love or volition engages in its life of sensing and its life of acting.* The reason love can neither sense nor act in the body apart from discernment, or any desire of love apart from the thinking of discernment, is that to all intents and purposes, love without discernment is blind, and desire without thought is in the dark. Discernment is the light that enables love to see. Then too, the wisdom of discernment comes from the light that radiates from the Lord as the sun. If the love of our discernment cannot see anything and is blind apart from the light of discernment, it follows that without discernment's light, our physical senses too would be immersed in blindness and stupidity—not only our sight and hearing, but our other senses as well. The reason this would apply to our other senses is that all our perception of what is true is a property of love within discernment, as already explained [§404],

406

and all our physical senses derive their sensitivity from the sensitivity of our mind.

The same applies to all our physical actions, since an action that springs from love apart from discernment is like something we do in the night without knowing what it is that we are doing. So there would be no trace of intelligence or wisdom in the act, and the act could not be called a living deed. An action, that is, gets its reality from love and its quality from intelligence.

Further, whatever power anything good has comes by means of truth, so what is good acts in and therefore by means of what is true. What is good is a matter of love and what is true is a matter of discernment.

We may then conclude that it is through the three unions discussed in §404 that love or volition engages in its life of sensing and its life of acting.

407 We can find striking support for this in the union of the heart with the lungs, since it is in the nature of the volition-heart and discernment-lungs correspondence that the heart acts with the lungs on the physical level the way volition acts with discernment on the spiritual level. This enables us to see what I have been talking about in a kind of visual image.

As for our lack of any sensory life, and therefore of any active life, when heart and lungs are not working together, this is evidenced by the state of a fetus or infant in the womb and the state of the same after birth. As long as the individual is a fetus or is in the womb, the lungs are closed. As a result, the individual has no sensation or action. The sense organs are closed, the hands are restrained, and so are the feet. After birth, though, the lungs are opened, and as they are opened we sense and act. The lungs are opened by blood that flows in from the heart.

We can also see from people who have fainted that if the heart and the lungs are not working together we are deprived of both sensory and active life. When people have fainted, only the heart is working, not the lungs—breathing has been taken away. Everyone knows that people who have fainted are deprived of sensation and action.

It is the same with people who suffocate, whether by water or because of something that blocks their windpipe and closes off the lungs' breathing passage. People then seem to be dead, having neither sensation nor action. Yet we know that the heart is still keeping them alive. They in fact return to both sensory and active life as soon as the blockages of the lungs are removed. In the meantime, blood has been making its circuit through the lungs, but only through the pulmonary arteries and veins, not through the bronchial arteries and veins; and these latter give us the ability to breathe.

It is the same with the inflow of love into discernment.

10. *Love or volition leads wisdom or discernment into every corner of its house.* By the "house" of love or volition, I mean the whole person, everything that goes to make up our minds; and since these things correspond to everything in our bodies (as already explained [§§374–377]), the "house" also means the whole [physical] person, everything that goes to make up our bodies, which we refer to as members, organs, and viscera. What has already been presented shows that the lungs are brought into these latter just the way discernment is brought into all the functions of the mind. See, for example, §402, "Love or volition prepares a home or bridal chamber for its spouse-to-be, wisdom or discernment," and §403, "Love or volition also prepares everything in its human form or house so that it can act in unison with wisdom or discernment." We can see from what it says there that the whole body and everything in it is connected by extensions from the ribs, the vertebrae, the sternum, the diaphragm, the peritoneum that is suspended from them, and the ligaments—so closely connected that when the lungs are breathing all the organs are impelled and carried along in a similar rhythmic movement.

Anatomy shows us that this respiratory rhythm penetrates right into the viscera, even to their deepest recesses, since the ligaments already mentioned are connected to the coverings of the viscera, and the coverings reach into the deepest recesses through their extensions just the way the arteries and veins do through their branches. We may conclude, then, that the lungs' breathing is completely united to the heart in the whole body and in all its parts. To make this union complete in all respects, the heart itself is involved in the respiratory motion. It rests in the lung cavity and is connected to it by its auricles, and it rests on the diaphragm, so that its arteries are also involved in the respiratory movement. Further, the stomach is similarly united because of the connection between its esophagus and the windpipe.

I cite these anatomical details to show what the union is like between love or volition and wisdom or discernment, and how the two of them in partnership are united to everything in the mind, since the [spiritual and physical] unions are similar.

11. *Love or volition does not do anything without wisdom or discernment.* Since love has neither sensory nor active life apart from discernment, and since love leads discernment into all the functions of the mind (see §§407 and 408 above), it follows that love or volition does not do anything

apart from discernment. What would it be to act from love apart from discernment? We could only call it something senseless. Discernment is what shows us what needs to be done and how it needs to be done. Love does not know this apart from discernment. As a result, there is so full a union between love and discernment that even though they are two functions, they still act as one. There is a similar union between what is good and what is true, since what is good is a matter of love and what is true is a matter of discernment.

There is the same kind of union in everything the Lord has created in the universe. Their function looks to what is good, and the form of their function looks to what is true.

It is because of this union that there is a right and a left to the whole body and everything in it. The right goes back to the good that prompts what is true, and the left to the truth that is prompted by what is good, so they go back to that union. This is why there are pairs in us—two brains [the cerebrum and the cerebellum], two hemispheres of the cerebrum, two ventricles of the heart, two lobes of the lungs, two eyes, ears, nostrils, arms, hands, legs, feet, kidneys, reproductive glands, and so on; and where there are not separate pairs, there is still a right side and a left side. This is because the good looks to the true for its manifestation and the true looks to the good for its existence. The same holds true in the angelic heavens and in the individual communities there.

There is more on this subject in §401 above, where I explained that unless it is married to wisdom or discernment, love or volition cannot accomplish anything through its human form. I will elsewhere discuss the inverse of the union of what is good and what is true, namely the union of what is evil and what is false.

410

12. *Love or volition marries wisdom or discernment to itself and arranges things so that wisdom or discernment marries it willingly.* We can see that love or volition marries wisdom or discernment from their correspondence with the heart and the lungs. Anatomical research teaches that the heart is engaged in its life motion before the lungs are. We learn this by experience from people who have fainted, people who have suffocated, embryos in the womb, and chicks in eggs.

Anatomical research also teaches us that while the heart is acting by itself, it forms the lungs and organizes them so that it can breathe in them, and that it also forms the other viscera and organs so that it can perform its various functions in them. It forms the organs of the face so that it can sense, the organs of motion so that it can act, and the other parts of the body so that it can fulfill the functions that answer to the desires of its love.

The main conclusion we can draw from this is that just as the heart brings forth such organs for the sake of the different functions it is going to undertake in the body, so love does the same in its vessel, which we call volition, for the sake of the different desires that make up its form—which as already noted [§400] is the human form.

Next, since the first and immediately following desires of love are the desire for knowing, the desire for discerning, and the desire to see what we know and discern, it follows that love forms discernment for these desires and actually enters into them when it is beginning to sense and act and when it is beginning to think. We can tell from the parallelism with the heart and lungs just mentioned that discernment makes no contribution to this process.

This in turn shows that love or volition marries wisdom or discernment and that wisdom or discernment does not marry itself to love or volition. We can also look at the knowledge that love gets because of its desire for knowing, the sense of what is true that it gets from its desire for discerning, and the thought it gets from its desire to see what it knows and discerns and conclude that these are products not of discernment but of love. Thoughts and perceptions and consequent knowledge do indeed flow in from the spiritual world, but they are not accepted by our discernment. They are accepted by our love depending on its desires in our discernment. It seems as though discernment were accepting them and not love or volition, but this is an illusion. It also seems as though discernment married itself to love or volition, but this too is an illusion. Love or volition marries itself to discernment and arranges things so that the marriage is mutual. The reason it is mutual lies in the marriage of love with it; so the union seems to be mutual because of the life and consequent power of love.

The same holds true for the marriage of what is good and what is true, since the good is a matter of love and the true is a matter of discernment. The good does everything. It accepts the true into its house and marries it to the extent that it is in harmony. The good can accept truths that are not in harmony, but it does this out of its desire for knowing, understanding, and thinking before it has settled on the functions that constitute its goals and are called its virtues. The reciprocal union—the union of what is true with what is good—is actually nonexistent. The reciprocity of the union comes from the life of what is good.

This is why the Lord looks at everyone, at us, at spirits, and at angels, in regard to our love or good. No one is seen in terms of discernment or of what is true apart from love or what is good. Our life is our love, as already explained [§§1–3]; and we have life insofar as we have lifted up our desires by means of truths, that is, to the extent that we have completed our desires by means of wisdom, since the desires of our love are lifted up and completed by means of truths and therefore by means of wisdom. Then love acts in unison with wisdom just as though it were acting out of wisdom. It is acting out of itself, though, and through wisdom as its form. That form derives nothing whatever from our discernment. It derives everything from some specific instance of love that we call a desire.

411 Love calls "good" everything it has that supports it, and it calls "true" whatever things it has that serve as means to that "good." Since they are means, they are loved and become objects of love's desires; and in this way they become formed desires. Consequently, truth is simply the form of love's desires. The human form is simply the form taken by the totality of love's desires. Beauty is its intelligence, which it acquires by means of the truths it gains through outer and inner sight or hearing. It is these that love arranges in the form of its desires. There are many variations on this form, but they all take some similarity from their common form, which is the human form. To love, all these forms are beautiful and loveable, but others are ugly and unlovable to it.

It also follows from this that love marries itself to discernment, not the other way around, and that the answering union comes from love as well. This is what it means to say that love or volition arranges things so that wisdom or discernment marries it willingly.

412 We can see and confirm what I have been talking about in a kind of image in the way the heart answers to love and the lungs to discernment as already described [§§371–393], since if the heart answers to love, then its limited forms, its arteries and veins, answer to desires, with the ones in the lungs answering to desires for what is true. Further, since there are other vessels in the lungs (called airways) that make respiration possible, these vessels answer to perceptions.

We need to be fully aware that the arteries and veins in the lungs are not desires and that the breaths are not perceptions and thoughts, but that they are corresponding functions. They are actually responsive or synchronized. It is the same for the heart and the lungs. They are not love and discernment, but are corresponding functions; and since they are corresponding functions, we can see one in the other. Anyone who knows the whole structure of the lungs from anatomy and makes a careful comparison with discernment can see quite clearly that discernment does nothing on its own. It neither senses nor thinks on its own, but does everything because of desires proper to love. The ones in discernment are called the desire already described for knowing, understanding, and seeing [what is true]. All the different states of the lungs depend on blood from the heart and from the vena cava and aorta; while the breathing that takes place in the bronchial tube occurs in keeping with their state, since breathing stops when the inflow of blood stops.

I could disclose a great deal more by comparing the structure of the lungs to the discernment that it answers to, but since not many people are familiar with the science of anatomy, and since it beclouds a subject to explain or support it by unfamiliar examples, I may not say more about this. I am wholly convinced by what I know about the structure of the lungs that love marries itself to discernment by means of its desire and that discernment does not marry itself to any desire of love. Rather, it is married willingly by love so that love may have a sensory and active life.

At all costs, we must realize that we have two forms of breathing, one of the spirit and one of the body. The breathing of the spirit depends on the fibers that come from the brain, and the breathing of the body depends on the blood vessels that come from the heart and from the vena cava and aorta.

Clearly, too, it is thought that gives rise to breathing and it is love's desire that gives rise to thought, since thought without desire is exactly like breathing without a heart—impossible. We can therefore see that love's desire marries itself to discernment's thought, as just stated. It is the same with the heart in the lungs.

13. *Because of the power given it by love, wisdom or discernment can be raised up, can accept things in heaven's light, and can grasp them.* I have already and often stated that we can grasp hidden treasures of wisdom when we hear them. This ability of ours is what we call "rationality," and it is ours from creation. This ability to see into things deeply and to form conclusions about what is fair and just, about what is good and true, is what distinguishes us from animals. It is also what I mean by the statement that discernment can be raised up, can accept things in heaven's light, and can grasp them.

We can also see a kind of image of this fact in the lungs, since the lungs correspond to our discernment. Looking at the lungs, we see that their substance comprises little chambers. These consist of the extensions of the bronchia all the way into the tiny sacs where the air is taken in when we breathe. Our thoughts act in unison with them because of their correspondence. It is characteristic of the substance of these little sacs that it has two ways of expanding and contracting, one in unison with the heart and the other almost independent of the heart. Its unison with the heart is

413

because of the pulmonary arteries and veins, which come directly from the heart. Its virtual independence is because of the bronchial arteries and veins, which come from the vena cava and aorta, vessels external to the heart. This happens in the lungs because our discernment can be raised above its own love, which answers to the heart, and accept light from heaven. Even so, when our discernment is raised above its own love it does not leave it completely behind. It takes along some of it, which we can call a desire for knowing and discerning for the sake of promotion, praise, or profit in this world. Some trace of this clings to each love like a coating. This gives the love a superficial glow; but for wise people, there is an actual translucence.

I cite these facts about the lungs to show that our discernment can be raised up and accept and grasp things in heaven's light. There is in fact a complete correspondence. To see from correspondence is to see the lungs reflected in our discernment and our discernment reflected in our lungs, and to find assurance in each at the same time.

414   14. *Love or volition can be raised up in the same way and can grasp things in heaven's warmth provided it loves its spouse, wisdom, to that degree.* I have explained in the preceding section (and often enough before that) that our discernment can be raised into heaven's light and gather in wisdom from it. I have also frequently noted that our love or volition can be raised up as well if it loves the things that are found in heaven's light, things that involve wisdom. However, our love or volition is not raised up by any concern for promotion, praise, or profit, but by a love of service—that is, not for our own sake but for the sake of our neighbor. Since this love is granted us only from heaven by the Lord, and since the Lord gives it to us when we abstain from evils as sins, this is how our love or volition can be lifted up as well; otherwise it cannot happen. Love or volition, though, is raised into heaven's warmth, while discernment is raised into heaven's light. If they are both raised up, a marriage takes place there that we call "the heavenly marriage" because it is a marriage of wisdom and heavenly love. This is why I said that love is raised as well if it loves wisdom, its spouse, to that degree. A love for our neighbor that comes from the Lord is a love for wisdom, or the human mind's real love.

The same thing is true of light and warmth in the world. There is light without warmth and there is light with warmth—without warmth in winter and with warmth in summer. When there is light with warmth, then everything blooms. The light in us that answers to winter light is wisdom apart from its love, and the light in us that answers to summer light is wisdom together with its love.

We can observe this union and separation of wisdom and love virtu- **415** ally imaged in the way the lungs are connected to the heart. The heart can be connected with the clustered little bronchial bladders by blood that comes directly from itself and also by blood that comes not from itself but from the vena cava and aorta. This makes it possible for our physical breathing to be independent of our spiritual breathing; though if the blood is coming only from the heart, the two forms of breathing cannot be separated.

Next, since our thoughts act in unison with our breathing because of their correspondence, we can also see from the double nature of the lungs' breathing that we can think one way and speak and act out our thoughts one way when we are with other people, while when we are by ourselves—that is, when we have no fear of damage to our reputation— we think another way and speak and act out our thoughts another way. Then we can both think and say things against God, the neighbor, the spiritual values of the church, and moral and civic values. We can act against these as well by deeds of theft, revenge, blasphemy, and adultery. All the while, when we are in public where we risk loss of reputation, we can talk, preach, and behave exactly as though we were spiritual, moral, and civic individuals.

We can tell from this that love or volition, like discernment, can be lifted up so as to receive things proper to the warmth or love of heaven provided only that it loves wisdom to that degree; while if it does not love it, they can part company.

15. *Otherwise, love or volition pulls wisdom or discernment back from its* **416** *height so that they act in unison.* There is earthly love and there is spiritual love. When we are engaged in earthly love and spiritual love together, then we are rational people. When we are engaged solely in earthly love, though, we can think just as rationally as spiritual people, but we are not really rational individuals. We do lift our discernment up into heaven's light, into wisdom, but the matters of wisdom or heaven's light are not objects of our love. It is our love that is making this happen, but behind it is a desire for respect, praise, and profit. However, once we realize that we are not getting any benefit from this elevation (as we do realize when we are thinking to ourselves on the basis of our earthly love), then we have no love for matters of heaven's light or wisdom. So our love then pulls our discernment down from its height so that the two will act in unison.

For example, when our discernment is filled with wisdom because it has been lifted up, then our love sees what justice, honesty, and chastity are, even what real love is. Earthly love can see this because of its ability to understand and ponder things in heaven's light. It can even talk about, preach, and describe these as both moral and spiritual virtues. When our discernment is not lifted up, though, then if our love is merely earthly it does not see these virtues. It sees injustice as justice, deception as honesty, lust as chastity, and so on. If we do think about the matters we discussed when our discernment was at its height, then we may make fun of them and think that they serve us only to ensnare people's minds.

We can therefore tell how to understand the statement that unless love loves its spouse, wisdom, to that degree, it pulls it down from its height so that they act in unison. (On love's ability to be lifted up if it does love wisdom to that degree, see §414 above.)

417   Since love corresponds to the heart and discernment to the lungs, what I have just said can be supported by their correspondence. That is, we can see how discernment can be lifted above its own love all the way into wisdom and how if the love is merely earthly it will pull discernment down from its height.

We have two kinds of breathing, one physical and one spiritual. These two kinds of breathing can be independent or coordinated. For people who are completely earthly-minded, especially for hypocrites, they are independent, while for spiritual and honest people they rarely are. This means that once their discernment has been lifted up so that they have a store of elements of wisdom left in their memory, people who are completely earthly-minded and hypocritical can talk wisely in public because their thinking is based on their memory. Still, when they are not in public they base their thinking on their spirit and not on their memory, which means they base it on their love. They breathe in the same way, since thinking and breathing are responsive to each other.

I have already explained [§§405, 415] that the structure of the lungs enables breathing to take place from blood directly from the heart and from blood not directly from the heart.

418   Most people think that wisdom is what makes us who we are; so when they hear someone speaking or teaching wisely, they believe that this is a wise individual. People even believe this of themselves at such times, since when they are speaking and teaching in public they are thinking on the basis of their memory. If they are completely earthly-minded people, then the source is the surface of their love, a desire for respect, praise, and profit. However, when these same people are by themselves, they think from the deeper love of their spirits—not wisely at all, but at times insanely.

This shows that no one is to be evaluated on the basis of verbal wisdom, but on the basis of life. That is, we are not to rely on verbal wisdom separated from life but on verbal wisdom together with life. Life means love: I have already explained [§§1–3] that love is life.

16. *If they are raised up together, love or volition is cleansed by wisdom in our discernment.* From birth, all we love is ourselves and the world, because this is all that comes into our view. So this is all we think about. This love is on the earthly, physical level: we may call it materialistic. Not only that, this love has become defiled by its separation from heavenly love in our parents.

419

This love cannot be separated from its impurity unless we have the ability to lift our discernment into heaven's light and see how we need to live in order to have our love raised up into wisdom along with our discernment. It is through discernment that our love sees—that we, in fact, see—which evils are defiling and polluting our love. This also enables us to see that if we resolutely abstain from those evils as sins, we love the opposites of those evils, which are all heavenly. We also see the means by which we can resolutely abstain from those evils as sins. Love sees all this—that is, we see all this—by using our ability to lift our discernment into heaven's light, which gives us wisdom. Then to the extent that love puts heaven first and the world second, at the same time putting the Lord first and ourselves second, love is cleansed of its pollutants and purified. That is, it is to that extent lifted into heaven's warmth and united to the light of heaven that surrounds discernment. Then the marriage takes place that is called the marriage of the good and the true, the marriage of love and wisdom.

Anyone can grasp mentally and see rationally that to the extent that we resolutely abstain from theft and cheating, we love honesty, integrity, and justice. To the extent that we resolutely abstain from vengefulness and hatred, we love our neighbor. To the extent that we resolutely abstain from adultery, we love chastity, and so on.

However, hardly anyone knows what is heavenly and divine about honesty, integrity, justice, love for our neighbor, chastity, and the other desires of heavenly love until their opposites have been removed. Once their opposites have been removed, we are involved in them, so we recognize and see them from the inside. Until that happens, there is a kind of veil in the way. It does let a little of heaven's light reach our love, but since that love does not love wisdom, its spouse, to that extent, it does not accept the light. It actually criticizes it severely and finds fault with it when it comes back down from its height, though the light is still attractive to it because wisdom in our discernment can be a tool that helps gain us respect, praise, and profit. Then, however, we are putting ourselves and the world first and the Lord and heaven second, and what we put second is loved only as long as it is useful to us. If it is not useful, we renounce and reject it, after death if not before.

This illustrates the truth that love or volition is cleansed in our discernment if they are raised up together.

420 There is an image of the same process in the lungs. Its arteries and veins answer to desires proper to love, and its respiratory motions answer to perceptions and thoughts proper to discernment, as already noted [§§405, 412].

There is ample experience to support the proposition that the heart's blood is purified in the lungs from what it has not digested and that it nourishes itself there with appropriate elements from the air that is drawn in. As for the blood being purified in the lungs from what it has not digested, this we can tell not only from the inflowing blood, which is venous and therefore full of chyle gathered from what we have eaten and drunk, but also from the moist breath we exhale and the odors others can smell. We can also tell from the fact that the blood that flows back into the left ventricle of the heart is diminished in volume.

As for the fact that the blood nourishes itself with appropriate elements drawn from the air, this we can tell from the immense variety of fragrances that are constantly given off by shrubs, flowers, and trees as well as from the immense variety of different kinds of salts and liquids from soils, rivers, and lakes. There is also the immense variety of gaseous emanations that both we and animals give off—the air is full of them. Undeniably, these enter our lungs with our indrawn breaths, so it is also undeniable that our blood absorbs elements that are good for it. The elements that are good for it are the ones that answer to the desires of our love. This is why in the tiny sacs at the center of our lungs there are so many little veins with minute pores that take these substances in. This is why the blood that flows back into the left ventricle of the heart is changed into arterial blood and is brilliant. All this shows that the blood is purifying itself from unsuitable elements and nourishing itself with suitable ones.

Until now, it has not been recognized that the blood purifies and nourishes itself in the lungs in a way that answers to the desires of our own nature, but this is common knowledge in the spiritual world. Angels in the heavens take pleasure only in odors that answer to the love of their wisdom. Spirits in hell, on the other hand, find pleasure only in odors that answer to a love that rejects wisdom. These are foul odors, while the others are fragrant.

It follows that we in this world are saturating our blood with similar elements depending on how those elements answer to the desires of our love. Whatever our spirit loves, our blood seeks out in response, and our breathing draws in.

It flows naturally from this correspondence that we are purified in our love if we love wisdom, and are defiled if we do not love it. All our purification happens by means of truths that constitute wisdom, and all our defilement happens by means of false beliefs that reject the truths of wisdom.

17. *Love or volition is polluted in and by our discernment if they are not raised up together.* This is because if the love is not raised up it remains impure, as noted in §§419 and 420 above. When it remains impure, it loves what is impure. It loves things like vengefulness, hatred, deceit, blasphemy, and adultery. These are what appeal to it then, what we call its cravings; and it rejects whatever springs from thoughtfulness, justice, honesty, truth, and chastity. **421**

I stated that love is polluted in and by discernment. It is polluted in discernment when love is influenced by these impurities. It is polluted by discernment when it makes matters of wisdom its own servants, and even more when it distorts, falsifies, and corrupts them.

There is no need to say more about the way this state answers to the heart or to its blood in the lungs than has already been said in §420. I may add only that the blood is polluted instead of being purified, and that instead of its being nourished by fragrant odors it feeds on stenches, just the way it happens in heaven and in hell.

18. *Love that has been cleansed in our discernment becomes spiritual and heavenly.* We are born earthly, but to the extent that our discernment is raised into heaven's light and our love into heaven's warmth along with it, we become spiritual and heavenly. Then we become like a Garden of Eden, bathed in the light and warmth of springtime. **422**

Our discernment does not become spiritual and heavenly. Our love does, and when it does it makes its spouse, discernment, spiritual and heavenly as well.

Love becomes spiritual and heavenly through a life in accord with the truths of wisdom, truths that discernment teaches and illustrates. Love absorbs these truths not on its own but by means of discernment, since love cannot lift itself up unless it knows truths; and it can know truths only by means of a discernment that has been lifted up and enlightened. Then love is lifted up to the extent that it loves these truths by doing them. It is one thing to discern, that is, and another to intend; or it is one thing to speak and another to act. There are people who understand truths of wisdom and utter them but still do not intend and do them. When love, then, puts into practice the truths of light that it discerns and utters, then it is raised up.

Simple reason shows that this is so. After all, what are we when we discern and utter truths of wisdom while we are living—that is, intending and acting—contrary to them?

The reason love becomes spiritual and heavenly when it has been purified by wisdom is that we have three levels of life, levels called earthly, spiritual, and heavenly. These were discussed in part 3 of the present work [§§236–241]. We can be lifted up from one to the next; but we are not raised simply by wisdom. We are raised by a life in accord with wisdom, because our life is our love. So to the extent that we live in accord with wisdom we love it; and we live in accord with wisdom to the extent that we purify ourselves from those unclean things we call sins; and to the extent that we do this, we love wisdom.

423 It is not that easy to see from the correspondence with heart and lungs how love is purified by wisdom in our discernment and becomes spiritual and heavenly because no one can see what the blood is like that keeps the lungs breathing. The blood can be full of impurities and still be indistinguishable from pure blood. Then too, the breathing of purely earthly-minded people seems very much like the breathing of spiritual-minded people. However, people can tell them apart very clearly in heaven. Individuals there breathe in keeping with the marriage of their love and wisdom; so just as angels can be identified by that marriage, they can be identified by their breathing. This is why when people who are not in that marriage arrive in heaven, they begin to feel chest pains and to struggle for breath like people in the throes of death. As a result, they hurl themselves down headlong and find no rest until they are with people whose breathing is like their own. Then, because of the correspondence, they are with people who feel the way they do and therefore think the way they do.

We can therefore tell that if we are spiritual, it is our purer blood, sometimes called the animal spirit, that is purified, and that it is purified to the extent that we participate in the marriage of love and wisdom. It is that purer blood that most closely answers to this marriage; and since it does flow into our physical blood, it follows that it also purifies that blood. The opposite happens for people whose love is defiled in their discernment.

As I have already noted, though, no one can investigate this by experiments with our blood, only by looking at the desires of our love, since these correspond to our blood.

19. *Love that has been polluted in and by our discernment becomes limited to nature, our senses, and our bodies.* An earthly love separated from spiritual love is opposed to spiritual love. This is because earthly love is love for ourselves and love for the world, and spiritual love is love for the Lord and love for our neighbor. Love for ourselves and for the world looks downward and outward, and love for the Lord looks upward and inward. So when an earthly love is separated from spiritual love, it cannot be raised away from our self-absorption. It remains immersed in it and even mired in it, to the extent that it loves it. If our discernment does rise up and see elements of wisdom in heaven's light, then our love drags it back down and unites it to itself in its self-absorption. There it either discards the elements of wisdom or distorts them or arranges them outside itself so that it can mouth them for the sake of reputation.

§424

Just as an earthly love can rise up by levels and become spiritual and heavenly, it can also go down by levels and become sensory and physical. It goes down to the extent that it loves being in control with no love of service, simply for love of ourselves. This is the love that we call demonic.

People involved in this kind of love can talk and behave like people involved in spiritual love, but at such times they are operating either out of memory or out of a discernment that has lifted itself into heaven's light. The things they say and do, though, are like fruit that looks lovely on the outside but is nothing but rot inside, or like almonds whose shells look intact but which have been completely eaten away by worms inside. In the spiritual world they summon up illusions that enable prostitutes (called "sirens" there) to look beautiful and to dress in attractive clothing. Once the illusions are taken away, though, they look like ghosts. They are like demons, too, who make themselves into angels of light; for when that physical love drags its discernment down from its height (which happens when we are alone) and thinks from its own love, then it thinks against God and for nature, against heaven and for the world, against the true and good values of the church and for the false and evil values of hell. That is, it thinks against wisdom.

This shows what the people we call "physical" are like. They are not physical as far as their discernment is concerned, but they are as far as their love is concerned. That is, they are not mentally physical when they speak in public, but they are when they talk with themselves in spirit. Further, since they are like this in spirit, after death they are like this in both respects, in both love and discernment. They become the spirits called "physical spirits." People who in this world absolutely loved being in control because of their self-absorption and were also intellectually a cut above others look physically like Egyptian mummies, and are crude and foolish mentally. Is there anyone in the world these days who knows that this is what this love is really like?

However, there is a love for being in control because of a love of service—a love of service not for the sake of ourselves but for the common welfare. It is hard, though, to tell this from the other kind, even though the difference between them is like the difference between heaven and hell. On the difference between these two kinds of love for being in control, see *Heaven and Hell* 531–565 *[551–565]*.

425   20. *There still remain that ability to discern that we call rationality and that ability to act that we call freedom.* I have discussed these two abilities of ours already in §§264–267. The reason we have these two abilities is so that we can become spiritual instead of earthly, which is being reborn. I have already explained [§§422–423] that it is our love that becomes spiritual and that is reborn; and the only way it can become spiritual or be reborn is by using discernment to learn what is evil and what is good and what is therefore true and what is false. Once it knows this, it can choose either one or the other. If it chooses what is good, then it can use discernment to learn about the means by which it can reach what is good. We are provided with all the means we need to reach what is good. Knowing and discerning these means depends on our rationality, while intending and acting depend on our freedom, freedom being our own intent to know, to discern, and to think about these matters.

People do not know about these abilities called rationality and freedom if they believe, as the church has taught, that spiritual and theological matters transcend understanding and are therefore to be believed without being understood. All they can do is deny the existence of the ability called rationality. Further, if people believe that we cannot do good on our own, as the church has taught, and that therefore we do not need to do anything good voluntarily for the sake of our salvation, they cannot help denying the existence of our other ability because of their religious principles. After death, therefore, people who have convinced themselves of these beliefs lose both abilities because of their beliefs.

They might have been in heavenly freedom, but they are in hellish freedom instead. They might have enjoyed angelic wisdom because of their rationality, but instead they are immersed in the insanity of hell. Strange as it may seem, they still recognize the gift of these two abilities in their evil behavior and their false thinking, not realizing that the freedom of doing evil is slavery and the rationality of thinking falsely is senseless.

However, we need to be quite clear about the fact that neither of these abilities, neither freedom nor rationality, is really ours. They are the Lord's gifts to us, and we are not to claim them as our own. They cannot really belong to us; they are constantly being given to us by the Lord. Still, they are never taken from us because we cannot be saved without them. Without them, that is, we cannot be reborn, as already noted [§264]. This is why the church teaches that we cannot think what is true on our own or do what is good on our own.

However, since our whole perception is that we do think what is true on our own, and that we do do what is good on our own, the idea that we only seem to think what is true on our own and only seem to do what is good on our own is clearly something we need to *believe*. If we do not believe this, then we neither think what is true nor do what is good, and we therefore have no religion whatever. Either that, or we think what is true as well as do what is good with our own strength, which is claiming for ourselves what belongs to Divinity.

On our need to think what is true and do what is good in apparent independence, see *Teachings about Life for the New Jerusalem* from beginning to end.

21. *When love is spiritual and heavenly, it is a love for our neighbor and for the Lord; while when it is limited to nature and our senses, it is a love for the world and for ourselves.* "Love for our neighbor" means a love for acts of service, and "love for the Lord" means a love for doing such acts, as already noted [§237]. The reason these loves are spiritual and heavenly is that loving acts of service and doing them because we love to is divorced from any concern for our own image. That is, when we love acts of service spiritually, we are not focused on ourselves but on others outside ourselves, others for whom we are doing something good. Love for ourselves and for the world are the opposites of these loves because they focus our attention on doing acts of service not for the sake of others but for our own sake. When we do this, we are turning the divine design upside down, putting ourselves in the Lord's place and the world in heaven's place. This means we are looking away from the Lord and

426

heaven, and looking away from them is looking toward hell. There is more about these loves, though, in §424 above.

Still, we do not have the same kind of feeling and sense of love for doing what is useful for its own sake that we have for doing what is useful for our own sake. This also means that when we are doing something useful we do not know whether we are doing it for its own sake or for our own sake. We might know, though, that we do what is useful for its own sake to the extent that we abstain from evils because to the extent that we do, the source of our acts of service is not ourselves but the Lord. Evil and good are opposites, so to the extent that we are not engaged in something evil, we are engaged in something good. No one can be in evil and in good at the same time because no one can serve two masters at the same time.

I mention this because it helps to know that even though we may have no clear sense of whether we are doing acts of service for their own sake or for ours—whether the acts are spiritual, that is, or merely earthly—we could tell by seeing whether we think evil deeds are sins or not. If we think they are sins and therefore do not do them, then our acts of service are spiritual; and once we begin abstaining from sins because they are distasteful to us, then we begin to have an actual sense of loving service for its own sake because there is a spiritual pleasure in service.

427   22. *It is the same for charity and faith and their union as it is for volition and discernment and their union.* There are two loves that are the grounds of a basic distinction in the heavens, namely heavenly love and spiritual love. Heavenly love is love for the Lord and spiritual love is love for our neighbor. The difference between these two loves is that heavenly love is a love for what is good, while spiritual love is a love for what is true. When we are moved by heavenly love, we do our acts of service out of love for what is good; while when we are moved by spiritual love we do them out of love for what is true. The marriage of heavenly love is with wisdom, and the marriage of spiritual love is with intelligence. Wisdom is doing what is good because it is good, and intelligence is doing what is good because it is true. This means that heavenly love acts out what is good, while spiritual love acts out what is true.

The only way I can describe the difference between these two loves is to say that people who are moved by heavenly love have wisdom written not on their memory but on their lives. This is because they do not talk about divine truths, they simply do them. In contrast, people who are moved by spiritual love have wisdom written on their memory, so they talk about divine truths and do them on the basis of the principles they hold in their memory.

Since people who are moved by heavenly love have wisdom written on their lives, whenever they hear something they know immediately whether it is true or not; and when they are asked whether something is true, they say either that it is or that it is not. They are the people referred to by the Lord's words, "Let your speech be 'Yes, yes; no, no'" (Matthew 5:37). Because this is their nature, they do not like it when people talk about faith. They say, "What is faith? Is it not wisdom? And what is charity? Is it not action?" If anyone says that faith is believing what we do not understand, they turn away and say, "That's crazy."

These are the people who live in the third heaven, and they are the wisest of all. People get that way in this world by applying whatever divine principles they hear directly to their lives with an aversion to evils as hellish and a total reverence for the Lord. Because they live in innocence, they look to others like little children; and because they never talk about truths of wisdom and there is no trace of self-importance in their conversation, they seem simple. However, when they hear others talking they can sense their whole love from their tone of voice and their whole intellect from what they are saying.

These are the people who are kept in the marriage of love and wisdom by the Lord. As already mentioned [§381], they also reflect the heart region of heaven.

In contrast, people who are moved by spiritual love, by love for their neighbor, do not have wisdom written on their lives. They do have intelligence, since as already noted [§427] it is characteristic of wisdom to do what is good because we are moved by what is good and characteristic of intelligence to do what is good because we are moved by what is true. People like this do not know what faith is either. If someone mentions faith, they hear "truth," and if someone mentions charity, they hear "doing the truth." If someone says something should be believed, they call it nonsense and say, "Who doesn't believe what is true?" They say this because they are seeing what is true in the light of their heaven. So in their eyes, it is either simplemindedness or folly to believe what we do not see. **428**

These are the people who make up the lung region of heaven, as also noted earlier [§381].

Some people, though, are moved by spiritual love on the earthly level. They do not have either wisdom or intelligence written on their lives, they simply have some element of faith drawn from the Word, to the extent that it is united to charity. Since they do not know what charity is or whether their faith is true, they cannot enjoy the company of **429** people in the heavens, people who are occupied with wisdom and intelligence. They find themselves with people who are occupied simply with information. Still, if they have abstained from evils as sins, they are in the farthest heaven, where the light is like moonlight at night.

Then again, if they have not become set in a faith in the unknown and have felt some attraction to truths, once they have been taught by angels (as far as their openness to truths and to a life by them allows), they are brought up into communities of people who are moved by spiritual love and therefore live intelligently. They become spiritual, while the others remain spiritual only on an earthly level.

However, if people have lived in a faith that is separated from charity, they are sent away and relegated to desolate regions because they are not engaged in anything worthwhile. This means that they do not participate in any marriage of what is good and true, the marriage characteristic of everyone in the heavens.

430 Everything I have said in this part about love and wisdom could also be said about charity and faith, provided only that charity is understood to mean a spiritual love and faith is understood to mean the truth that leads to intelligence. The same would hold true if we spoke of our volition and discernment, or our love and intelligence, since our volition is the vessel of love and our discernment is the vessel of intelligence.

431 I should like to add a matter of interest. All the people in heaven who are engaged in being of service because they enjoy doing it derive from their collective body a wisdom and happiness greater than that of others. As far as they are concerned, being of service means being honest, fair, proper, and faithful in whatever task is appropriate to their station. This is what they call "charity," and they refer to their acts of formal worship as emblems of charity. Anything else is a duty or a good deed. They say that whenever they do the tasks proper to their station honestly, fairly, properly, and faithfully, the collective body takes on substance and permanence in their good work. This is what it means to be "in the Lord," since everything that flows into them from the Lord has to do with service; and it flows from the members into the collective body and from the collective body into the members. The members there are angels, and the collective body is their community.

432 *The nature of our first stage after conception.* No one can know what our first or primal stage in the womb after conception is like because we cannot see it. Further, it is composed of a spiritual substance that is not visible in physical light. Some people in this world are inclined to focus their minds on our primal stage, the father's semen that is the agent of conception, and many of them have fallen into the error of thinking that we are complete humans from the very first and then reach completeness simply by getting larger. For this reason, some angels to whom the Lord had revealed it showed me what this first or primal stage of ours is like with respect to its form. Since they had made this a matter of their wisdom and since the delight of that wisdom was to share what they knew with others, they were given permission to present a representation of that initial form of ours to my own eyes in heaven's light.

It was like this. I saw what seemed to be a tiny image of a brain with a sort of face drawn faintly on its front, with no appendages. On its upper convex part, this primal form was a composite of closely connected little balls or spheres. Each sphere was made up of still smaller spheres, and each of these of spheres still smaller. This meant that there were three levels. Something that looked like a face was outlined on the front, concave part.

The convex part was enveloped by a very thin, transparent meningeal membrane. The convex part, the miniature image of a brain, was also divided into what seemed to be two lobes the way the full-scale brain is divided into two hemispheres. I was told that the right lobe was the vessel of love and that the left lobe was the vessel of wisdom, and that by some incredibly intricate connections they were like partners or roommates.

In the light of heaven, a radiant light, the angels also showed me that inwardly this composite structure of a miniature brain was in the design and form of heaven with respect to both its setting and its flow, while the outer composite structure was opposed to that design and that form.

Once I had seen what they showed me, the angels said that the two inner levels, the ones that were in the design and form of heaven, were vessels of love and wisdom from the Lord, while the outer level, the one that was opposed to heaven's design and form, was a vessel of hellish love and madness. This is because we are born into all kinds of evil because of our hereditary imperfection, and these evils are located in our outermost natures. These flaws cannot be eliminated unless our higher levels are opened, the levels that are vessels of love and wisdom from the Lord, as already noted. Further, since love and wisdom are the essential person, love and wisdom being the Lord in essence, and since this primal stage of ours is a vessel, it follows that there is in this primal stage a constant striving toward the human form, a form that it gradually takes on.

THE END

Biographical Note

E MANUEL SWEDENBORG (1688–1772) was born Emanuel Swedberg (or Svedberg) in Stockholm, Sweden, on January 29, 1688 (Julian calendar). He was the third of the nine children of Jesper Swedberg (1653–1735) and Sara Behm (1666–1696). At the age of eight he lost his mother. After the death of his only older brother ten days later, he became the oldest living son. In 1697 his father married Sara Bergia (1666–1720), who developed great affection for Emanuel and left him a significant inheritance. His father, a Lutheran clergyman, later became a celebrated and controversial bishop, whose diocese included the Swedish churches in Pennsylvania and in London, England.

After studying at the University of Uppsala (1699–1709), Emanuel journeyed to England, the Netherlands, France, and Germany (1710–1715) to study and work with leading scientists in western Europe. Upon his return he apprenticed as an engineer under the brilliant Swedish inventor Christopher Polhem (1661–1751). He gained favor with Sweden's King Charles XII (1682–1718), who gave him a salaried position as an overseer of Sweden's mining industry (1716–1747). Although Emanuel was engaged, he never married.

After the death of Charles XII, Emanuel was ennobled by Queen Ulrika Eleonora (1688–1741), and his last name was changed to Swedenborg (or Svedenborg). This change in status gave him a seat in the Swedish House of Nobles, where he remained an active participant in the Swedish government throughout his life.

A member of the Royal Swedish Academy of Sciences, he devoted himself to studies that culminated in a number of publications, most notably a comprehensive three-volume work on natural philosophy and metallurgy (1734) that brought him recognition across Europe as a scientist. After 1734 he redirected his research and publishing to a study of anatomy in search of the interface between the soul and body, making several significant discoveries in physiology.

From 1743 to 1745 he entered a transitional phase that resulted in a shift of his main focus from science to theology. Throughout the rest of his life he maintained that this shift was brought about by Jesus Christ, who appeared to him, called him to a new mission, and opened his perception to a permanent dual consciousness of this life and the life after death.

He devoted the last decades of his life to studying Scripture and publishing eighteen theological titles that draw on the Bible, reasoning, and his own spiritual experiences. These works present a Christian theology with unique perspectives on the nature of God, the spiritual world, the Bible, the human mind, and the path to salvation.

Swedenborg died in London on March 29, 1772 (Gregorian calendar), at the age of eighty-four.